Early Identification of Emotionally Handicapped Children in School

Publication Number 734
AMERICAN LECTURE SERIES®

A Monograph in
AMERICAN LECTURES IN PSYCHOLOGY

Edited by
MOLLY HARROWER, Ph.D.
Professor of Research in Clinical Psychology
Department of Psychiatry
Temple University School of Medicine
Philadelphia, Pennsylvania

Early Identification of Emotionally Handicapped Children in School

Second Edition

By

ELI M. BOWER

Consultant, Mental Health in Education
National Institute of Mental Health
Bethesda, Maryland
Formerly
Deputy Director, Liaison and Prevention Services
California State Department of Mental Hygiene
Sacramento, California

CHARLES C THOMAS · PUBLISHER

Springfield · Illinois · U.S.A.

Published and Distributed Throughout the World by
CHARLES C THOMAS • PUBLISHER
BANNERSTONE HOUSE
301-327 East Lawrence Avenue, Springfield, Illinois, U.S.A.
NATCHEZ PLANTATION HOUSE
735 North Atlantic Boulevard, Fort Lauderdale, Florida, U.S.A.

First Edition, 1960
Second Edition, 1969

With **THOMAS BOOKS** *careful attention is given to all details of
manufacturing and design. It is the Publisher's desire to present
books that are satisfactory as to their physical qualities and artistic
possibilities and appropriate for their particular use.* **THOMAS
BOOKS** *will be true to those laws of quality that assure a good
name and good will.*

Printed in the United States of America
N-10

To

Barbara who no longer sharpens the pencils,
Kenneth who no longer eats the erasers, and
Phyllis who still does the work.

PREFACE TO THE SECOND EDITION

THE FIRST EDITION expired quickly and gracefully about a year
ago. Both conscience and publisher have conspired to convince me
it would be worth the time and effort to update the materials, the
concepts, and the research. In this age of frenzied activity and
people saturation, one seldom has time to read a book, much less
write one. Writing grates my patience, snags my social life, and
wearies my gluteus maximus. I was most impressed during a visit
to Goethe's rebuilt house in Frankfurt to discover that in those
days some desks were constructed so that one could write in a
standing position. Supposedly the creative parts of the brain
functioned more effectively when the body was upright. This may
have been true for Goethe, who took over fifty years to finish one
book, but my feet seem to tire long before the creative parts of my
mind swing into action. So sit I must.

With all these booby traps and personal obstacles, why a second
edition? In the ten years since the research on early identification
was completed, concern and interest has grown in this type of preventive, educational, and mental health activity. There have also
been significant new contributions to the research, to the conceptual approaches, and in the screening materials themselves.
Such materials and related aids have been significantly revised and
are replicated and described in the revised Appendix. At present,
these materials plus a Manual for School Administrators and
Teachers, a Technical Report, and assorted recording and descriptive aids are contained in a kit called "A Process for In-school
Screening of Children With Emotional Handicaps" which is
available to qualified personnel from the Office of Special Tests,
Educational Testing Service, Princeton, New Jersey. In California,
the materials are available from the State Department of Education, Sacramento, California.

This second edition has also attempted to include and react to
some of the new research on early identification, but no attempt

has been made to cover all that has happened in this field since the first edition. The new material is aimed at giving readers more perspective on the basic assumptions in the research and reducing to normal the surprising number of misconceptions, misunderstanding, and misuse of the materials. The process described herein is not and is not intended to be a clinical diagnostic procedure for differentiating emotionally disturbed children from so-called normals or for identifying the future mentally ill. I have tried to rewrite some of the material so that all conceptual and operational boundaries are heavily lined and visible.

Lastly, I have taken the time to patch and mend because I feel the problem this book addresses itself to is desperately important to man and his survival. The horror the entire world experienced the afternoon of November 22, 1963, was fulminated by one small boy who could not be helped to function successfully in school but who could learn to shoot a high-powered rifle with consummate skill. In a world where elbowroom and margins for error are rapidly diminishing, civilizations cannot permit even one child to fail to become a fully functioning adult human being.

Revision and publication of the materials and manuals included in *A Process for In-School Screening of Children with Emotional Handicaps* could not have been accomplished without the help of many of my research colleagues in the California State Department of Education and Educational Testing Service. Mrs. Nadine M. Lambert, Assistant Professor of Education, University of California, Berkeley, collaborated in the development of the manuals and the revisions of the materials. In this task we wish to acknowledge the encouragement and specific help of John Dobbin, Henry Dyer, Scarvia Anderson, and Frank Nulty, all of Educational Testing Service, Princeton, New Jersey.

Bethesda, Maryland   E.M.B.

PREFACE TO THE FIRST EDITION

EDUCATION CAN be regarded as a process for increasing the degrees of freedom of human behavior. Such freedom, however, depends not only on the knowledge and information an individual can obtain, but on the restrictive or enhancing characteristics of his emotional processes. Emotional conflicts and defects limit perceptual and behavioral alternatives, restrict intake of information, and distort aspects of an individual's knowledge. Individuals emotionally disabled to a minor, moderate, or severe degree are unable, to that degree, to profit from their educational experiences. Therefore, children whose educational progress will be handicapped by emotional conflicts or defects need to be identified early to reduce the cumulative and concomitant effects of the disability.

The social problems posed by individuals with moderate or severe emotional handicaps are generally recognized as a major social concern. Yet, one would be hard pressed to discover any major specific effort to reduce or prevent the occurrence of mild, moderate, or major emotional maladjustment in the citizens of our society. One can almost assume that the sum and substance of present creative social and scientific thought is to encourage disabling emotional conditions to develop fully so that professional energies can then be expended on long-term treatment or hospitalization.

Luther Woodward, at a meeting of the American Orthopsychiatric Association, described an ancient Cornish test of insanity as follows: The subject to be tested was placed in a room in which there was a pail of water directly under a water faucet. The water was turned on and the subject given a ladle and asked to bail the water from the pail. If he first turned off the faucet before beginning to bail, he was considered sane. If he continued to bail with the water still running into the pail, he was declared insane.

In addition to the question of where or how do we begin to turn off the flow of human maldevelopment and emotional defectiveness, we need to ask, Are we really interested in doing so? The answer must be sought in deeds which are specific in intent and evaluation, and are practical possibilities in a free society.

This book describes one way of beginning. It is a book written primarily for teachers, school administrators, and school trustees about what the schools can do to increase, to some degree, the emotional strengths of children. The major purpose of the research study described herein is to present a usable and useful method by which teachers can be helped to be more effective "suspecticians" about the emotional development of children. Research on this problem is continuing with authorization and support by the California State Legislature and the California State Department of Education.

Many persons assisted in the research study and its implementation; among these were Carl A. Larson, Peter J. Tashnovian, Donald E. Kitch, Thomas A. Shellhammer, and Helen Heffernan, all of the California State Department of Education. Thomas W. Smith, Director of Research and Pupil Personnel Services, Covina Elementary Schools, helped with material on socioeconomic status and mental health. Nadine Lambert, Phyllis Van Vleet, Gilbert Whitney, and Konrad Fischer, research consultants in the present state research project on the problems of educating emotionally disturbed children, were of invaluable assistance.

Grateful acknowledgment is made to the California State Department of Education for permission to reproduce instruments and rating scales used in the research study and to revise chapters in a previous bulletin for this publication. Parts of Chapters 1 and 2 were published in the September, 1959, issue of *Exceptional Children* and used with the permission of the journal.

This book could not have been written without the help of the 271 California teachers who participated in the research study on which this book is based. Each contributed much time, effort, and work. This book is dedicated to them and other teachers of children.

Sacramento, California   E.M.B.

CONTENTS

xi

Contents

Early Identification of
Emotionally Handicapped
Children in School

Chapter 1

PREVENTION AND THE TASK AHEAD

This book describes one way of helping schools to be more effective in educating children with "emotional handicaps." The rationale of the helping process is essentially to call the schools' attention to the problem before the problem itself does, thereby permitting more successful intervention on behalf of the child.

What does *emotional handicap* mean and why use the term? It means children-in-school whose learning and behavior difficulties seem destined to result in school failure. The term *emotional* suggests that the child's difficulties do not lie primarily in a lack of learning capacity, in health or sensory handicaps; his relative potential for effective cognitive-affective functioning in school is good however this is determined. The term also implies that school failure is not taken lightly by children; their inability to do the things demanded of them in school are high priority irritants on tender egos. Whatever the causes of the initial difficulty, the term *emotional handicap* encompasses the circularity of failure to function in school and negative feelings about self.

Emotional handicap can be used interchangeably with *educationally handicapped,* or any other term suggesting a child with potential ability who is not making it in school. The handicap or disability referred to is exclusively school related and is not intended to be a clinical or medical diagnostic label nor does it mean a mild or moderate form of psychopathology.

Failure to function in school is not tantamount to failure in life but it comes perilously close in this day and age. Moreover, it appears that as we pitch headlong into the Industrial-Knowledge State, persons without educational competence will be able to muster only a few degrees of occupational or social freedom. They will be highly restricted in the kinds of jobs in which they can function and in the kinds of symbolic media from which they can process information. It is probable, therefore, that such groups will

3

contain greater numbers of malfunctioning or nonfunctioning citizens, including criminals, drug addicts, the mentally ill, the alcoholic, the drifter, the dependent, the accident prone, the unhappy, the lonely, and the poor.

The task, therefore, is to prevent a wastage of human beings by helping to make one of our key integrative systems, the school, a more effective system. Bringing the word *emotional* into the hallowed intellectual halls of learning is not suggesting that schools be anything other than they are or do anything other than they do. It does seem fairly clear that children are unable to neutralize their feelings about learning and about the tasks and values espoused by the school and the greater society. When they succeed in a meaningful task, they feel good. When they feel good about a task, they often succeed. The purpose of this process of early identification is not to hasten children to child guidance clinics as early as possible but to hasten them into more effective learning and behavior programs *in school*. The basic premise of the preventive effort discussed in this book rests on the notion that it is only in helping primary institutions such as the family, the school, health, recreation, and religious agencies to carry out their goals more effectively for more children that we prevent human failure.

However idealistic and wide-eyed we may be about prevention, families, communities, cities, and states are all overburdened by the vast numbers and the cost of caring for and helping functionally disturbed and inadequate persons. While it is true that certain types of patients or prisoners are helped by certain kinds of treatment, the mental health professionals are somewhat disheartened by what von Bertalanffy calls the *methodological helplessness of psychiatry* to come up with any significant therapeutic approaches to the problem.[145] In a short period of time, treatment for the emotionally disturbed or mentally ill has swung back and forth between drilling holes in the brain, electric shock, insulin shock, drugs, and talk, to name but a few approaches. So little of what is done to help the confused or disturbed individual seems to be effective it would seem almost mandatory that we look for preventive approaches.

Prevention is a word with many shades and dimensions of meaning. Somewhere in the history of the United States Public Health Service there is described a program to prevent yellow fever in the city of Philadelphia. The program consisted of repeated firings of a cannon from the steps of city hall. To many scientists of the day, this appeared to be too much of a shotgun approach. A few suggested the program lacked a precise plan for evaluating the results since no one was able to ascertain how many mosquitoes were killed by this bombardment.

Prevention as a concept has carried the opprobrium of being something that *blocked* a disease or a disorder. Its value rested on *not allowing something to happen*. Prevention in the context of this book is what one does to enhance or promote growth. It is what is done in some positive way to help each human animal to grow up to become the most creative, spontaneous, thoughtful, healthy human being he is capable of becoming.

To many, preventive goals are wild, starry-eyed, and too "cloud nineish" to make any operational sense. Some point to the specific magic of prevention in man's relationship to nasty viruses, bacteria, and protozoans. Smallpox *is* prevented by a nick on the arm, and polio by several shots. Little in the way of such magical nicks or shots exists for the prevention of living and learning disorders. Some beginnings have been made in this wilderness by Office of Economic Opportunity programs such as Project Head Start and Office of Education programs of compensatory education for disadvantaged children. The War on Poverty is an example of one direct assault on a large segment of a highly vulnerable population. Yet such programs hang by a thread in each succeeding congressional year.

One would not need to be a Sherlock Holmes or Hercule Poirot to suspect that there is more than a conceptual and research abyss in prevention. One can, if one wishes (and I do), make a good case for the existence of explicit and implicit societal resistances to the prevention of human failures. Delineating some of these antagonisms toward preventive programs which exist in all of us may help one understand the specific possibilities of success of programs in early identification.

Antagonisms Toward Preventive Programs

A common conception of prevention often obfuscates thinking and action, namely, that little can be accomplished short of major social overhaul. Prevention of functional emotional disorders is seen as the exclusive result of the abolition of injustice, discrimination, economic insecurity, poverty, slums and illness. To seek less is to attempt to fell a giant sequoia with a toy axe. Any effort, therefore, that is not aimed directly at major social change is viewed as an inadequate and inconsequential attack at the problem. A corollary of this notion is that prevention involves wheels within wheels within wheels. Thus, any possible action is perceived as if it were a combined luncheon check presented by an inexperienced waiter to a group of women at the end of an a la carte meal. The alleged magnitude of the complexities and the ungeared wheels within wheels perceived are also major deterrents to biological and social scientists who can, with little effort, find more digestible problems to define and solve. Other scientists who see some value in pursuing this kind of "elusive Pimpernel" search in vain for something akin to Archimides' lever with which the whole of the problem can be moved. Many believe one should concentrate on immediate needs such as the care, treatment and rehabilitation of mental patients. Such problems are real and specific. If one means to do anything in this field, "they" say, let's start with this problem. Small beginnings, however, need to be made on many fronts. There is a *need* and there is a *problem*. The need to care and treat the inadequate and the ill is a major concern, yet it is fairly obvious that all the king's horses and all the king's men will have little effect on the problem — how to reduce the development of inadequacy or illness in the first place.

A second and related phenomenon that influences preventive efforts in the mental health field is the high, often impregnable, fortress of personal privacy — the right and privilege of each person, and family, in a free society to mind his own business and have others mind theirs. If prevention of any kind includes early effective intervention in the lives of persons in the population at large, then the intervention must take place prior to such time as the person is singled out for special help. Where it can be shown that such intervention is necessary, indeed mandatory for the common good, as it is in automobile use, school attendance and physical hygiene and sanitation, acceptance may be given. Yet, in polio inoculations and water fluoridation, invasion of personal privacy is still a major issue. Our deepest values have historical roots in individualism although our frontier ancestors quickly discovered survival required giving up some privacy for health and safety.

Laws providing sanctions for intervention by an agency or person in the private life of an individual are therefore clearly and with sound reason limited to situations that endanger the life or health of the person or his neighbors. In essence, one can only stop minding one's own business and become one's brother's keeper when "brother" is in pretty sad shape. Nevertheless, few persons would be prepared to sacrifice the values of a free society on any nebulous, preventive altar.

Yet, some primary institutions are actually mobilized and authorized to help the family in a positive and potentially preventive manner. For example, the well-baby clinic and the public school are given informal and official sanction to interfere and meddle — the former, in relation to the child's health, the latter, in terms of the child's educational progress or lack of it. However, these institutions must also be alert to the dangers inherent in such sanctions. The school must find its leverage in its assigned task of educating children and carefully define and demonstrate the role of auxiliary services such as health examinations, psychological testing, and mental health consultation as necessary in carrying out this assignment. The health and educational progress of children represent to most parents important and highly significant achievements; almost always, there is a strong motivation to do whatever is necessary to work with the school or well-baby clinic in enhancing their child's health or educational success.

Another major social resistance to prevention, pointed out by Ruth Eissler, lies in the realm of the reduction of criminal and antisocial behavior:

> . . . modern society, with all its dazzling technological progress has
> not been able to protect itself from individual or mass aggression
> against property or life. Must we assume that this helplessness is acci-
> dental and has no psychological basis? If we take the standpoint that
> society needs its criminals in the same way as the mother of my de-
> linquent patient needed his delinquency, then we understand the ex-
> istence of two general tendencies. The first is the seduction of individ-
> uals into criminal acting-out. The second is the interference with or
> the prevention of anything which promises to prevent delinquency.[41]

One explanation advanced for this phenomenon is related to
cultural values in which success lies with virtue and failure with
sin. In a free society each person has equal opportunity with his
fellows to show his mettle as a conscientious, hard-working, and
therefore successful citizen. If he chooses not to be conscientious
and hard-working, he has only himself to blame for the consequences. Such competition in games, school work, business, and
life can only be perceived as successful for all when it is unsuccessful for some. As Don Alhambra sings it in *The Gondoliers:*

> In short, whoever you may be
> To this conclusion you'll agree
> When everyone is somebodee
> Then no one's anybodee.

To a great extent, the ritual of the television-western, in which
good wins over evil fair and square, celebrates this notion at least
once or twice each evening. On the other hand, increasing clinical
and research evidence supports the notion that those individuals
who find positive satisfactions and relationships in family, neighborhood, and school also find these satisfactions and relationships
as adults; and that those who find frustration, failure, and defeat
in these primary institutions also tend to be defeated in adulthood.
This unconscious sponsorship and enhancement of defeat and
alienation in and among groups of children and adolescents is
often spelled out in terms of pseudo-Darwinian theory.[73] Yet the
idea of equalitarianism is in our historical bones. How have we
come to place equality for all and excellence for all as one-dimen-
sional opposites? Gardner states the problem more succinctly:
"How can we provide opportunities and rewards for individuals

of every degree of ability so that individuals at every level will realize their full potentialities, perform at their best and harbor no resentment toward any other level?"[50]

Who Bells the Cat?

As a specific activity, prevention still has the major problem of interesting and involving members of the professions dealing with dependency, criminal behavior, alcoholism, and mental illness. Clinicians trained in treatment, rehabilitation, and adjunctive therapies in a one-to-one relationship naturally find this more rewarding than they find plunging into the misty arena of prevention. The physician is responsible for the health of his patient, particularly when such health is threatened. As Fox points out, "Curative medicine has generally had precedence over preventive medicine: people come to the doctor to be healed, and most practicing physicians still think of prevention as subsidiary to their main task which is to treat the sick. Though they subscribe intellectually to prevention, they really feel more at home when the disease has 'got going.'"[47] Often, the mental health worker, be he psychiatric technician, nurse, psychologist, social worker, or psychiatrist, is deeply impressed by the mountainous obstacles to effecting positive, healthful changes in clients or patients and consequently finds it difficult to comprehend how other less intensive types of experiences might have prevented the illness.

Yet, one is often surprised by the range, variety, and quality of human experiences and human relationships that can and do produce significant changes in personality. Sanford's experience and research lead him to conclude that marked and profound changes do occur in students during the college years:

> Some students undergo in the normal course of events changes of the same order as those brought about by psychotherapy. Not only may there be expansion and reorganization in the ego, with increased sophistication, broader perspective, increased flexibility of control but, also, there may be changes in the relations among the ego, the id, and the superego. The question is, what makes these changes occur and can be done deliberately to bring them about. There is a common notion that changes so profound as to involve the relations of id, superego, and go can be brought about after adolescence only by means

as thoroughgoing as psychoanalysis or deep psychotherapy. I'm suggesting that changes of a pretty fundamental kind can be brought about by regular educational procedures or by events, provided we know enough about what makes changes occur.[124]

In bringing prevention into the ken of the psychiatrist, clinical psychologist, or social worker, one may need to recognize and deal with the minimization or depreciation of change processes other than a depth peeling of defenses. Stevenson, in his study of direct instigation of behavioral changes in psychotherapy, finds that some patients often improve markedly when they have mastered a stressful situation or relationship and that by helping such patients manage a day to day problem, change is brought about.[135] In the early relationships of the mental health professions and the parents of retarded children, it was often assumed that being a parent of a retarded child necessitated intensive psychological help or mental health counseling. Yet, many such parents were more puzzled and distressed by a lack of information and skill in basic home management of the child and were often best helped by simple instruction in how to help retarded children learn to feed and dress themselves.

It is possible, as Sanford suggests, *that our overemphasis on individual therapy as a major community resource retards to some degree our interest in or our giving priority to prevention.* The fact is, primary prevention is the concern of all of our professions, but the responsibility of no one group. Much preventive gold can be mined from clinicians and therapists by encouraging them to translate their clinical experiences and knowledge into programs with preventive possibilities. Such translations, however, must be within a framework of what is operationally feasible within one of the "key integrative systems" of our society. Gardner Murphy may well be right: "The ultimate keys to the understanding of mental health will come, not through exclusive preoccupation with the pathological, but with the broader understanding of the nature of life and of growth. Perhaps the understanding of resonant health and joyful adaptation to life will help us to understand and formulate the issues regarding the prevention of mental disorder."[110]

Prevention of What?

Lastly, there is the knotty problem of defining the goals of prevention. Do such goals include the development of individuals who can more easily be helped by community resources, a reduction in hospitalized schizophrenics, or making persons more amenable to psychotherapy? If our purpose is the promotion of emotional robustness, what exactly does this mean and how can this goal be translated into specific, positive and, hopefully, measurable objectives of health? Dubos notes, "Solving problems of disease is not the same thing as creating health. . . . This task demands a kind of wisdom and vision which transcends specialized knowledge of remedies and treatments and which apprehends in all their complexities and subtleties the relation between living things and their total environment."[38] The lack of specificity as to what constitutes mental illness, plus the changing character of such illnesses, make this baseline difficult to define or use in evaluating programs. Yet, where living is equated with and therefore measured by degrees of illness rather than health, one can easily perceive the world as a giant hospital peopled by patients whose only health lies in discovering how sick they are. Nevertheless, reliable measures or indexes of health or illness of a community are the *sine qua non* of any preventive program.

A Framework for Primary Prevention

No single problem in primary prevention has a solution deserving of greater priority than the development of a platform or position from which one can begin to organize and act. One cannot exert leverage on any field of forces except from some fixed position. Without such a theoretical framework little can be done in developing hypotheses, testing them, and further developing or, if need be, abandoning them.

Primary prevention of living and emotional disorders is any specific biological, social, or psychological intervention that promotes or enhances the functional and emotional robustness or reduces the incidence and prevalence of functional or emotional illnesses in the population at large. In this framework, primary preventive programs are aimed at persons not yet separated from the general population and hopefully at interventions specific enough to be operationally defined and measured.

Measured how? along what dimensions? and by what value systems? To be sure, some types of primary prevention can be specified in relation to specific diseases or impairments. In such illnesses as phenylketonuria or pellagra psychosis, an appropriate diet initiated at an appropriate time may prevent some of the serious complications of the illness. Other types of disabilities, however, may come about as the cumulative effect of a myriad of interacting social and biological causes and be relatively uninfluenced by any single intervention. Yet, if one assumes that emotional robustness is built on the interactive elements of a healthy organism with enhancing life experiences, one must consider how one could increase those social forces in a community that help the population at large to cope with normal problems, rather than to defend against them, to deal with stress effectively, and to be less vulnerable to illness, including the emotional and functional disorders.

Almost all of us live our lives in the primary or key integrative social systems of our society. In our early life, these consist of home, school, social health, safety, and recreation systems. As we get older, work and political agencies come more strongly into the picture. Under normal biological and social conditions, we learn to function fairly adequately in these institutions. Occasionally for most of us, or more often for some of us, other agencies or services of a secondary nature are required: if ill, a hospital; if delinquent, a special school; if disturbed, a child guidance clinic. These are the services or agencies which attempt to help us when we are in temporary health or social trouble. When we come into this arena we are usually asking for help from physicians, attorneys, courts, pastoral counselors, social agencies, or special schools. The chances are rather good that our stay in these secondary agencies is only temporary and that we will soon return to life in the primary institutions. However, should our troubles increase, we may find ourselves living in institutions characterized by a singular lack of freedom or privacy, these are mental hospitals or prisons. As one moves from living in primary institutions to secondary or tertiary institutions, one gives up degrees of freedom until in the tertiary institutions few if any remain.

The point of all this for any society is to devise primary institutions which have sufficient flexibility and effectiveness to keep more and more citizens out of secondary or tertiary institutions. Children who fail in school have little choice but to seek help in secondary and eventually in tertiary institutions. Processes of early identification of such children are more apt to produce effective interventions since the problems of the children have not yet been set concretely. The procedure outlined in this book is only one way to help the school increase its flexibility and its educational potency for children beginning to flounder.

Prevention and the School

One of the major accomplishments of American public education has been the development and implementation of educational services for all children. Yet to many educators and lay persons this accomplishment is regarded with mixed feelings and some surprise. The expectations of most communities in America today are that all children of school age in the community will attend school. Diffused and interspersed with these expectations are values which tend to define education as a somewhat selective process in which only the able and willing can function. The money and effort spent in the education of the less able and often unwilling student is often regarded as necessary, but on a hierarchy of values, less necessary than other services.

Conflict of Values in the School

The continuous and dynamic mixture of these values creates a major psychic split in policy makers, school administrators, and teachers. Is the school and community responsible for the education of children who come to school resistant and antagonistic to the values of the school? Like marriage, education is a process which can only be accomplished with the consent of the learner. If some children do not "choose" to give such consent, can the school reasonably be asked to educate them? To what extent does the school act as a social irritant for the nonsuccessful learner?

Looking at the problem from a more positive point of view, can the school identify problem children early enough to plan successful curriculum and counseling programs for them? Can schools be equipped with staff and the inclination to deal with the beginnings of problems, rather than with the results of the problems? Is intervention in the life of a child who is not yet a problem, but is rapidly becoming one, acceptable in a free society?

The Strategic Position of the School

The school is seen as a logical place to immunize the child more vulnerable to emotional disorders. In actual practice, however, the school may face the Scylla of keeping emotionally handicapped children in school and educating them in some type of adjusted program or the Charybdis of sending them out into the community with little supervision, control, or guidance. Schools which accept the responsibility of educating the emotionally handicapped child have a legal and professional right to ask, "How do we do it?" The legal mandate of compulsory attendance for all children placed on the school district can only be implemented when the school has the professional know-how and staff to carry out the law and its intent.

One area of possible effective impact and strategic action by a society lies in early detection of the more vulnerable child followed by appropriate remedial steps. The school is an agency which has regular and continuous contact with a child and his family over a long period of time. Most teachers are well educated about the personality development of children and are professionally experienced in observing a variety of children under stress and ease. The teachers' day to day experience with a variety of normal behavior gives them an unequaled perspective for appraising inappropriate or deviant behavior. In addition, the school is an institution affecting all children and is usually seen by most families as positive and helpful.

How can the more vulnerable children be identified? Can the teacher be helped to screen, in an economical and productive manner, those children who are developing marked or severe emotional problems? This book will present a research study the aim of which was to answer these and other questions relating to helping teachers detect emotionally handicapped children early in their school life.

Chapter 2

THE WHYS AND WHEREFORE OF THE CONCEPT *EMOTIONALLY HANDICAPPED*

M OST DEFINITIONS, like Mt. Everest, are hazardous to attempt. The danger lies in the fact that when we use words to define abstract concepts we often become caught up in our own tautology. Living, as a process, seems to be made up of objects, events, and inner experiences which differ only in degree (with the possible exception of pregnancy). Until such time as some creative behavioral scientist comes up with a more precise symbol system, we will need to convey as best we can with words what we mean by *emotionally disturbed or handicapped,* and why we have gone through the trouble of defining this term and differentiating these children from others.

It is important to consider that any classification of children in school does exactly that — accentuates differences while keeping similarities constant. There is one overriding reason for going through the whole process of collecting and organizing data for the purpose of such differentiation: It is the hope that such classification will lead to some positive action or program on behalf of such children. If a school system considers it worthwhile to identify children with retarded mental development, children with hearing loss, or children with emotional handicaps, it must be prepared to do something positive on behalf of the children so identified. It therefore becomes necessary for diagnostic and classificatory systems to be useful to the system in which the classification is made. In the past, such differentiation was made primarily on medical or psychiatric models so that the results were more often translatable into medical or psychiatric action. A child with a serious emotional problem was studied diagnostically to determine if he had a primary behavior disorder, a reactive neurosis, a psychopathic personality, or a Bach fugue. These would be more meaningful tags if one were planning a medical or psychiatric

intervention. A school is not, however, a hospital. Its key personnel are teachers whose dreams, both night and day, consist of
visions such as, How do I manage this child? How do I teach him?
What is he prepared to learn? How do I get him to pay attention?
Therefore, the kinds of differentiations and classifications needed
by schools are those related to what schools can do to educate
children more effectively.

Magic Definitions

There are many definitions which crop up as magic phrases
to explain learning and/or behavior problems of children in
school. Benton points out that the concept of *minimal brain injury* seems to enjoy increasing popularity among psychoeduca-
tional workers:

> The term, as some psychologists and psychiatrists use it, not only
> does not have any direct reference to the condition of the brain—it
> has no reference at all to it. It refers to behavior—typically to behav-
> ioral deviations short of mental deficiency, psychosis or severe motor
> impairment, which are referable to brain damage. These relatively
> minor behavioral deviations are translated into a concept of relatively
> minor brain damge. This equating of behavior with the state of the
> brain has no foundation in fact. . . . The psychological examiner of
> children should abandon this rather preposterous habit. He can some-
> times make inferences regarding the presence or absence of brain
> damage in children. But, except in the case of low-grade defectives,
> he has no basis whatever for assessing the amount of brain damage
> in children.[6]

Man as a Mediating Organism

It seems clear that man's knowledge about himself strongly
suggests that his personality contains an active ingredient called
ego processes which serve to define, interpret, and mediate stimuli
from the inner and outer environments. Between stimulus and
response stands a scanning, organizing, protecting, selecting, and
acting component of the organism. By what magic then do we de-
prive "minimally brain-injured" or "neurologically impaired"
children of these human qualities? Certainly brain tissue destruc-
tion if present in any organism affects behavior most probably by
lowering the homeostatic resiliency of the organism. But this

lowered capacity to adapt may be managed in a variety of ways and result in a multitude of different behaviors. Let me suggest an analogous position in the so-called pure environmentally derived disorders. Conjure up a test to classify all emotionally disturbed children "rejected by their parents" at the .01 level of significance. Because all these children have a common etiology, parental rejection, let us classify them as having the same learning and behavior problems. But, you say, these children cannot all have the same educational needs and problems. Consider then for a moment why rejected children cannot be so classified but so-called minimally brain-injured can.

It seems probable that when we separate a group of distractable, hyperactive, perceptually impaired, figure-ground-confused, confabulated children, there are many roads by which each child travelled to this destination. Many of us have sat in on clinical teams of physicians, psychologists, nurses, and teachers loaded with neurological, EEG, and developmental histories trying to decide whether or not a particular child did or did not have cerebral disrythmia or lesions. Have we considered the "why" of such deliberations? What "truth" is revealed by a six-to-four vote deciding that the child has "minimal brain injury" or a seven-to-three vote that he has not? Or if drugs are indicated for hyper-reactivity, does a positive or negative vote affect the prescription either way?

There is little doubt that brain or nervous tissue can be injured or damaged and that such damage can affect the learning and behavior of human beings. It is also probable, as many obstetricians and pediatricians have pointed out, that almost every baby suffers some brain injury at birth as a result of the physical strain and pressure changes during the birth process. If minimal brain injury were a unitary, singular, and exclusive cause of specific learning and behavior disorders, I suspect we would be dealing with a highly selective and unique group of *Homo sapiens*.

The notion of special educational programs for children with special problems has been based on what kinds of educational intervention can best help the child learn, rather than on any specific medical etiology, be it organically or environmentally derived. We educate mentally retarded children in separate groups because they lack the ability to handle abstract symbols with the speed and effectiveness of others. I know of no programs where such children are grouped on the basis of medical or psychosocial etiology of the retardation. On the other hand, some children with obvious brain injury, as in cerebral palsy, who show normal learning potential should be educated with their normal peers.

There is probably as much heterogeneity in the personalities and educational needs of children diagnosed as "minimally brain-injured" as those diagnosed "neurotic." In all cases what the teacher will be striving to change are the mediating or informa-tion-processing components of the child's personality — those aspects of the child's self which interpret, modify, utilize, organize, and bind information within self.

If behavioral diagnosticians insist on getting into the school game, they must find ways of helping teachers and parents make effective decisions about children in the context of the social sys-tem of the school. There is no objection to placing "suspected brain injury" in the array of facts about a child; there is objection to its utilization as a magic phrase which reduces the individual child to an autonomic nervous system and helps remove the more sticky human learning problems from messing up a neat simple "solution."

The Many Faces of *Emotionally Handicapped*

Certainly *emotionally handicapped* doesn't provide the teacher with anything more useful than *minimal brain damage*. Its use, however, is necessary to provide a basis for describing children who need extra help and differentiate them from other children who may already get such help in other special education pro-grams. Not only does one need a scientific, understandable defini-tion of the term prerequisite for research action, but one needs to be mindful of legal, financial, legislative, operational, and paren-tal perceptions of any definition. If schools receive extra funds for educating emotionally handicapped children, an auditor in a de-partment of finance will want to know which children are legally entitled to consideration as an emotionally handicapped child and why there are differences in relative numbers of such children among school districts. A school administrator will want to know how he may differentiate among the children who have problems those who are emotionally handicapped. A parent might well ask, "There have been times in my life when I could have been called emotionally disturbed. Does this mean I would be a member of the group called emotionally handicapped?"

The complexity and difficulty of defining are increased by attempting to define the beginning of a process and not the ending — the sniffles and sneezes, as it were, rather than the full fever. One can communicate with some success the pronounced symptoms of a condition in which the characteristics are often sufficiently marked to be observed. In trying to differentiate early symptoms one runs the risk of defining characteristics which are more or less true of almost everyone.

The Use of the Term "Emotionally Handicapped"

Our language, with its subject-predicate structure, tends to define as black or white, qualities which are seldom neither. The use of the term *emotionally handicapped,* for example, in place of *emotionally disturbed, socially maladjusted* or other similar terms is designed to reduce somewhat the semantic problems inherent in delineations of states of emotion. The term *handicap* has a more lasting and persistent quality; disturbances are often seen as transitory or temporary. The use of *disturbance* is usually indicative of the acting out, overtly aggressive child; therefore, one tends to perceive emotional problems as resulting in one type of behavior. In addition, the term *emotionally disturbed* is often associated with a formal psychological or psychiatric appraisal; *emotionally handicapped* has less of the black or white connotation of a disease and is more illustrative of the degree nature of emotional problems. Lastly, the term *emotionally handicapped* is often more realistically descriptive of the disability and is not an attempt to gild the lily. Part of the problem, however, of any attempt at an adequate description or definition of the term, lies in the difficulty in cognitively describing the complex affective state, called emotion. Indeed, one dictionary states, "emotion is virtually impossible to define except in terms of conflicting theories."[42]

Feelings and emotions are synonymous to most persons. Both are regarded as vague, misty things, highly variable and situational. In part this may be a result of not having any measurement devices or techniques comparable to those employed in measuring intellect, sight, hearing acuity, or academic achievement. Unlike sensory, intellectual, or physical handicaps which exhibit themselves along a single dimension primarily as a deficit, emotional handicaps can only be inferred from behavior which may be overly aggressive, inappropriate, overly withdrawn, or combinations of these. One can, for example, be just as handicapped by an overabundance of emotion as by a lack of emotion. One can be said to be emotionally handicapped by demonstrating "normal" emotional behavior at inappropriate times, as one can show apparently "normal" grief at the death of a loved one — for twenty years. One may consistently develop strong and overwhelming emotions in one relationship and be relatively self-contained in another. In addition, one can be economically successful because of an emotional handicap or in spite of such a handicap, just as one can be a blatant failure without benefit of neurosis or emotional conflict.

Handicap as Restriction of Choices

The definition which would be of greatest use to the school would be one which is operationally related to the possibility of early detection and intervention in the school. One is trying to define and predict which children in the school population will be markedly handicapped by emotional problems as adolescents or adults. In this sense, perhaps, the term *handicapped* can best be understood as an increasing restriction of choice or alternatives of behavior. To be able to choose behavior freely and responsibly rather than being driven by impulses or emotion is a sign of healthy emotional development. When one's choices are severely limited by emotional lacks or injunctions, one's behavior can be regarded as handicapped. The reduction of possible behavioral alternatives serves to reduce further the individual's degrees of freedom in social and educational endeavors. In addition, this reduced maneuverability or inflexibility in a changing world of mobile peers and events increases an individual's susceptibility to behavior difficulties and interpersonal friction. The emotionally handicapped child is therefore circumscribed as one having a higher degree of vulnerability to behavior problems and one who, as an adult, will exhibit this vulnerability in general health problems, poor interpersonal relationships, inability to function sexually or economically, inability to profit from experience or lead a happy life. In its more pervasive form this vulnerability may lead to psychosis, neuroses, suicide, repetitive automobile accidents, alcoholism, narcotic addiction, or criminal behavior. One can therefore describe the emotionally handicapped child as a child who is unable or will be unable to take the slings and arrows of life without caving in, becoming immobilized, or exploding.

Definition of Emotionally Handicapped Children

In terms of their visibility to the teacher, emotionally handicapped children can be perceived as children who demonstrate one or more of the following characteristics *to a marked extent* and *over a period of time:*

1. *An inability to learn which cannot be explained by intellectual, sensory, or health factors.* An inability to learn is perhaps the single most significant characteristic of emotionally handicapped children in school. Such nonlearning may be manifested as an inability to profit from experience as well as inability to master skill subjects. The nonlearner seldom escapes recognition. Achievement tests often confirm what the teacher has long suspected. If all other major causative factors have been ruled out, emotional conflicts or resistances can be ruled in.

2. *An inability to build or maintain satisfactory interpersonal relationships with peers and teachers.* It isn't getting along with others that is significant here. Satisfactory interpersonal relations refers to the ability to demonstrate sympathy and warmth toward others, the ability to stand alone when necessary, the ability to have close friends, the ability to be aggressively constructive, and the ability to enjoy working and playing with others as well as

enjoying working and playing by oneself. In most instances, children who are unable to build or maintain satisfactory interpersonal relationships are most visible to their peers. Teachers are also able to identify many such children after a period of observation.

3. *Inappropriate types of behavior or feelings under normal conditions.* Inappropriateness of behavior or feeling can often be sensed by the teacher and peer groups. "He acts funny," another child may say. The teacher may find some children reacting disproportionately to a simple command such as "Please take your seat." What is appropriate or inappropriate is best judged by the teacher using her professional training, her daily and long-term observation of the child, and her experience working and interacting with the appropriate behavior of large numbers of normal children.

4. *A general, pervasive mood of unhappiness or depression.* Children who are unhappy most of the time may demonstrate such feelings in expressive play, art work, written composition, or in discussion periods. They seldom smile and usually lack a *joie de vivre* in their schoolwork or social relationships. In the middle or upper grades a self-inventory is usually helpful in confirming suspicions about such feelings.

5. *A tendency to develop physical symptoms, pains, or fears associated with personal or school problems.* This tendency is often noted by the school nurse and parent. Illness may be continually associated with school pressures or develop when a child's confidence in himself is under stress. In some cases, such illnesses or fears may not be apparent to the teacher; peers, however, are often aware of children who are sick before or after tests or have headaches before recitations. Speech difficulties which may be the symptoms of emotional distress are usually most visible to the teacher and parent.

The significant characteristics of children indicating a need for closer scrutiny by a teacher are inability to learn, unsatisfactory interpersonal relationships, inappropriate behavior, unhappiness, and repetitive illness.

These characteristics can, of course, be said to be true of all children to some degree at different times. There seems to be little likelihood of bypassing the "how much is too much" issue in any descriptive attempt at separating the more vulnerable child from others. A more satisfactory analysis can be made by assessing classes by some standardized process in which perceptions by teacher, peers, and self can be combined. Such a procedure has been employed and is reported in some detail later in the book. .

Differentiating Between Difference and Pathology

A major caution in the use of descriptive definitions of the behavior of children to infer causation is the problem of differentiating incipient pathology from normal behavioral deviation. Marked differences in behavior are noted in children who *choose* to behave somewhat idiosyncratically. Perhaps the key in differentiating the child whose behavioral deviation is caused by emotional problems and the child whose behavior is socially different is one of determining the source of the behavior. The behavior of the emotionally handicapped child is, to the extent of his handicap, not a matter of choice but of necessity. The degrees of behavioral freedom for the emotionally handicapped individual may be restricted by internal conflicts or by a lack of inner controls. In any case, strange, unconventional, or deviant behavior cannot in and of itself be regarded as a sign of an emotional handicap. The film *Shyness** contains an excellent illustration of the difficulty in inferring causes solely on the basis of observed behavior. Of the three children in the film referred to as being shy and withdrawn, only one could be said to be emotionally handicapped. On the other hand, Clare, in *Feelings of Hostility,*† although a successful and competent business woman, had pervasive feelings of loneliness and hostility toward men. Her overt behavior would hardly suggest the depth of intensity of her problems.

---

*Shyness, 16 mm. Sound. McGraw-Hill Book Co., 330 W. 42nd St., New York 36, N. Y.

†*Feelings of Hostility,* 16 mm. Sound. McGraw-Hill Book Co., 330 W. 42nd St. New York 36, N. Y.

Relationship of Definition to Personality Theory

Teachers with the help of peer and self-perceptions are in the best position to act as "suspectician." They may note children whose behavioral temperature is rising or those who show no normal reaction under stress. In the final analysis a diagnosis of emotional handicap rests on an inference of motivation of behavior based on personality dynamics. The energy source of the behavior is the basic sought-after ingredient. Is the behavior motivated primarily by transient environmental forces or by personality factors?

Personality is at best an inference of the dynamic organization of needs, motivations, and drives of the child. Behavior can be regarded as an interaction of personality and environmental factors mediated or defined by personality processes commonly called the self or ego. The driving forces in personality are often well masked from the observer as well as from the organism. The root of the word personality, *persona,* had reference to a theatrical mask.[42] In any case, appraising children to distinguish normal behavioral differences from incipient emotional pathology must be based on inferences relating to an inference of personality dynamics and relationships.

What kinds of observations about personality would be most helpful in making inferences or professional guesses as to causes of deviant behavior? To the teacher or principal, the behavior of the emotionally disturbed child will be "driven" behavior, i.e. the energy level of the child will seem to be inappropriate or disproportionate to the task or situation. The child may play with an intensity and frenzy which bodes ill to anyone or anything interfering. He may be unable to obey rules in school even after repeated and varied contacts with accepting or disciplining adults. The emotionally handicapped child has relatively little freedom to adapt. He is often regarded as especially stubborn and recalcitrant since the usual influence techniques of reward, punishment, recognition, praise, etc., are relatively ineffective in influencing his behavior. Or he may be regarded as a "real pushover," i.e. influenced almost completely by the wishes and ideas of others. Here the self or ego may be regarded as underdeveloped as compared to other emotionally handicapped children who are immobilized or driven by inner conflicts.

In healthy emotional development, the individual has sufficient ego strength to vary his *persona* appropriately in accordance with the situation and at the same time to maintain a sufficient core of self in all situations. For example, one is not expected to be the same at church as at a party, yet the differences cannot be so radical as to involve complete changes in personality.

The emotionally handicapped child seems not to profit from experience and appears to behave in an automatic, repetitive pattern. His ideas about the teacher or his peers may be somewhat distorted. For example, he may see the teacher as a punishing, threatening adult, and classmates as unfair competitors constantly outdoing him in reading, drawing, or sports. One would infer that in the relatively unhandicapped child, behavior is motivated by forces at relatively greater levels of awareness; conversely, behavior motivated primarily by unconscious forces would be characteristic of the emotionally handicapped child. Thus, as Kubie notes:

> . . . . the essence of normality is flexibility, in contrast to the freezing of behavior into patterns of unalterability which characterize every manifestation of the neurotic process whether in impulses, acts, thoughts, or feelings. Whether or not a behavioral event is free to change depends not on the quality of the act itself, but upon the nature of the constellation of forces that has produced it . . . Wherever unconscious forces play the preponderant role in this constellation . . . then behavior . . . is subject to a tendency to automatic and obligatory repetition.[89]

While the emotionally handicapped child might be characterized as having a greater load of problems and conflicts, in some cases he may appear to have little conflict, little concern with others, and little if any conscience. Such individuals deal with emotional tensions by rapid action rather than by internalizing the subsequent anxiety. Whereas most children develop a core of self or ego processes which mediate forces in the environment and in the organism, some children may have a deficiency of such processes. This may be manifest by an absence of normal anxieties about behavior or misbehavior and a pattern of behavior which is stereotyped, childish, and relatively uninhibited. A large number of these emotionally handicapped individuals are found among juvenile delinquents.

The Degree of Emotional Handicap

Emotional handicaps may be displayed in transient, temporary, pervasive, or intensive types of behavior. To complete the definition, it would be necessary to establish a continuum in which the degree of handicap can be perceived and perhaps estimated, especially as it relates to possible action by the school. One could begin such a continuum with (1) children who experience and demonstrate the normal problems of everyday living, growing, exploration, and reality testing. There are some, however, who can be observed as (2) children who develop a greater number and degree of symptoms of emotional problems as a result of normal crisis or stressful experiences, such as death of father, birth of sibling, divorce of parents, brain or body injury, school entrance, junior high school entrance, or puberty. Some children move beyond this level of adjustment and may be described as (3) children in whom moderate symptoms of emotional maladjustment persist to some extent beyond normal expectations but who are able to manage an adequate school adjustment. The next group would include (4) children with fixed and recurring symptoms of emotional maladjustment who can with help profit by school attendance and maintain some positive relationships in the school setting. Beyond this are (5) children with fixed and recurring symptoms of emotional difficulties who are perhaps best educated in a residential school setting or temporarily in a home setting.

Chapter 3

PROBLEMS IN EARLY IDENTIFICATION OF EMOTIONALLY HANDICAPPED CHILDREN

A DULTS AND CHILDREN usually have a nostalgic and pleasing remembrance of things magical. In most adults there lingers the magic of childhood omnipotence and the feeling that science and technology are in some way related to doing what seems impossible. Consider what can be done by the flick of a switch, the turn of a dial, or the push of a button. Science, to some extent, has indeed provided man with "magic" solutions to highly technological problems. It is not surprising, therefore, to find human beings seeking sleight-of-hand solutions for complex social or personal problems. Such attitudes may be most unrealistic and unproductive of magic solutions when the problem is complex, where little scientific knowledge regarding possible solutions is available, and where the problem concerns human personality. No problem is at present less subject to solution through necromancy or magic spells than the antisocial and asocial behavior of individuals in this society.

The Magic of the School

The search for a kind of psychological penicillin by which personality problems and their associated disabilities might be prevented has been and continues to be particularly intriguing. This search generally leads to the public school as the agency with the greatest potential for providing the needed immunization. Public school services are available to all the children in the community; public schools employ professional personnel educated to understand the personality development of children; the relationship of the school to its children is a natural and positive one; teachers have opportunity to work with parents; teachers observe children over a longer period of time and in a greater variety of situations than persons in any other profession; and schools normally employ specialists to assist in providing services to the more vulnerable

28

child and his family. All this is true in varied degrees and qualities. It is not surprising then for professional and lay individuals concerned about the mental health of future citizens to look to the school as perhaps one avenue for reducing the rate of psychological morbidity in our population. One of the most common and specific requests made of the school is to identify emotionally handicapped children early and to provide the help they need in the school or community. However, the effectiveness of such programs rests on a number of implicit theoretical assumptions.

The Effect of Early Identification

One basic assumption is that if a child with a developing emotional disorder can be detected early, he can be helped most economically and effectively. Although the truth of this assumption seems logical, its psychological or scientific validity needs to be pinpointed. Stevenson,[136] for example, discusses a variety of assumptions, still unproved, related to the supposed greater plasticity and malleability of the child over the adult. It may not always be true that the younger an individual is, the more economical and effective his treatment. For example, some psychotherapists who are reluctant to treat adolescents feel that the results are more effective and lasting if treatment is started at a later time.

A study of children identified and helped early was made in the Cambridge-Somerville areas of Massachusetts.[116] In this study 650 children, ages nine to eleven, all of whom were showing problem behavior in school or in the neighborhood, were divided into two comparable groups. One group received the services of nine trained professional persons for a period of eight years (1938 to 1945). During these eight years, the service teams studied the children, counseled the families, and applied their professional skill and training to prevent delinquent behavior by the children. The other group of 325 children did not receive any special help or counsel. Despite the extenuating circumstances and difficulties of the project, especially during the war years, Witmer and Tufts concluded:

> . . . . this experiment seems to indicate that the provision of the kind of friendly guidance and other service the C.S.Y.S. [Cambridge-Somerville Youth Study] afforded will not reduce delinquent acts or

keep chronic delinquency from developing . . . . The chief importance of the Cambridge-Somerville Youth Study, so far as evaluation
is concerned, is its use of a control group for checking results. Had this ⎤
been lacking, much greater claims for the effectiveness of the program ⎟
as a delinquency prevention measure might have been made . . . . ⎦
It was only when the delinquency records of the treatment and control groups were compared that the inability of the study to prevent
or reduce delinquency was revealed.[153]

There is, however, a valuable lesson to be learned by this
evaluation study. One is to avoid blanketing all kinds of "friendly
guidance and other services" under one roof and assuming that
whatever was happening to the experimental children was the
same experience to each child. Indeed, it could have been entirely
possible for some children in the experimental group to be helped
a great deal but their progress lost in the total statistical comparison. That this may have happened is indicated by further research
on the Cambridge-Somerville children, now adults, by the Mc-
Cords and Zola.[104] They found that, as adults, the court records of
the boys who had received treatment did not differ significantly
from the control boys; nor did the number of counselors, length of
treatment by first counselor, or total length of treatment seem to
show any qualitative differences. However, when the children were
separated on the basis of intensity of contact with any counselor,
it was found that those seen at least every week had a significantly
smaller incidence of criminality. Other factors which were significantly related to the reduction of criminality were age at which
treatment was begun and sex of counselor at the adolescent period.
The research findings of this study corroborated the general in-
effectiveness of those forms of counseling which consisted in family
assistance plus infrequent interaction with the boy. However, the
findings strongly suggest that frequent counseling contact with a
predelinquent child — particularly if begun when the child is
under ten, or by a female counselor after the boy has reached
adolescence — may effectively prevent criminality.

Other studies similar to the Cambridge-Somerville Youth
Study have produced positive results. For example, the reduction
of delinquency among Jewish minors in New York City when the
overall rate of delinquency was increasing was justifiably attri-

buted to the comprehensive program of psychological outpatient clinic facilities for psychotherapy and in-patient treatment centers developed by the Jewish Board of Guardians.[99] As Bovet points out, "The suggestion that this organization, the Jewish Board of Guardians, has contributed to the remarkable diminution of child delinquency in the Jewish community of New York is very possibly correct."[14]

Visibility of Developing Emotional Handicaps

A second assumption implicit in any school program for early identification of children with emotional difficulties is that personality disorders in adulthood are the result of a progressively developing condition *visible* in children's personalities and behaviors. Indeed, the recognition of normal personality growth, to say little of its measurement, is a problem of which the surface has only been scratched. Where normal behavior is equated with average behavior it may be difficult to differentiate the child who is different from the child who it basically ill. Therefore, any appraisal of children with suspected emotional handicaps must differentiate between behavior pathology and the wide range of normal behavior. Jahoda[78] and other professional workers in mental health have emphasized that the criteria for mental health must be such that they do not automatically exclude everything but average behavior. To complicate this matter further, one can equate modal or average behavior with normal behavior but not necessarily with healthy behavior. For example, such disabilities as the common cold or dental caries cannot be regarded as a healthy state despite their vast prevalence.

Value Differences in Appraising Behavior

Another problem in identifying children with serious personality difficulties is that the same behavior may be interpreted as having different meanings under different circumstances and at different times. What is considered maladjustment in one phase of development may be considered normal in another. For example, a boy who is being hostile and rebellious toward his parents when he is eleven years old may be considered a problem until he reaches the age of thirteen when he finds himself in a peer group where hostility and rebellion against adults is expected behavior. As has often been pointed out, cultural and subcultural values tend to circumscribe the definition of mental illness and normality. Temporal change in values in our own culture have also affected our concept of normality. Whyte,[151] for example, describes as an emergent social value the belief in the group as the moving force in our society. To belong to the group and to work well with a group is behavior which is seen as good, i.e. normal behavior. The rugged individualist of the early years of the century would undoubtedly be perceived differently under the present concepts of normal or different behavior.

Often, one may observe a child who seems to be experiencing little difficulty until a psychological crisis initiates what appears to be an unexpected eruption. Management of emotional difficulties may be possible under the protective environment of a school, but environmental changes may trigger a coiled spring. For example, a study of high school students who became psychotic showed that some of them made excellent school records but ran into difficulty almost immediately after graduation.[17] The progress of a slow-learning child might well be within normal limits in the earlier years of elementary school, but may fall off sharply in the fourth or fifth grades when reading and arithmetic skills become the *sine qua non* of school success.

Effect of Past Experiences of Observer

The past experiences and unconscious conflicts of adults undoubtedly play a large role in determining which behavior is perceived as normal or abnormal. Adults who have had problems involving authority figures may be more sensitive to children who elicit authority-related problems. Some adults are upset by boys who appear to act effeminate or overly athletic. Others are more upset by children who don't work or prefer other interests than the schoolwork presented to them. Early studies by Wickman[152] and others which seemed to indicate a lack of congruity between teachers and mental health experts in evaluating problem behavior have been negated by recent studies which indicate a close relationship between the two perceptions. For example, it was found in the present study that teachers perceived as emotionally disturbed or maladjusted about the same children seen as emotionally disturbed by psychologists and psychiatrists.

In addition to the problem of determining what it is that is to be evaluated, one needs to know how early is "early" in evaluating a child's mental health. Is early recognition often too late, too costly, or too ineffective if it is made after the child has completed the fourth grade? What should schools attempt by way of early recognition of mental health problems? Which factors are most important in helping teachers to accept the role of "suspectician" comfortably and understandably? Does the process of identification carry with it the seeds by which the identified are helped? Are school systems and teachers able, realistically, to undertake a program designed for early identification and correction?

Some research on these questions has been done. The next chapter will present some of the findings of such research.

Chapter 4

THE DIRECTION AND TRENDS OF
PAST RESEARCH

I T IS PERHAPS NOT surprising to find only a paucity of major research studies on the problem of early identification of emotionally handicapped children in school. Among the first, however, was a study by Olson[114] of 1,537 first grade children in the Minneapolis public schools. The children were rated by experienced raters on a Behavior Problem Record — a rating scale developed and used by Haggerty, Wickman, and others. Olsen noted that grades in which pupils had the highest average ability tended to have a lower problem tendency score, that there were significant differences in the number of problem children among schools, and that the overage group of children in each grade showed the greatest amount of problems. Olson also found the relationship between achievement and problem tendencies to be negative, i.e. the lower the achievement the higher the problem tendency, or the higher the achievement the lower the problem tendency.

A Study of Multiple Indices

Ten years later, Rogers[121] set out to determine what proportion of Columbus, Ohio school children were showing evidences of poor mental health. His methodology included the following steps: (1) developing several objective criteria indicative of maladjustment or of influences causing maladjustment, (2) applying the criteria to the normal classroom group, and (3) identifying as maladjusted those children who were selected by several of the criteria.

The nine indices used by Rogers and his co-workers were chronological age, mental age, reading achievement, school failures, truancy, behavior scale ratings, personal index or California Test of Personality, a "Guess Who Game," and observer ratings. Reading achievement was used twice, once in comparison to mental age and again in comparison to the median achievement of the class. If a child was found to be significantly different from his group in any one of the indices, he was considered a "misfit" in that index. For example, a child who differed from the median age of his classroom group by more than one year was considered a misfit in chronological age. If his mental age was more than one year below or two above the median of the class, he was considered a misfit in mental age. Not all the nine indices could be applied at all grade levels. However, ratings for at least six of them were obtained on approximately 1,500 of the 2,000 children in this study.

After clinical studies of some of the children who were selected on the basis of four or more indices, Rogers concluded that the method actually screened those who were sufficiently maladjusted to make them excellent candidates for jails, state hospitals, divorce courts, and relief agencies within a few years. According to Rogers, each of the indices might be fallible or roughly indicative of some aspect of a child's adjustment; when taken together, however, he felt they provided a sound base for evaluating a child's future mental health and adjustment.

Rogers found that 12 per cent of the children studied showed evidence of poor mental health, and another 30 per cent showed a moderate degree of poor adjustment. He also found that there were three times as many boys as girls with serious mental health problems; that children in the fifth grade were the most maladjusted; that children in the higher socioeconomic neighborhoods had the fewest serious mental health problems, and that the child who was most like his group was least likely to present mental health problems. Some of the findings of Rogers' study indicated that there were differences in the degree of maladjustment of children in the different schools. He expressed his reaction by concluding his study with the following questions: "Are there discernible differences in educational policy which might account for the fact that in one school problems tend to increase and in another school they tend to decrease? Does this finally indicate that the school is a very potent force in creating and controlling maladjustment?" As is the case with most questioners, Rogers goes on to answer his questions as follows:

> There seems to be evidence from this study that educational poli-
> cies serve to create and increase mental health problems or to prevent

and decrease them . . . . Educational policies and procedures, in other words, have direct and potent influence on the mental health of the children . . . . It becomes clear that a suitable program of mental health in the schools cannot be something extraneous to the educational structure, but must be an integral part of administrative and classroom policies and procedures if it is to be effective.

Identification Using Teachers, Peers, and Self-ratings

Approximately ten years later, Ullmann[144] surveyed the nature and extent of the mental health problems presented by a group of children in the ninth grade of a public school system. He was also interested in finding out to what extent the judgments of teachers could be relied upon as a means of identifying children who needed psychological assistance. Another question Ullmann wanted to answer was, To what extent are children who have been identified as maladjusted by the teacher the same as those who would be considered maladjusted by their classmates? He found a high correlation between the judgments of teachers and clinicians, and concluded that teachers and mental hygienists are at present much closer together in their judgments of the behavior problems of children than perhaps earlier studies had noted.

Ullmann obtained six kinds of information for each of the 810 pupils studied to determine each student's emotional adjustment. The information used included (1) ratings by teachers of the adjustment level of the child, (2) rating by teachers on a forced choice test of pupil adjustment, (3) the self-score on the California Test of Personality, (4) the social score on the California Test of Personality, (5) the basic difficulties score on the Youth Inventory, and (6) a sociometric rank converted to a standard score. In comparing the results of his study with those of the studies done by Wickman in 1927 and by Rogers in 1940, Ullmann found the per cent of severe maladjustment to be 8 compared to Rogers' 12 and to Wickman's 7. On the basis of the results on the Youth Inventory, Ullmann found that boys tended to resolve their problems outwardly and were concerned with doing something actively about life's situations as a means of releasing tension, while girls were more preoccupied inwardly with their feelings and their symptoms. Ullmann also found that teachers' ratings of adjustment showed a much closer relationship to sociometric ratings than to scores on personality tests. In using the teachers' appraisal of the adjustment status of children, Ullmann found that their ratings were more accurate when the teachers were not functioning under anxiety or pressure. He also noted that increasing the emphasis upon the use of data which were available to the teacher had the effect of increasing the breadth and depth of the teachers' understanding of the child.

This study and others indicate that teacher ratings, self-descriptive data, and peer ratings when combined give the clearest, most comprehensive, and economical picture of the adjustment status of children. Teacher ratings were found to be better predictors of maladjusted children when the resultant behavior was manifested overtly or acted out; self-descriptive data appeared to be better for evaluating that aspect of maladjustment which had to do with feelings, attitudes, and inner tensions of self.

A Study of Children Referred by Teachers

Another study[33] of children referred by teachers for mental health services found that approximately 11 per cent of the school population was moderately or severely emotionally handicapped. Of this number, roughly two boys for every one girl were referred. In some school districts of this county as many as 35 per cent of the children enrolled were included as "emotionally disturbed" while in others, only 5 per cent of the total enrollment were referred. There was a consistently smaller percentage of emotionally handicapped children at the kindergarten age level, and a slight increase in the eighth grade. It was also found that a high percentage of the children who were referred were enrolled in special training classes for mentally retarded.

The Santa Barbara teachers used the terms *withdrawn* and *fearful* frequently in their descriptions of some emotionally handicapped children and did not seem to overlook nonaggressive children in their referrals. Whether teachers are at present more sensitive to problems relating to passive, withdrawing types of behavior or more aware of the present climate of professional functioning remains to be seen.

Studies of Delinquents

There are a number of studies which deal more specifically with early identification of predelinquents. *Delinquency* is a legal term designating children or adolescents who have violated laws. Not all delinquents can be said to be emotionally handicapped in terms of the definition proposed in Chapter 2. A recent work by Kvaraceus and others[92] contains a comprehensive discussion of the etiology of delinquency including the extent to which emotional factors are involved in such behavior. There is little doubt that a great proportion of juvenile delinquents have a marked degree of emotional disturbance and could be classified as emotionally handicapped. However, it should be kept in mind that *delinquency* is primarily a legal term while *emotional disturbance* is an inferred, descriptive one.

In a monumental study by the Gluecks,[56] five hundred delinquents were compared with five hundred nondelinquents similar in age, IQ, ethnic origin, and residence in underprivileged neighborhoods. The Gluecks discovered that five factors could be used for predicting eventual delinquency. These were (1) discipline of boy by father, (2) supervision of boy by mother, (3) affection of father for boy, (4) affection of mother for boy, and (5) cohesiveness of family. Although these factors may be difficult to define or assess accurately, their use by trained investigators seems to have been fruitful.[56,57] However, teachers' use of these factors for the purpose of identifying delinquents has many limitations. First, the appraisal of families and of such highly abstract states as affection, supervision, discipline, and cohesiveness would present problems of reliability and validity of observation and inference; indeed the definition of love is in itself a major undertaking of some duration. To make such an appraisal, the teacher would have to spend some time in the home of the child and be prepared to work through the facade which the family would undoubtedly produce for the teacher's benefit.

Glueck, in a refinement of her earlier study demonstrated a way of discriminating between true delinquents and pseudo-delinquents. This, the paper suggests, would be helpful to school personnel faced with a baffling array of behavioral difficulties "and who wish to know whether they are dealing with children who already are or who are likely soon to become delinquents."[54] I would submit that as far as school people are concerned, this kind of discrimination has no "critical action" possibilities since what teachers want to know about children with behavior problems are mainly how to teach and manage them in the classroom. Discrimination between delinquents and pseudo-delinquents might be extremely useful to probation officers and judges who because of the state of the art have to make professional guesses on whether or not a particular delinquent act is a unique or uncommon prank or the beginning of serious antisocial behavior.

It is most important therefore in any program for early identification that the data collected be data ordinarily collected by the system itself, that it be useful in doing something to make the child more effective in the system, and that it be related to the goals and processes of the system, in this case, the school.

There are some professional and lay persons who question the wisdom of a program of early identification, especially where the identification entails a prediction of mental illness or delinquency. This kind of early "stigmatization" has arisen from time to time in connection with Glueck's Social Prediction Scale which attempts to predict delinquency at school entrance utilizing assessments of such factors as (1) supervision of boy by mother, (2) discipline of boy by mother, (3) cohesiveness of family, (4) recreational preferences, (5) attitude toward school. It has been suggested that the civil rights of students and their families may be infringed by such procedures, especially those who have high delinquency prediction scores but turn out not to be delinquent (false positives). Others suggest that in some cases children may turn out to be delinquent only because someone predicted it. As J. R. Lowell suggested, "Don't ever prophesy—unless ye know for sure."

The excellent and extensive research of the Gluecks in attempting to prevent delinquency has had enthusiastic coming-out parties but little in the way of meaningful collaborative proposals with schools and communities. In part, the problem is that the collection of the data would require a large cadre of trained nonschool personnel, would require this carde to visit the homes of all children, and would entail making extremely difficult judgments of highly complex family interactions.

The New York State Study

The New York State Youth Commission in 1952[118] attempted to select delinquent-prone children through the use of multiple criteria in a procedure such as the one utilized by Rogers. The results secured in studying 5,299 pupils in grades three to eight indicated that the greatest concentration of future delinquents was represented by the truants. Another good measure of the adjustment capacity of the child found in the New York State study was the measure of social isolation. It was also found that about one-fifth of the delinquents showed no undesirable behavior symptoms on the adjustment scales.

Some Recent Studies on Use of Multiple Criteria

All researchers from Olson and Rogers down to the present found fairly consistently that much information obtained by the teacher in an effort to do a better job of teaching could be used for predicting the adjustment status and future of children. Ullmann,[143] in a later study, examined the hypothesis that teacher ratings were better predictors of that aspect of maladjustment which had to do with acted-out behavior and that self-descriptive data were better predictors of what the person himself will choose to do. Using honor roll attainment and withdrawal from school as criteria, he found that ratings by teachers and ratings by peers were better predictors than self-descriptive data. He also found, as have other investigators, large sex differences in the predictive and criterion measures. Ratings by peers, for example, were found useful in predicting withdrawal from school by boys but ineffective in predicting withdrawal from school by girls. Personality tests, however, were useful in supplementing teacher ratings for the prediction of withdrawal from school by girls. Overall, Ullmann found self-descriptive ratings had the poorest predictive ratings of adjustment when compared to teacher and peer ratings but did add a necessary substance to the total appraisal.

Smith[131] investigated the validity of six group-administered personality and adjustment tests for children. He concluded that none of the tests discriminated well enough to be used singly. However, he noted that several of the tests had group differences extensive enough to allow for a limited amount of applicability when the test data were combined with other information. Satterlee[125] found a low but definite correlation between sociometric choice of individuals in a group and the individual's self-appraisal. He concluded that sociometric and self-appraisals are measuring different aspects of personality and that a relationship between the two measures might be indicative of an individual's reality testing. Gronlund and Holmlund[67] studied sociometric scores of high school students as related to scores received in the sixth grade. They found that pupils with low sociometric scores in the sixth grade do not blossom out in high school and that sociometric status is highly predictive of the high school adjustment of students. Tindall[142] urged caution in using one type of measure for assessing the mental health of students and suggested that a number of indices were usually more effective than one.

Next to teacher judgment, research points to peer perception as the most valid and reliable indicator of pupil adjustment and maladjustment. There are a host of studies,[13,26,45,64,65,66,68,90,115] in addition to the ones already mentioned, which confirm the effectiveness of peer responses in noting those children who are becoming or have become alienated from self or group. There is also much evidence indicating that teachers are, in general, valid observers and raters of children's emotional status.[1,46,76,93,108,112,126,138] Other factors related to the prediction of school adjustment have been found to be IQ,[81,132,149] achievement in school subjects,[2,20-22 35,45,118] age-grade relationship,[3,60] socioeconomic status[5,48,49,61,74,98] and truancy.[56] The two school factors most closely related to the prediction of delinquency in the New York State study were over-age and poor achievement in arithmetic.

The Culturally Deprived

A recent overview of the field of prevention by Bolman and Westman[12] groups such programs under three headings: (1) child-centered prevention — measures aimed at individual children; (2) family-centered prevention — measures aimed at maintaining and restoring the integrity of child-rearing units; and (3) society-centered prevention. While this conceptual arrangement makes for neat packaging, it presents little in the way of an overall rationale or strategy for prevention.

This overview does contain an up-to-date list of references including studies on prevention related to the "culturally deprived." Here again, it is assumed that the problem in helping culturally deprived families is the problem of *developing and maintaining a therapeutic contact* with each family. On the other hand, it may well be such families want some help in bucking the social system and want to learn the social and individual skills which make women effective wives and homemakers, make men available for a variety of meaningful employment, and make children effective in play and school learning. The utilization of the therapeutic model as "remediating ill health" may need to be modified to one of changing primary social systems so that all members of society can learn the necessary social skills for effective participation in it. I am reminded of a young mother of a retarded child who came to me a little concerned with her experiences at a diagnostic clinic for retarded children and their families. She had been referred to the clinic because she wanted to know more about how to feed her mongoloid child. Before this young lady could state the specific nature of her concern, she found herself in a weekly parent group led by a psychiatric social worker who constantly reminded the group to express their true frustrations and feelings about being a parent of a retarded child. While this parent admitted she did have some unresolved feelings about being the mother of a mongoloid child, this was not as much a concern for her as knowing how and what to feed the child. She had come to me to find out if there were somewhere else she might go to get this kind of help. Mental health agencies have to be careful to give people what they ask for before selling them their favored products.

Research in England

Studies conducted in English schools show trends and results similar to those found in the United States. A publication of the

Ministry of Education[63] includes summaries of the results of three pilot studies. In the Sumerset Survey of 1952, approximately 11 per cent of the children were found to be emotionally maladjusted, with more boys maladjusted than girls. In the six-year-old group of maladjusted children, however, girls and boys were equally represented. On the basis of all studies, the Committee concluded that 8 per cent of school children in England needed psychiatric treatment.[63] Teachers were found to be in general agreement with psychologists in their ratings of maladjusted children.

Wall[147] compared eight investigations of maladjustment in school children and found the incidence of seriously maladjusted children ranged from 4 to 12 per cent. He concluded that present evidence tends to indicate that both serious maladjustment and states of developmental difficulty were more common in children than was generally supposed.

Conclusions

Past research in the early identification of emotionally handicapped children tends to point in the direction of teacher-collected information as a reliable and profitable point of focus. Research confirms the usefulness of different kinds of information relevant to the child's development and adjustment in making appraisals of a child's future adjustment. Different combinations of peer, teacher, and self-ratings plus achievement and age-grade relationships were shown to be effective in separating emotionally handicapped children from others.

There is little doubt that emotional maladjustment or adjustment cannot be studied as a discreet illness such as pneumonia or scarlet fever. It can only be regarded as a complex, interwoven relationship of the organism with himself and his environment. However, it was noted that by providing a teacher other perceptions of a child exclusive of his own, one can help him obtain a somewhat more comprehensive picture of each child. The ability of a teacher to assimilate and use perceptual information other than that filtered through his self-will help him to be more accurate in confirming or rejecting suspicions about children. Therefore, early identification of children more vulnerable to emotional handicaps must be regarded as a process administered by a professional person, in this case, the teacher, in which standardized data from other, easily available sources can be synthesized into a total perceptual look at the child. All the teacher may be able to say is, "On the basis of what information I have at this time, it looks as if . . . . may be true. Let's have a closer look at this child to find out if my guess is correct."

Research points to the fact that teachers can, with some help, make good judgments about the adjustment capacities of their pupils. The problem is how to synthesize the different kinds of information and put the various perceptual parts, like Humpty Dumpty, back together again.

Chapter 5

OBJECTIVES AND METHODS
OF THE STUDY

W HATEVER METHODS are employed in identifying emotionally handicapped children early, they would have to be initiated by the teacher. Therefore, it was felt vitally important to consider as relevant the teacher, his role expectancies, his instructional pressures, and his perception of the task along with the validity and reliability of the instruments and information to be collected. Consequently, in deciding what techniques and data were to be used, major consideration was given to the following eight factors:

1. The information to be collected by the teacher should be usable with large samples of school children. In other words, it should be obtainable by group administration in the regular classroom.

2. The information or data to be collected should be defined in an operational manner so as to have the same meaning to all teachers.

3. The information or data to be collected should not involve direct psychological or psychiatric assessments.

4. The collection of the information, the administration, scoring, and interpretation of tests should require a minimum amount of time and work.

5. The information or data should be obtainable as part of regular classroom routine and not involve the teacher in extra-classroom duties, excessive home visits, or the administration of individual tests.

6. The information or data should be aimed at obtaining a comprehensive picture of the behavior and personality of the child from as many different sources as are economically possible.

7. The information collected should be of such a nature that in collecting and analyzing the data, the teacher would be helped to understand and teach the individual children better.

8. The process of collecting and anlyzing the data should motivate and direct the teacher to seek further help for children most vulnerable to emotional handicaps.

Research Steps

The method employed in making the study involved a succession of discrete steps. In outline form, these steps were as follows:

1. Identification of approximately sixty school districts and offices of county superintendents of schools where the services of a social worker, psychologist, psychiatrist, or clinical team were available.

2. Selection by the psychologist, psychiatrist, or clinical team of children in the fourth, fifth, or sixth grades who in the judgment of the clinician could be designated as moderately or severely emotionally handicapped.

3. Selection of classes in which one or more of the designated emotionally handicapped children were enrolled, *not revealing to the teachers of the classes the reasons for the selection of the class.*

4. Gathering and recording of information on all the pupils in the class by the teacher. Such information was recorded on a single sheet provided by the research staff. The information recorded by the teacher on each child in his class included (a) a score on a group intelligence test, (b) scores on a reading and arithmetic achievement test, (c) "Thinking About Yourself" — a personality inventory prepared by the California State Department of Education, (d) "A Class Play" — a type of sociometric technique prepared by the California State Department of Education, (e) the amount of absence in a four-month school period, (f) the age-grade relationship, (g) the socioeconomic status of the family as indicated by father's occupation, (h) a rating by the teacher of the physical status of each child, and (i) a rating by the teacher of the adjustment status of each child.

5. Completion on a special form by the psychologist, psychiatrist, or clinical team of all clinical information available about each selected emotionally handicapped child. These were mailed separately to the State Department of Education.

6. Tabulation and analysis of the data by the State Department of Education.

The study was conceived in three parts. The first part consisted of the selection of the emotionally handicapped children; the second part, the collection of information by the teachers in whose classes these children were enrolled and an analysis of the data to determine to what extent the information could be used to differentiate the emotionally handicapped child from the others. A third part* involves the development of a screening process based on the study and its use in selected schools to determine the degree of accuracy of the technique and its usefulness and usability to teachers.

Problems in Selection of Criterion Group

The first step in making the study involved the selection of school districts that had well-developed psychological or psychiatric services and which were broadly representative of school districts in the state. Regional meetings were then held for the psychologist, guidance counselors, and others who were responsible for the selection of emotionally handicapped children. In these meetings the general outline of the study was presented and discussed with the group. The participants were asked to select children who were enrolled in the fourth, fifth, or sixth grade who had been studied by them or by others on their staff and who could at present be clinically designated as emotionally handicapped. Such selections were not to be revealed to the teachers.

In the discussions of the criteria to be used in selecting emotionally handicapped children and an agreed-upon definition of an emotionally handicapped child, it was suggested that the clinicians differentiate wherever possible those children who were situationally or sociologically maladjusted from those with psychological or emotional difficulties. For the purpose of this study it was suggested that the clinically designated child be one whose primary problem was emotional. The crux of the differential diagnosis was to be a determination of whether or not the child's perception of himself, his ego processes, or personality integration were major factors in his behavior. Jahoda's[78] definition of mental

*This is part of the present research study by the California State Department of Education, authorized by Senate Bill 62 of the 1957 California State Legislature.

health, as well as several of the concepts of emotional handicaps presented in Chapter 2, were presented for discussion. Children with moderate or severe ego conflicts and those whose ego or self-development had never prospered were generally included in the criterion group. However, emphasis was placed on the clinician's use of his clinical experience and professional judgment in selecting each emotionally handicapped child. Other criteria for selection were also discussed. Each child selected was to be enrolled in a regular class. No mention was made of sex, racial, or ethnic factors in the selection of the criterion group.

At the conclusion of these meetings, each clinician was asked to select in the district he served a number of emotionally disturbed children who would be representative of the disturbed children in the school district. Large school districts were asked to select more children than small school districts; offices of county superintendents of schools in large counties were asked to select more than were those of small counties. The smallest number of emotionally handicapped children chosen by any one district or county superintendent of schools was five; the largest number, fifty.

The emotionally handicapped children were selected in the spring of a school year. The following fall, the teacher of the emotionally handicapped was contacted and asked to participate in a general study of emotionally handicapped children but was not told why his class was chosen. Many more teachers than were necessary for the purpose of the study volunteered. In most cases, the teachers selected to collect information were perhaps above average in ability and interest in the problem. Some, however, participated because of administrative pressures.

The purpose of the study, as explained to the teachers, was to study all the children in their classes with the idea of identifying the emotionally handicapped children in each class. Although the teachers know that some children in their classes may have been studied by a school psychologist or in the school clinic, none of them knew why his class was selected for participation in the study. This information was withheld to gain as unbiased a judgment by the teacher as possible. The biases, it was felt, would not come about by a teacher knowing that a child had been to see the psychologist but by knowing that a class had been selected to participate because a particular child was in the class.

Major Aims of the Study

The major purpose of this study was to select an emotionally handicapped child according to the judgment of a clinician who was experienced and trained for such work and to determine the extent to which information available to the teacher in his day-to-day instruction with his class could be used to identify such a child. Teachers were therefore asked to collect the prescribed information about each child in their classes without any direct help from psychiatric or psychological personnel. It was believed that the mental health of children would be most accurately assessed through the utilization of multiple criteria, that is, using as many different perceptions or different aspects of the individual's behavior in school as possible. Information obtained by the teacher for each child in his class would be analyzed in such a way that children with poor mental health and children who were becoming emotionally maladjusted would be identified. It was hoped that in this process teachers might gain increased insight regarding the problems involved in identifying children who need help.

In this study, emphasis was given to determining significant differences in patterns from expected individual or group patterns of behavior as a means of identifying individuals who were emotionally handicapped. It should be noted that in using this procedure, the teacher is not interested in classification or diagnosis but in screening. Also, it should not be assumed that deviations in testing or behavior patterns are in every case the result of emotional difficulties; nor can one assume that conformity to a group norm is synonymous with good mental health or nonconformity with poor mental health. However, there is much evidence to indicate that the individual with persistent, nonadjustive or nonadaptive behavioral characteristics may have emotional problems somewhat greater than those of other individuals.

Instruments and Rating Scales

The information to be collected by the teacher was discussed by the research staff and the clinicians participating in the study. In certain instances dissatisfaction was expressed about various instruments that were available for obtaining desired information. The personality inventory, "Thinking About Yourself," and the sociometric instrument, "A Class Play," were devised as a result of suggestions made by several of the clinicians. There was little agreement regarding the best instruments for obtaining group IQ's and achievement test scores; however, for the purposes of the study, one test was selected and used by almost all the schools.

A form was developed so that the information collected by the teacher could be recorded and used directly for tabulating purposes. Information obtained by the teacher, therefore, had to be in some manageable quantitative score. Although there were many excellent personality inventories and sociometric techniques available, none provided the quantitative score necessary for the purposes of the study. A description of the father's job for rating socioeconomic status and ratings of any physical disabilities of the child were the only two types of information that teachers recorded in words rather than in numbers. Information was collected in approximately 75 school districts by about 200 teachers for approximately 5,500 children. There was at least one clinically designated emotionally disturbed child in the class of each of the 200 teachers. Altogether there were 162 boys and 45 girls in the group of emotionally disturbed children.

Answers Sought by the Study

As a first step, an analysis was made of the data collected to determine to what extent each kind of information collected helped to differentiate the emotionally handicapped child from other children in his or her class.

In addition to meeting the more immediate purposes of the study, securing answers to some of the following questions was envisioned as an important outcome: To what extent is a teacher's perception of an emotionally handicapped child like the perception of the school clinician? To what extent do the children in a class identify the emotionally handicapped child as being different? How do emotionally handicapped children see themselves? What are the differences in the patterns of maladjustment between boys and girls? To what extent is socioeconomic status a factor to be considered in attempting to identify emotionally handicapped children? Are emotionally handicapped children overage in comparison to their peers in the class? Are they children who generally underachieve in reading and arithmetic? How do they stand in comparison to their classmates in intelligence? Are they likely to have sight, hearing, or speech difficulties?

If the information regarding emotionally handicapped children collected by teachers proved useful in formulating conclusions regarding methods of identification, then certain other questions might be answered: Could the amount of maladjustment be lessened by in-service or child study programs? Would the amount of maladjustment be reduced as a result of specific mental health projects or activities which are aimed specifically at helping all children become more emotionally mature? What relationships are there between school policies such as grade placements, reporting, semiannual promotion and the amount of maladjustment? Are there valleys and peaks in the mental health problems experienced by children as they progress through the grades? What effect would participation in the process of early identification by the teacher have on her relationship to the children in the class and on her own understanding of the behavior problems in the class? Might such participation prove useful in providing teachers with a systematic, meaningful procedure for using the information collected in verifying or rejecting hypotheses about children's behavior? Can such participation help a teacher become a more effective inquirer into the meaning of maladjustive behavior? It is possible for this kind of participation to be helpful in the teacher-clinical staff relationship, that is, would it be possible for this process to assist in developing greater team effectiveness between the teacher and the guidance staff?

Chapter 6

RESEARCH RESULTS AND THEIR
IMPLICATIONS FOR SCREENING

T WO HUNDRED fourth, fifth, and sixth grade classes, each of which contained at least one child who could be clinically designated as "emotionally handicapped," were studied. Each teacher collected and recorded the following information on each child in his class: (1) the child's chronological age, (2) the amount of absence in any four-month school period, (3) the father's occupation, (4) standardized test scores in reading achievement and arithmetic achievement, (5) a group IQ test score, (6) a score on a personality self-measure, "Thinking About Yourself," (7) score on a sociometric technique, "A Class Play," (8) teachers' rating of each child's physical and emotional characteristics.

When the data on all the approximately five thousand children were completed each of the separate kinds of information was analyzed to obtain an answer to the question, To what extent does this information, i.e. IQ, rate of absence, etc., differentiate an emotionally handicapped child from his classmates? A full statistical analysis is presented in *A Process for Early Identification of Emotionally Disturbed Children.*[18] The major findings will be presented and their relationship to the process of screening emotionally handicapped children amplified and discussed.

Chronological Age

In this study the emotionally handicapped children were found to be older than their classmates. However, the differences were not found to be great enough to be useful in predicting differences in the adjustment of children.

Relationship to Screening Process

Research and common sense seem to agree that children who are significantly overage for their grade usually have a greater number of social and emotional problems. For example, in a study by Bedoian,[3] the mental health of overage pupils were found to be markedly inferior to underage pupils. Goodlad[60] studied the effects of nonpromotion on the adjustment of children and found that repeating a grade did not induce children to try harder or effect a change in their academic achievement. In addition, he found that in general it was detrimental to the social and personal development of children.

Most school systems and policies regard nonpromotion as a highly individualistic course of action to be utilized only after a total case study of the child indicates the results will be positive. Some children may be retained in a grade if they are found to be too immature for their peers or for the next level of work. Only in extreme cases, however, are children retained for two grades in the elementary school. As will be noted later, the differences in achievement highlight what would happen if children were promoted on the basis of "cutting the mustard" in each grade at grade level.

Rate of Absence

The rate of absence was greater for the emotionally handicapped child than for his classmates. However, the differences did not turn out to be great enough to be used in differentiating the emotionally handicapped child from his classmates.

Relationship to Screening Process

In this study of the amount of absence, both excused and unexcused absences were included in the comparison since it was felt that in some cases emotional difficulties result in a pattern of minor illnesses. Consistent unexcused absences or truancy is perhaps one of the strongest predictive signs of maladjustment usually leading to delinquency because of compulsory attendance laws. In most cases, however, a pattern of truancy is not developed until late preadolescence. In the Gluecks' study,[56] the delinquent group as a rule initiated consistent truancy sometime about the age of nine or ten. In the Gluecks' control group, when truancy occurred, it was initiated during puberty or adolescence. Since truancy is difficult to define and appraise in younger children and often does not begin to be consistent until the child is in adolescence, and since there are other ways children can avoid attendance including complaints, illness, or malingering, total absence, instead of unexcused absence, was utilized as perhaps a more productive measure of maladjustment.

In an analysis of factors associated with superior school attendance[109] when scholastic ability was held constant, it was noted that superior attenders established this pattern early and received higher grades. Poor attenders showed a lack of strong positive motivation toward school plus a less favorable total life situation.

A larger number of truancies and absences are more true of children from lower socioeconomic classes than of middle class children. Rogers[121] found less than .5 per cent truants in the more favored neighborhood schools as against 7 per cent in the less favored neighborhood schools. Middle class children have been more prone to a type of problem behavior called school phobia,[24,140,146] a disturbance characterized by extreme panic when in school, chronic lateness, school vomiting, crying, or dizziness. Investigation has produced as the most significant factor in the genesis of this behavior, mothers who were oversolicitous, overanxious, immature, and domineering. In such cases, the child's fear seems to be a reflection of the mother's conflict about the school's intrusion on the parent-child relationship with the possibility that the child will transfer his affection or dependency to a teacher.

Children who are absent in excess should be referred for further study on the basis of other data to rule out major psychogenic factors as a contributing cause.

Socioeconomic Status (Father's Occupation)

The distribution of the occupations of fathers of emotionally disturbed children, when compared to the occupations of the fathers of the other children in the class, showed no significant differences. In addition, no differences were found between the socioeconomic background of the emotionally handicapped children when compared to the California population as classified in the 1950 census report. The assumption, then, that the socioeconomic backgrounds of the emotionally handicapped children *se-*

lected for this study were not significantly different from the rest of the population was sustained.

Relationship to Screening Process

Father's occupation was obtained as the best single index of the socioeconomic status of the family. There seems to be little doubt that socioeconomic factors are of prime importance in evaluating the mental health status of children. The relationship of social class status and maladjustment has been studied extensively. As Leacock points out, "Although the studies of socioeconomic status and mental illness are not strictly comparable (some employ occupation; some, income; some, neighborhood or style of house as their criterion, depending on the data available), the general trend is clear and consistent enough to be meaningful. Rates for all illness increase as one goes down the socioeconomic scale."[98]

Other studies[48,49,74] show that the diagnosed prevalence of psychiatric disorders is significantly related to an individual's position in the class structure. In any one school class, however, a child who comes from a home which is to some degree different from the homes of the other children may be more likely to develop problems in school. As Rogers noted, the child who is most like his group is least likely to present personality difficulties. He also found that the type of mental health problems children developed were closely related to the type of neighborhood they came from. In the less favored neighborhood, children tended to "act out" their difficulties in various forms of delinquent behavior; in the more favored neighborhood children tended to internalize their problems.

Several real advantages are associated with the use of occupational indices as a measure of socioeconomic status. The first is that the information is usually available in school records. Secondly, the rating or ranking of occupations can be done objectively. Other advantages are associated with time and utility. For example, indices which depend on securing data about income or level of education may be inaccurate or incomplete since some persons are sensitive about revealing this type of information. In addition, ratings of type of neighborhood, dwelling, or home furnishing require a certain amount of training and professional skill which varies from person to person. Occupational indices also have the advantage of extensive research studies in which this kind of socioeconomic classification has been used. Occupation of father has also been found to be about the most valid single index of social class. In addition, publishers of widely used tests report norms based on the per cents of different occupational groups which were included in the devlopment of the norms. By using the occupation of father, schools may compare their test population with the standardization group used by the test publisher.

There are different systems of using occupation in classifying socioeconomic classes. In 1949 Lloyd Warner[148] described a system for ranking occupations in which the prestige enjoyed by the occupation as well as the skill and training required for the job were used in the classification. The United States Census Bureau revised a scale developed by Edwards in 1937[40] for use in the 1950 census. There are advantages in both types of classifications. The use of the 1950 census classification system has the advantage of greater objectivity and ease in rating; there is also available census tract data for counties and areas within counties for comparison purposes. This enables a teacher to examine the socioeconomic status of her class and compare it to the community or neighborhood from which the school draws its children.

Since the rating of socioeconomic status by occupation of father is based on a single factor, it lacks the comprehensiveness of other kinds of classifications. Also the use of occupation as an index of socioeconomic status should be evaluated in relation to the known composition of the community. For example, salesmen, clerical workers, and skilled workers residing where there is a large concentration of professional and managerial home owners may be subject to class influences far different than the same group in a more modest area. Another difficulty in the use of occupation as a socioeconomic index is the instability and mobility of jobs and people. It should be noted that the degree of mobility from unskilled to skilled jobs is greater than the mobility from skilled

to professional occupations because of the heavy training require-
ments for the latter.

Research on the relationship of school adjustment and social
class indicates that children of fathers whose occupations are in a
professional area score higher on mental tests and are more acceptable to their peers. Children of professional fathers were found to
be more dominant, extraverted, and had more emotional stability,
while children from semiskilled families had more worries.[102] In a
study of achievement and socioeconomic status for 108 sixth grade
pupils, Gough[61] found a respectable correlation between status and
achievement with the exception of arithmetic where the relationship was almost zero.

In this study, father's occupation was used to compare the class
status of the emotionally handicapped child with other children.
No significant differences in socioeconomic status were found,
probably due to the selection of a variety of emotionally handicapped children by the psychologists and psychiatrists. This finding has no relevance to the relationship of socioeconomic status to
maladjustment in the population at large. Teachers, however, need
to be aware of the significant role of socioeconomic status as it
affects the values, motivations, and emotional conflicts of children.
The use of father's occupation and the 1950 Census Bureau scale
will assist the teacher in gaining a more sharply focused socioeconomic look at her group.

Achievement in Reading and Arithmetic

In this research study, emotionally disturbed children were
compared to other children on reading and arithmetic achievement tests at the fourth, fifth, and sixth grade levels. In each grade,
the scores of the emotionally disturbed child on reading and
achievement tests were significantly below the scores of the other
children in the class.[18] The differences between the emotionally
handicapped child and other children were greater in arithmetic
achievement than in reading achievement. In addition, the differences in achievement between the emotionally handicapped child
and others in his class became increasingly divergent with each

succeeding grade level. In essence, the rich get richer while the poor get poorer.

Relationship to Screening Process

The "meat and potatoes" of education are reading and arithmetic. All children recognize that mastery of these skills by pupils is a highly valued objective of the school. Effective learning, however, entails an ability to apply effort of self and to manage the symbols of language and mathematics successfully. Often the first observable sign that something is wrong is an inability to learn. In a survey of problems referred to a child guidance center, Gilbert[51] found that the most frequently cited reason for referral was "academic difficulties." The relationship between achievement in reading, arithmetic, and school adjustment often becomes gyroscopic and mutually reinforcing. Those children who are able to be successful are rewarded, find wholesome satisfactions in applying effort, are friendly to the school and its values, and are encouraged to invest more of themselves in their school activities. Conversely those who are not successful in academic activities find little reward in them, perceive themselves negatively, are perceived by thir peers negatively, and are thereby unable to relate to the school or its activities in any constructive manner. The school to them becomes an unfriendly, often hostile institution with little opportunity for real satisfactions. Children's perceptions of non-achievers illustrate this cause and effect relationship. In a study by Buswell[22] of the interrelationship of achievement and adjustment, achievement as a basic factor in adjustment was found to precede rather than follow social acceptability. Buswell demonstrated that in kindergarten, before academic values as such are stressed, the future achiever is not perceived any more positively than the future nonachiever. In the first grade, however, when academic achievement is becoming an important school activity, those children who are achieving success are also the most socially acceptable. If social adjustment preceded successful achievement, those who had been the most acceptable in the preceding spring should be the ones to show the best school achievement in the fall. This, however, did not take place.

Olson's study,[114] discussed in Chapter 5, demonstrated that the relationship between the amount of problem tendencies and achievement was negative, i.e. the higher the amount of problem tendencies, the lower the achievement. He found this relationship to be influenced only slightly by intelligence. In the study by the Gluecks[56] significant differences were found between the delinquent and control groups in reading and achievement. Although some of the delinquents in the study may not have been emotionally handicapped children, it is highly probable that the same relationship between achievement and school success exists for predelinquents.

Differences in arithmetic achievement as compared to reading achievement were noted in the emotionally handicapped group. The larger differences in arithmetic achievement between the emotionally handicapped child and other children may in part be due to the reading difficulties on certain of the arithmetic tests where reading is an integral part of the problem. It is also possible that arithmetic is more abstract and less meaningful to the emotionally handicapped child than it is to other children and is a skill that requires greater concentration and attentiveness than reading. The learning of mathematics in general may require a greater degree of freedom from anxiety and inner concern than does reading. Jastak,[79] working with an individually administered achievement test, found that a high reading score coupled with a low arithmetic score tended to occur in abnormal mental states of a developmental nature in adults. In children he found that the neurotic and disorganized child is usually more proficient in reading than in arithmetic. He also noted that failure in arithmetic and failure in reading in the same child may be caused by entirely independent factors.

There have been numerous studies of the relationship of reading achievement and personality. Studies by Axline[2] and Bills[8] are indicative of the trend of most of the research on this relationship. Poor second grade readers who were placed in a therapy group for three and a half months made achievement gains up to sixteen months with an average gain of about five months.[2] In a study of factors which best predicted delinquency conducted by the New York State Youth Commission, the investigators found that arithmetic failure was one of the two school factors most closely related to delinquency.

Not all reading or arithmetic failures can be said to be the result of emotional problems. Buswell's study cited before would indicate, however, that reading difficulties may precede emotional difficulties. In any case it would be difficult to divorce value-laden skills such as reading and arithmetic from the emotional consequences of failure. In school, failure to learn can be a most disastrous emotional event and a most significant one for the child's future.

Intelligence Quotient

In this research study, the mean group IQ score of the emotionally handicapped child was found to be significantly lower than other children in the class—92.9 compared to 103.2. However, on individually administered tests such as the Standford Binet and Wechsler Intelligence Scale for Children, their scores were not significantly different from the scores of other children. Further, the scores made by the emotionally handicapped children on the Wechsler Intelligence Scale for Children was less related (r = .58) to their scores on the group tests than were their scores on the Stanford Binet (r = .74). The normal relationship (correlation) between a group test and an individual test is about .85. The results indicate that the emotionally handicapped children have a greater variability of relationship between their individual and group test scores than do other children but that they usually make higher scores on individual tests which are in content less related to school subjects.

Relationship to Screening Process

Intelligence or IQ commonly refers to a person's ability to deal with abstractions, to learn, and to solve problems. Wechsler[149] defines IQ as encompassing the ability to achieve and the ability to adjust. Like Janus, IQ has two sides which need to be borne in mind in evaluating intellectual ability in relation to the child's personality development. In children governed largely by emotional needs, intellectual efforts will be bent or directed by these needs. Emotion can imprison the intellectual capacities of a child or free it. Emotional factors can direct the intellect into paths of self-defensiveness and timidity or provide the necessary freedom for task-oriented, creative accomplishment. In all cases it provides the setting and direction for the operation of intellectual abilities. Klopfer[86] illustrated this relationship in a fourteen-year-old boy with an above average IQ who conspicuously failed an item on the Stanford-Binet which asks the subject to explain what "tall" and "short" have in common. This boy answered as follows: "If a short boy walks with a tall girl and doesn't mind it, it makes no difference." In explaining what heavy and light have in common he said, "If a task is heavy and you don't mind doing it, then it is light." What can one say about the failure of this boy on this item as a function of his intellect? What is the meaning of the stimulus question to him? Is failure a result of not knowing? It is relevant to consider in this connection the work of Wechsler[149] who attempted to identify the total amount of intellective factors in tests of intelligence. He found that the intellective factors seldom exceeded 60 per cent of the total factors. Wechsler concluded that general intelligence could not be equated with intellectual ability alone but must be regarded as a manifestation of the personality as a whole.

The differences between the emotionally handicapped child and other children as manifested on a group intelligence test may reasonably be attributed to nonintellective factors. Goldfarb,[59] Skodak,[129] and others have shown the significant effects produced by a variety of social and environmental factors on IQ scores. Bills[8] illustrated this relationship more positively by placing emotionally handicapped children in play situations where some of the emotional difficulties could be worked out and obtained substantial gains in the intellectual functioning of the children. In a study of three hundred children who were tested individually twice a year from age two and one-half until fifteen, significant changes in IQ levels were found for some of the children. In analyzing the groups who gained the most and lost and most, the authors concluded that "inadequate attention has possibly been paid to the role of lesser levels of anxiety on all kinds of performances. Anyone who has suffered a moderate degree of free-floating anxiety is perfectly aware of the fact that while he may be able to perform his daily routines, he loses much in his ability to remember telephone numbers and street addresses, etc., and to reason to the level of his full capacity. Free-floating anxiety is probably just as frequent in children and just as devastating to their performance as it is in adults. . . ."[132]

The investigators in the above study suggested that there was a spiral relationship between motivation on a test and previous experiences of success. Children who find opportunity for successful mastery of problems, reasonable competitiveness, and who obtain positive feedback for their efforts tend to perform progressively better. Such satisfactions and anticipation of success should produce a lower level of test anxiety and a higher score.

Another aspect of the effect of motivation on test results is illustrated in the same study by a group of late "downers" (individuals whose successive tests showed lowered scores), all of whom were adolescent girls. The girls were studied individually and were found to be undergoing what the investigators called a "flight into femininity." What seemed to happen was a change in values so that competition and achievement were no longer of primary importance per se but were perceived mainly in relation to being more feminine, more charming, more subject to admiration. School attainment or success on tests no longer became necessary for emotional comfort.

Intelligence as a concept cannot be equated with intellectual factors alone, as intellectual capacity cannot be regarded as something measured by quantity alone. Personality and intellectual factors interact in such a way that each takes on some of the qualities of the other. The tendency to isolate intellect as an independently existing trait or group of traits may be the artificial results of designing tests which create the trait. This is not to deny the descriptive or predictive value of a well-administered individual test or group test to children eager and motivated to do well. Positive personality factors in most children aid and abet the accuracy of the test. Negative personality factors as found in the emotionally handicapped child, however, become strong reins on the child's real ability. Nevertheless the loss of points on group IQ tests of children with emotional handicaps, whatever the cause, is sufficiently significant to enable the classroom teacher to use the results in screening if the score is appraised along with other known factors including, where possible, the child's performance on an individually administered test.

Perception* of Self, "Thinking About Yourself"

The comparison of the emotionally handicapped children and others indicated that emotionally handicapped boys exhibited greater self-dissatisfaction than other boys about their life and showed significantly greater discrepancies between self and wanted self. In general the content of their dissatisfaction related directly to their difficulties in school. However, the items which showed the greatest discrepancy between self and wanted self for the emotionally handicapped boys were the same items of greatest discrepancy for other boys. The differences lay in the degree of discrepancy.

Emotionally handicapped girls showed a more passive relationship between self and wanted self than did their male counterparts. In many cases other girls voiced a greater degree of dissatisfaction than did the emotionally handicapped girls. Emotionally handicapped girls related their difficulties and dissatisfactions more to personal and family matters than did the emotionally handicapped boys. The differences in the responses between the emotionally handicapped boys and girls were consistent with the culturally assigned roles of each. The boys reacted to their difficulties in a direct, forceful and nonintrospective manner. The girls were perhaps more insightful and thoughtful but less inclined to voice or act upon their difficulties. Undoubtedly these differences in personality play a large part in making emotionally handicapped boys more numerous and more difficult problems in an institution such as a school. Test re-test reliabilities were computed for

---

*Perception, as used throughout this section, refers to the process of assigning meaning to that which is seen, heard, felt, tasted, smelled or touched. In short, it refers to the interpretation of events or stimuli by the experiencing person.

approximately 150 boys and girls and found to be .82 for boys and .88 for girls.[95]

Relationship to Screening Process

Two standardized measures of self-concept are obtained on children: One is "Thinking About Yourself," an intraindividual type of personality questionnaire; the other is a comparison of roles assigned to a child by his peers and roles chosen for himself on "A Class Play." As was mentioned by Smith,[131] self-measures can be helpful in understanding and screening children who need help if used along with other information and data.

When one perceives, one not only "sees," but one interprets and experiences what one has seen. The self of an individual is a learned concept made up as it is of the multitude of relationships and interactions of the child with other persons. A child's concept of self is not however a fixed and unchanging picture; it can and does vary depending on the situation and the persons present. Block,[11] for example, found that a secretary's concept of herself varied in relation to the person she was with at the time but that a core of self was always present. He found that roughly 50 per cent of self was somewhat flexible and 50 per cent could be considered somewhat basic. One can surmise that persons with an overabundant core might be unable to shift gears to meet the changing social and personal conditions in which one finds oneself; on the other hand, persons with little or no core would have little or no anchor to drag or hold on and might be described as an organism with little self. In any case, the self is the window through which the environment, other people, and the organism are perceived.

When a child is asked to communicate about self he may not communicate what one may feel is an accurate self-concept. Accuracy of self-perception necessitates the reaction of other selves who have windows of their own to consider. At times the child may not be too clear about his self-concept, especially when he is asked to delineate it via a paper-and-pencil questionnaire. To some extent a child who communicates a confused or fragmented self may be reflecting an inability to see himself clearly. In some cases a child's self-concept may include a need to deny problems. In such children what may be communicated may be what the child can comfortably reveal. From the point of view of the teacher, such children may not be "truthful"; such denials, if they are appraised as such, may be a significant fact in understanding the child. Also the degree to which a child is able to communicate how he feels may be helpful to himself as well as to the teacher. As other perceptions of self are made available to the teacher, inconsistencies in perceived self may become apparent. Such inconsistencies are part of the structure of self. Behavior may appear to the teacher to be erratic or unpredictable at times, but if one could know how a child perceived the situation, his behavior might be understood as consistent and meaningful.

It should be emphasized that the psychological processes of children are subject to neither moral nor logical restrictions. A child whose experiences tend to communicate to him that he is unworthy or inadequate will develop a self which will accept only those perceptions which confirm or are consistent with these feelings. To change a child's attitude entails some change in his perception of self. The same kind and degree of failure in two apparently similar children may elicit two different responses. In one case the child may quit trying, become sullen, angry, and despondent. In the other, the child may bounce back with a new attack on the problem. The difference between saying, "I failed" and "I am a failure," is often the difference between healthy personality growth and emotional maladjustment.

The relationship between perception of self and perception of others may help explain why children who have negative concepts of themselves show up as isolates on sociometric techniques. Sheerer[128] found a definite and relatively high correlation between acceptance and respect for self and acceptance and respect for others. Stock,[137] in an independent study, confirmed Sheerer's results. Both investigators found a regular increase in acceptance and respect for self and others in individuals who had had a successful counseling experience. Sullivan described the relationship between a person's perception of himself and his perception of others as follows: "If there is a valid and real attitude toward the self, that attitude will manifest as valid and real toward others. It is not that as ye judge, so shall ye be judged, but as you judge yourself, so shall you judge others."[139]

The personality questionnaire, "Thinking About Yourself" (see appendix, p. 187), and Part II of the "Class Play" utilize intraindividual measures of self. The scores obtained are not based on comparing answers to a norm or how other children have answered the item. The scoring is based on the premise that the larger the difference between wanted or desired self (Do you want to be like him or her?) and present self (Are you like him?), the greater is the child's dissatisfaction with his present status. This is not to suggest that little or no differences are optimum. Teachers should look at children where the congruence between self and wanted self is inordinately congruent as well as those in which great differences occur. The scoring procedure described on page 190 is based on this concept.

The self-measure on "A Class Play" (p. 170) consists of comparing the choices of peers with that of self. Does the child choose himself for parts in the play very much like those he is chosen for by his classmates? If there are differences, wherein do they lie? How do you explain such differences?

As has been suggested in analyzing the results on "Thinking About Yourself," some attention should be paid to children whose self and wanted self are almost entirely congruent as well as those who have high discrepancy scores. It is possible for the responses to the question, "Do you want to be like him?" to range in the thinking of the child from immediate situational needs to highly developed fantasies. For example, the more weak or helpless a child's concept of himself may be, the more imperious or overwhelming may be the demands of the environment. As a consequence, the desired or wanted self may be built out of a strong need to live in fantasy.

Studies[9,70] have shown that adults who scored low on acceptance of self also had high discrepancy scores between the self and wanted or desired self. In one study[70] of the congruence of self and wanted or ideal self in relation to personality adjustment it was noted that the correlation between the two aspects of personality tends to be positive and somewhere between .33 and .46.

The results of this study suggest the relevance of measures of self and ideal self as a measure of personality maladjustment. Seldom is one completely satisfied with himself and few are completely dissatisfied. Some children are too frightened to express a wanted self that is any different from self. Others are so disturbed that they cannot help but be greatly dissatisfied with the way things are going. An optimum relationship between self and wanted self would depend on many factors including how much insight the child had about himself.

Children with good reality testing usually feel comfortable about themselves and their future. Children who are disturbed may hesitate to express a wanted self different from self or may express a wanted self greatly different from self.

The results on "Thinking About Yourself" should be considered along with the results on "The Class Play" and other relevant data. The wanted or desired self on the personality inventory may be a more direct expression of self needs or wishes. It is often productive for the teacher to compare the kinds of roles a child thinks other children will select for him on "A Class Play" with the items on the personality inventory which show the highest discrepancy between self and wanted self. In a study[115] of the relationship of personality tests and sociometric choices, the results demonstrated that children who were perceived positively by peers had the "best" scores on the personality test while those with few positive choices and many negative ones had the poorest personality test scores. Children with few or no negative choices on the sociogram as compared with those who had many negative choices had better adjustment scores on the personality test. The investigators found that peer perceptions can be helpful in understanding the results of a personality inventory and conversely a child's concept of himself as revealed on a personality inventory can be helpful in understanding his positive or negative valuation by the class. Therefore, in the use of this technique by teachers, it would be profitable to evaluate the results on "A Class Play" and "Thinking About Yourself" together.

Peer Perception, "A Class Play"

Certain of the parts in "A Class Play" were chosen as representative of negative roles and others of neutral or positive roles. The appellation of "negative" to a role is based on commonly accepted cultural perceptions. For example, Snow White would be chosen as a positive role while her stepmother would be chosen as a negative role. In "A Class Play" (see page 170), the negative parts are even numbered while the positive or neutral parts are odd numbered. Test re-test reliabilities of 180 children were found to be .92 for total selections and .90 for total even selections.[94]

Not only are the roles chosen for emotionally handicapped children most often negative ones, but these children are seldom seen as boys or girls who would play any of the positive or neutral parts of the play. The differences in the perception of the emotionally handicapped group and other children are highly significant. In comparing the peer choices for the emotionally handicapped child and his self-choices, one can make some helpful inferences about the meaning of the child's behavior.

Relationship to Screening Process

The Teachers' Worksheet for A Class Play (p. 256) enables a teacher to tally and evaluate peer and self-selections. What is done in tallying and evaluating Section I and II is operationally similar. After tallying the choices of peers and self-choices, the teacher adds the total choices. This total can be utilized as a rough index of the social impact of the child in the class (Column A, p. 256). Next, the teacher tabulates the total negative choices. This can be utilized as a rough index of the negative impact of the child in the class (Column B). By dividing the number in Column B by the number in Column A, one can get a fairly good approximation of the quantity of visibility of the child by his peers and the quality of this visibility. The same analytic process holds for tabulating and evaluating the second section, self-perception. The percentage obtained in Section I (peer perception) can be compared to that obtained in Section II (self-perception) for each child as follows:

a. The child who is seen positively by his peers and who sees himself positively.

b. The child who is seen by his classmates as a negative child but who sees himself positively.

This child may need to distort reality somewhat or have difficulty in appraising how others see him. Many of the emotionally handicapped children showed this or the following pattern of self-peer relationship.

c. The child who is seen by his classmates as a negative child and who also sees himself negatively.

Some of these children show delight in playing negative roles. Some are quite realistic in appraising how they are seen by others. Most of these are emotionally handicapped children.

d. The child who is seen positively by his classmates but who sees himself negatively.

Such relationships are rare but do occur in children who are academically and socially successful but who feel they are not living up to some internalized expectations. Such children may have personality problems which are seldom noted in a typical classroom. Only few of the emotionally handicapped children in this research study showed this peer-self relationship.

e. The child who is not seen by his classmates at all.

This group includes children who are quiet, slow learning, or mentally retarded, nonintrusive personalities, and a core of children who have actively withdrawn from the group because of emotional problems. It is well to note IQ score in analyzing the meaning of a low social impact score. Children with above average IQ's who are found in this category should be reviewed for possible emotional problems. In addition to IQ score, self-perception on "A Class Play" and on "Thinking About Yourself" should be studied to obtain clues about the meaning of absence of peer perception.

f. A child who is seen by his classmates as a mixture of positive and negative roles.

These children have great role versatility in the eyes of their peers. Often they are children who are mildly irritating but not sufficiently so to provoke hostility or rejection of the child by his peers.

Another factor that may be relevant to an analysis of the results on "A Class Play" are the choices of those who do not perceive the children in their class as others do. This idiosyncratic perception may be caused by such things as poor reality testing, late entrance into the class or poor intelligence. In any case, the teacher should not only be aware of how a child is chosen but how he chooses. It is often helpful to discuss results with other teachers who have known the child or with the school psychologist, guidance counselor, or principal. Individual study should be sought if the information obtained confirms other suspicions.

In appraising the relationships of peer and self-scores on "A Class Play," one should be aware of a fundamental concept of mental health often referred to as "reality testing." Reality testing is the ability to perceive others and oneself accurately and to be free to test the accuracy of one's inferences about the environment in which one lives. It is often helpful to know to what extent a child sees himself as others do. To what extent does a child need to use fantasy to change the nature of reality? To what extent does a child need to deny the realities of his peer relationships?

Studies by Sears[127] and Rogers, Kell, and McNeil,[122] and Davids and White[34] may be helpful in understanding the relationships of perceptions elicited by this technique. For example, Sears studied children who experienced continual success in school as compared to children who had a long history of school failure and found that the former set goals at levels which indicated good reality testing while the latter set their goals with little regard for their possible fulfillment. Rogers and his co-workers found that in a group of delinquent children for whom there was an adequate amount of diagnostic information, the self-understanding factor had the greatest predictive value for later adjustment. A follow-up study by Rogers proved that realistic perception of self was the best predictor of future behavior.

Publications by Taba,[141] Jennings,[80] and others on the analysis of groups may be helpful to teachers in learning to use this technique. Grambs[62] has listed some of the basic assumptions in the development and understanding of such techniques as "A Class Play." In the final analysis, this technique, like any other classroom procedure, can only serve to verify, reject, or initiate hypotheses about children. It provides a point of view for looking at behavior. Along with other reference points, it can give the teacher a more sharply focused picture of what the child is really like.

The effective use of this technique, along with the other techniques, depends on the professional skill of the teacher and her willingness to examine the meaning of the results in light of other data. This technique along with other types of sociometric instruments adds an important dimension to the total perception of the child. Teachers and others have a tendency to overjudge the acceptance of children they like best and underjudge the status of those they least prefer.[66] When sociometric choices differ from teacher judgment, the differences in the perception should not be regarded as an indication that one or the other perception is wrong. Both perceptions may be right, i.e. accurate. Peers do not perceive children from the same value system as do teachers. A teacher may learn much about herself by comparing other perceptions of a child with her own. In the study by Gronlund[66] no relationship was found between the ability to judge a child accurately and the teacher's experience, age, years of college training, size of class, marital status, or length of time with class. The only factor which differentiated the best judges from the poorest was the taking of a volunteer in-service course in child development. Those teachers who had taken the course were significantly better judges than those who had not. Whether or not this is a result of greater curiosity about children, interest in them, or increased insight as a result of the in-service program would be hard to say. Since the course was voluntary, it may well be that those teachers who enrolled for the course already had greater insight, interest, and skill in appraising children.

"A Class Play" is a highly valid instrument for screening emotionally handicapped children. For boys, fourteen of the fifteen items were found to discriminate between emotionally handicapped and others; for girls, ten out of fifteen were found to discriminate.[94] If only one method for class analysis were permissible, this would undoubtedly be the best single procedure. In addition, the results can add much to the teacher's understanding of the child's problem. For example, in one class a highly intelligent fifth grade girl who was chosen for many negative and hostile roles by her classmates also perceived herself chosen for negative roles by her teacher and classmates. In answer to the question, "Which part would you like to play?" she chose the heroine role. Later she confided to the teacher that she recognized that her classmates had difficulties with her, but that "she knew what she was up against and was working on it." Another teacher described a boy who received eight positive and eight negative choices by the class. He found that his nickname among the children was "Little Pest." This seemed to represent how the group felt about him — an honest mixture of affection and irritation. The child perceived himself much like the class did and accepted the appellation "Little Pest" with good grace. Other data about this child helped the teacher come to a better understanding of this child's role selection and perception.

Almost all studies of peer perception point to a strong relationship between emotional adjustment and peer judgments. Most, if not all, confirm the reciprocity of school adjustment and school success. The child who is most accepted by his peers gets the best grades, has the higher IQ, comes from a higher socioeconomic level, and has fewer emotional problems. Conversely the child who is least accepted by his peers gets the poorest grades, has the lowest IQ, comes from a lower socioeconomic class, and has more emotional problems.

Teacher Ratings

Teachers reported 4.4 per cent of all children and 26 per cent of the emotionally handicapped children to be overly aggressive or defiant "most of the time." In the total group, boys were rated overly aggressive "most of the time" twice as often as girls; in the emotionally handicapped group the ratio was 7:1.

Of all the children, 6.1 per cent were rated overly withdrawn or timid "most of the time" while 11 per cent of the emotionally handicapped children were so rated. In the total group, twice as many girls as boys were rated overly withdrawn "most of the time"; in the emotionally handicapped group, twice as many boys as girls were so rated.

Of the total group 5.4 per cent (compared to 38 per cent of the emotionally handicapped group) were rated as control problems most of the time. The ratio of boys to girls was 4:1 for the total group and 9:1 for the emotionally handicapped group.

Of the total group, 10 per cent were rated as instructional problems most of the time. Of the emotionally handicapped group, 52 per cent were so rated. Twice as many boys as girls in the total group were rated control problems compared to a ratio of 4:1 in the emotionally handicapped group. About 70 per cent of the emotionally handicapped group were rated as an instructional problem "quite often" or "most of the time."

When teachers were asked to rate the adjustment of all children in their class as being (1) among the best, (2) average, (3) among the poorest, the ratio was approximately 1:2:1. However, 87 per cent (179 out of the 206) of the emotionally handicapped children were rated as being among the most poorly adjusted.

Five of the 206 emotionally handicapped children were rated as being among the best adjusted. When teachers were asked to select the two most maladjusted children in their classes, 154 of the 206 emotionally handicapped children (74 per cent) were selected.

Teachers rated emotionally handicapped girls as slightly underweight. They also reported 1.1 per cent of all children to have marked difficulty in vision, and 2.8 per cent of the emotionally handicapped group to have marked difficulty in vision.

Teachers reported 4.7 per cent of all children to have some physical disability and 11 per cent of the emotionally handicapped children to have some physical disability. This was the only significant difference in the ratings of physical status.

Relationship to Screening Process

The adequacy of teachers to identify children with poor mental health has been a question of much concern and interest to mental health specialists, as well as educators. The publication of a study by Wickman,[152] in 1928, in which he found that ratings by teachers correlated zero with ratings of mental health specialists on the seriousness of fifty behavior traits, seemed to indicate that teachers did not perceive behavior from a mental health point of view. Wickman, however, was careful to point out that the instructions to the teachers were distinctly different than those given to the mental health specialists. Teachers, for example, were told to rate in such a way as to secure response to *present* problems and the seriousness of the amount of difficulty produced by a particular type of troublesome behavior. The instructions given to the mental health specialists were exactly reversed from those given the teachers. Down through the years, the differences in instructions given the teachers and mental health specialists by Wickman have at times been overlooked in analyzing the results.

The "fact" that teachers were ostensibly unable to recognize serious problems in the classroom probably led to a greater emphasis on mental health in the classroom and some changes in teacher attitudes toward problem behavior. In any case, other studies were focused on the same problem with modifications in the administrative directions so that both groups received essentially the same instructions. Mitchell,[108] in 1940, reported a correlation of .70 between teachers and mental hygienists; in addition, he found a shift in the opinions of the mental health specialists from those utilized in the Wickman study.

Ullmann[144] found that differences in the two groups were not a matter of contradiction but resulted when one group considered an item important while the other group regarded it as neutral, equivocal, or unratable. Items on which the two groups differed tended to be those on which teachers had less information and less confidence in their ratings, such as home or social relationships, passive behavior, and intrapsychic or "worry" items. Teachers felt that politeness and obedience were characteristic of good adjustment; the clinicians felt these characteristics were of uncertain significance.

Persons interested in the results of other studies on this problem are referred to summaries by Schrupp and Gjerde,[126] and Hunter.[76] Most present-day studies have found teachers much more in agreement with the attitudes of clinicians than was formerly thought to be true. It should be emphasized that perfect congruity of the perception of teachers and clinical mental health specialists may be realistically undesirable since the teacher needs to be concerned with the group and the effect of disturbing behavior on the group. The fact that teachers are able to select with a marked degree of accuracy those children in need of psychological or psychiatric treatment is born out by adult follow-up studies of such children.[46]

Teachers' ratings of pupil adjustment seem to show closer relationships to sociometric ratings than to intrapersonal data, such as those derived from personality tests. There is also some evidence indicating that teachers have greater difficulty perceiving the patterns of maladjustment in girls than in boys. Undoubtedly the manifest overt symptoms in boys permit teachers to be more confident about their perception of acting-out behavior.

What about the teacher's own adjustment and its effect on his perception of children? Teachers have needs and problems; it would be unrealistic to assume that these are deposited in the principal's office while the teacher meets with his class. Teachers with overwhelming or serious personality difficulties are often able, like other persons, to transfer their anxieties or hostilities to children. On the other hand, some teachers with mental health problems may manifest such problems by being unenthusiastic, overconforming, or rigid. Perhaps to do a good job as a teacher, a small amount of anxiety or a foolish glimmer in one's eyes is desirable. It is equally as difficult to define the good or mature teacher as it is to define good mental health.

Perhaps most critical in effective judgment of behavior is the level of self-awareness and the extent to which the teacher is able to gain insight of self. A teacher who is fearful of any type of behavioral deviation in his class may need to resort to a type of blind spot to reduce his own anxiety. Another teacher may feel that children need a Prussian kind of control because his parents employed it successfully. Still another may find himself faced with a group of children who need a kind of rational authority. Unless one knows something about the personality constellation of each teacher it would be difficult at first glance to differentiate the emotional climate in each of the three classrooms. In addition, programs of professional growth in understanding children and mental health might have different results on each of the teachers mentioned above. The teacher who has a great amount of anxiety about himself may perceive an experience aimed at helping him understand children as a threat to his system of control and values.

When a teacher's personal and emotional difficulties cloud or distort his perception of children, he may resist or uphold values which will keep him from accepting help. In some cases, the teacher may feel hostile toward the whole idea of understanding behavior or in-service programs aimed at helping him gain insight into children's behavior. Dr. Lyman, the disgruntled, disturbed teacher in *Bus Stop*, summed up this point of view as follows: "Educators have despaired of ever teaching students anything so they have decided the second best thing to do is to understand them . . . I graduated magna cum laude from the University of Chicago, I studied at Oxford on a Rhodes Scholarship and returned to take my Ph.D. at Harvard. I think I have the right to expect my students to try to understand me."[77]

Gronlund's[66] study, mentioned before, demonstrated that a teacher's ability to judge children accurately was not related to experience, age, education, marital status, or length of time he had been in contact with the class. The only criterion which diffierentiated the poor teacher-judges from the good judges was voluntary participation in an in-service child development program by the latter group.

The complexities of demands made on teachers have fragmented the teacher's professional "self" into a number of "selves." For example, teachers are asked to be parent surrogates to some children, confidantes to others, ego supporters for withdrawn children, targets for hostile children, group leaders, and representatives of the do's and don'ts of society. The whole area of professional purposes and motives may be dimly perceived by some teachers, since the role expectations are often diffused and inconsistent. The demands of the children, parents, administrator, school board, and the profession may be inconsistent and confusing. For example, in a teacher's education and professional training, the concept of individual differences of children is strongly stressed and illustrated. In actual practice, the teacher may face classes and pupils in such rapidity and in such numbers that trying to adhere to a principle, however true, may be unrealistic. He may also have trouble reconciling the concept of "giving help where it is needed most" with the principle that singling out children for special help is playing favorites.

One possible result of the confusion and inconsistencies of role expectations and what is asked of teachers, coupled with teachers' high standards, is perhaps reflected in the mental health problems of teachers themselves. A study[130] at the Mayo Clinic of neurotic disturbances in its patients found teachers had the highest incidence among the various occupations represented in the sample of 1,164 patients. Fenton,[44] in a study of 241 teachers in California, found 187 or 77.6 per cent to be in reasonably good mental health, 54 or 22.5 per cent to be suffering from some form of personality disturbance. In 17 of these cases, the teachers were found not to be seriously handicapped in their classroom work. In 37 of the 54, their professional work showed evidences of their personal difficulties.

The more confidence a teacher has in himself and in his professional competency, the more freedom he has in learning about himself and others. This study has shown that teachers evaluate children with personality difficulties much as they are evaluated by clinicians. When a teacher is able to verify or compare his perceptions of children with other information, he may become more aware of his own blind spots and help himself to become a more accurate perceiver of behavior. The opportunity for verifying or rejecting his judgments on a more scientific basis may help strengthen his relationship to the clinician and enable him, through this relationship, to gain a better understanding of self. This is a long way around but may be the shortest road to increasing teaching effectiveness. The values of using this screening technique "in fitting information about a child together,"[71] is in the long run one way of helping teachers to be more effective teachers.

Summary of Findings

A brief summary of the aspects of the information collected by each teacher which differentiated the emotionally handicapped children (those selected by the clinicians) from others in the classes follows. (In all the statements the word "significantly" means that there is only one chance in a hundred that a difference as large as the obtained difference would occur by chance.)

1. The emotionally handicapped children scored significantly lower on group IQ tests. On psychological tests given individually, they approached the mean score of all children included in the study.

2. The emotionally handicapped children scored significantly lower on reading and arithmetic achievement tests. The differences were greater and more significant on arithmetic achievement. The higher the school grade, the greater were the differences between the emotionally handicapped child and his classmates.

3. The emotionally handicapped boys differed significantly from the other boys in the classes in their self-perception. Emotionally handicapped girls showed less dissatisfaction with self than the rest of the girls in the classes.

4. On "A Class Play," the other children in the classes tended to select emotionally handicapped children for hostile, inadequate, or negative roles and failed to select them for the the positive roles. Hostile children particularly were selected for roles consistent with their behavior.

5. The emotionally handicapped children in this study came from homes which were not significantly different in socioeconomic level from those of other children generally.

6. Altogether, 87 per cent of the clinically known emotionally handicapped children were rated by their classroom teachers as among the most poorly adjusted children in the class. As perceived by teachers, 4.4 per cent of all the children in the classes were overly aggressive or defiant most of the time, while 6.1 per cent were overly withdrawn or timid most of the time.

In conclusion, one might note the following:

1. Children's judgments of other children's personality were surprisingly accurate and predictive.

2. Teachers' judgments of emotional disturbance were very much like the judgment of clinicians.

3. Teachers selected about the same number of children as being overly withdrawn or timid as overly aggressive or defiant.

4. At least three children in each average classroom could be regarded as having emotional problems of sufficient strength to warrant the appellation "emotionally handicapped children."

5. The differences between emotionally handicapped children and their classmates increase in each succeeding grade level.

Chapter 7

ADDITIONAL RESEARCH RESULTS AND FOLLOW-UP STUDIES

Los Angeles County Study

A SURVEY OF MENTAL HEALTH needs and problems in Los Angeles County[106] attempted to get some idea of the extent of the problem of emotional handicaps in school children. Using a short, concise questionnaire and working hard to enlist the cooperation of all schools and teachers, the survey tried to discover (1) which children, in the judgment of the teachers, were emotionally handicapped to the degree that they should be referred for psychiatric help, and (2) which children, in the judgment of the teachers, were emotionally handicapped to the degree that they required a disproportionate share of the teacher's time. The results are given in Table I.

Kindergarten and first grade, more than upper grade teachers, tend not to like to find problems in children and are often loath to evaluate children as needing help. By the first grade, however, we get close to the average of children needing help. The percentages remain remarkably constant in the middle grades, falling off a little in the eleventh grade and sharply in the twelfth as many emotionally handicapped children drop out. It is worthy of note that while the overall percentage of Types I and II for the regular grades remains at about 9.5 per cent, the degree of emotional handicaps in special education classes is 55.1 per cent.

Follow-up Study of Screened Children

One often wonders what happens to children with emotional handicaps as they pursue their difficult pathways through the educational labyrinth. Certainly a few are helped to move in a more positive direction by individual teachers, counselors, or life situations. Unfortunately, research indicates that the majority lose more and more ground as they seek to find their way in the school system.

TABLE I
Enrollment in Selected School Districts in Los Angeles County and Per Cent of Pupils with Emotional Disturbances, by Grades, 1958*

Grade level	Total enrollment	Per cent of pupils disturbed		
		Type I**	Type II***	Total
ELEMENTARY THROUGH GRADE SIX (27 districts)				
Kindergarten....................	57,374	1.1	5.0	6.1
First...........................	61,411	2.0	7.3	9.3
Second.........................	56,834	2.2	7.9	10.1
Third..........................	54,660	2.8	8.1	10.9
Fourth.........................	52,587	2.7	8.3	11.0
Fifth..........................	51,184	3.0	8.0	11.0
Sixth..........................	45,797	2.6	7.6	10.2
Total......................	379,847	2.3	7.4	9.7
GRADES SEVEN THROUGH TEN				
Seventh (21 districts)	39,754	2.4	7.0	9.4
Eighth (21 districts)	39,777	2.5	7.8	10.3
Ninth (6 districts)	35,079	2.4	6.6	9.0
Tenth (6 districts)	34,023	2.1	6.9	9.0
Total......................	148,633	2.4	7.1	9.5
GRADES ELEVEN AND TWELVE (2 districts)				
Eleventh.......................	1,643	2.8	4.4	7.2
Twelfth........................	1.304	0.8	2.0	2.8
Total[1]........................	2,947	1.9	3.3	5.2
SPECIAL EDUCATION				
Elementary grades (4 districts)	147	23.8	23.1	46.9
Secondary grades (3 districts)	993	29.9	26.4	56.3
Total[2]........................	1,140	29.1	26.0	55.1
TOTAL[3]...................	532,567	2.4	7.3	9.7

*Source of data. *Mental Health Survey of Los Angeles County*, 1960. Sacramento: State Department of Mental Hygiene, Ch. VII, p. 309.

**Type I. Children judged by their teachers to be emotionally disturbed and who have been or probably should be referred for psychiatric help.

***Type II. Children who are not seriously emotionally disturbed but whose behavior is such that the children require more than their share of the teacher's time and attention.

[1]The marked drop in the per cent of emotionally disturbed in grade twelve over grade eleven may be accounted for by the fact that students may leave school legally at the age of sixteen, and maladjusted students tend to do so.

[2]Special class enrollments include only boys and girls who are handicapped physically or mentally. The enrollments therefore include a high per cent of emotionally disturbed.

[3]The 532,374 enrollment does not include 4,209 individuals who were reported as disturbed but not as Type I or Type II, nor according to their grade placement. If this number were included the total enrollment would be 557,875, and the number of emotionally disturbed would be 56,065 or approximately 10 per cent of the total enrollment.

TABLE II

Comparison in 1960 of Pupils Identified in the 1955-56 School Year as Emotionally Handicapped with Pupils Identified at That Time as not Emotionally Handicapped

Basis of evaluation	Per cent of group		Sig. level	Interpretation
	Emotionally handicapped $N = 28$	Not emotionally handicapped $N = 43$		
A. School adjustment in the 1959-60 school year	$N = 30$	$N = 70$		
1. Final grades (C average or better) ...	50	17	.01	1. The emotionally handicapped group is seriously below average in school achievement.
2. Referrals to vice principal (1 to 14 referrals)	50	17	.01	2. More emotionally handicapped pupils are sent to the vice principal for disciplinary action.
3. Referrals to school counselor (1 to 20 referrals)	64	63	NS	3. The school counselor sees both emotionally handicapped and not emotionally handicapped pupils to a similar extent.
4. Number of program changes (1 to 8) .	54	22	.01	4. The referrals to the school counselor more often involve changes in school programs.
5. Of those pupils remaining, per cent that will graduate on the basis of counselor judgment	57	86	.01	5. Only about half of the emotionally handicapped pupils remaining in high school will graduate from high school — many have already dropped or been dropped.
6. Number of full-day excused absences (1 to more than 18)	82	67	.01	6. Emotionally handicapped pupils have more full-day excused absences than pupils who are not emotionally handicapped.
7. Number of full-day unexcused absences (1 to more than 9)	43	28	.05	7. Emotionally handicapped pupils have more full-day unexcused absences than pupils who are not emotionally handicapped.
8. Number of part-day excused absences (1 to 16 absences)	47	44	NS	8. Emotionally handicapped and not emotionally handicapped pupils have similar rates of part-day excused absences.

	N = 52	N = 78		
9. Number of part-day unexcused absences (to to 12 absences)	39	26	.05	9. Emotionally handicapped pupils have more unexcused absences than pupils who are not emotionally handicapped.
B. In-school referrals for special services..				
1. Referral to health office during 1959-60 school year (nurse and doctor) 1 to 11 referrals	71	44	.01	1. Emotionally handicapped pupils are more frequently referred to health office for illness, rest, or discomfort.
2. Referral to school guidance office (anytime during the individual's school life)	67	4	.01	2. Emotionally handicapped pupils need and receive a significant amount of attention from school guidance personnel.
3. Referral to child welfare and attendance office	19	8	.05	3. More home calls are made by child welfare and attendance workers to check on emotionally handicapped pupils than on other pupils.
C. Delinquency rate				
1. Number of entries in central Juvenile Index[1] (1 to 12 entries)	24	12	.05	1. Emotionally handicapped pupils have a greater incidence of contacts with police than other pupils.
2. Date of first entry in central Juvenile Index (before 1957; before or during junior high school)	46	10	.01	2. Emotionally handicapped pupils more frequently have contacts with police before high school.
3. Number of pupils who are or have been on probation	15	4	.01	3. Emotionally handicapped pupils are more likely to be on probation.
4. Proportion of all penal code violations committed by each group[2]	81	19	.01	4. Emotionally handicapped pupils commit more penal code violations.
5. Proportion of all vehicle code violations committed by each group[2]	67	33	.01	5. Emotionally handicapped pupils commit more vehicle code violations.
D. Referrals to local child guidance clinics.	61	1	.01	Emotionally handicapped pupils need the assistance and are referred more frequently to local guidance clinics.

[1]Los Angeles County Record of juveniles who have violated the law and have been required to account for the act.

[2]Prorated according to size of group to secure comparison.

In 1960, a follow-up study was made by Lambert[29] of fifty-two students who had been screened as being emotionally handicapped while they were in grades four, five, or six. The follow-up was accomplished by identifying the emotionally handicapped students selected in 1955 in Los Angeles County and two classmates at random who had been selected by teachers as having average adjustment. The records of these students were compared in 1960, five years later (Table II).

As one can see, the emotionally handicapped children are significantly different from their classmates in committing vehicle code and penal code violations (and getting caught), in police contacts, in referral to guidance clinics, health offices, school guidance personnel, in school achievement disciplinary actions, and absences. There is strong support in this kind of data for programs in early identification and intervention.

Subsequent Studies of the Screening Process

Additional funds were provided in 1958 by the State of California to design, develop, and test out special programs and procedures in the education of emotionally handicapped children. In the carrying out of this project, the screening procedures developed earlier were revised and tested out with large populations of students. The validity of the screening procedures was subjected to a variety of tests. One such procedure was to study a selected group of screened students individually. In this study nine out of ten who were identified by the screening process were found to have moderate to severe emotional problems on the basis of such individual studies (Table III).

Another study was launched to determine if the screening process was picking up children already visible and known to teachers and the school. The important consideration in this study was to find out if such visibility and knowledge had produced some form of school action and if so what kind. It was found that seven out of ten children with moderate to serious emotional problems who were identified by the screening materials had not been referred to the principal or school psychologist. Such referrals are, of course, a product of the teacher's anxiety about a child and his assessment of whether or not anything will happen to help him. Nevertheless, it was evident that without some screening procedure a significant number of children who needed individual attention because of emotional difficulties would be missed.

TABLE III
Effectiveness of Screening Procedure in Identifying Pupils with Various Types of Emotional Handicaps

	Assignment			
	Boys		Girls	
Behavior classification[1]	Number	Per cent	Number	Per cent
Extremely poor interpersonal relations; bizarre, eccentric behavior	24	14	4	7
Shy, inhibited, timid, fearful	44	26	20	36
Generally aggressive in many situations.	42	25	9	16
Socialized delinquency, primarily a cultural problem where a child gets along with his gang but not with other groups	8	5	1	2
Organic — possible constitutional rather than emotional instability ...	7	4		
Other[2]	44	26	22	39
TOTAL	156	100	56	100

[1]Behavior classification system based on work of Richard L. Jenkins and Maurice Lorr as reported in "Patterns of Maladjustment in Children," *Journal of Clinical Psychology*, IX (January, 1953), 16-20.

[2]Pupils in this classification: 6 per cent were mentally retarded, 33 per cent had no problems or minor problems, and 61 per cent were handicapped by a variety of problems and could not be placed in any one of the other five classifications.

There was also some question about the ability of the screening procedures to identify children with different types of emotional difficulties. For example, how would the shy, quiet child fare in a screening procedure of this kind? Table V indicates that the procedures are sensitive to all kinds of emotional handicaps.

Another inquiry into the validity of the screening procedures was carried out by asking two experienced clinical psychologists to test thirty pairs of pupils without any prior knowledge of the school or case history of any of the students. In each pair, one pupil had been selected by the screening procedure and the other at random from the same class. Table VI indicates that the psychologists were able to identify twenty-seven out of the thirty children who were selected by the screening process.

TABLE IV
Extent to Which the Study Screening Process Identified Emotionally
Handicapped Pupils Previously Referred to School
Psychologist or Principal

Screening procedure results with pupils identified by specialists as emotionally handicapped	Per cent of pupils at each grade level		
	Primary	Elementary	Secondary
Scores on all instruments indicated emotional handicap	66	64	88
Scores on one instrument indicated emotional handicap and scores on the other instruments indicated a borderline case	25	26	10
Scores on instruments indicated borderline case..		6	
Not identified	9	4	2
TOTAL	100	100	100

The idea that early identification is a process of finding the most economical or efficient predictors must be expanded to include the notion that data used in prediction must be helpful and meaningful to the key persons in the system in planning educational changes for the identified child. Prediction in this sense is not a cold, dispassionate correlation of variables and weights but a sizing up of variables with teacher roles and tasks and judging which will be the best educational fit. The notion that early identification is basically cold prediction led Maes[103] to replicate the study discussed in this book in order to find more efficient predictors.

Maes studied forty emotionally disturbed children and their 548 normal classmates in twenty-two different classrooms using the same variable as in the original Bower study. Using a multiple regression method, Maes found that the variables most predictive of emotional disturbance were teacher rating (behavior), arithmetic achievement, group intelligence score, "A Class Play," teacher rating (physical status), and reading achievement. The prediction achieved with teacher rating and IQ score was considered as effective as the use of six variables.

Such predictions may be efficient but they provide sparse data to the teacher for planning educational interventions on behalf of the child. The consequences of prediction are not only as clean a separation of those who might need extra help from those who

TABLE V

Distribution of Pupils on the Basis of Screening Results Obtained Through Combinations of Teacher, Peer, and Self Ratings, According to Behavior Patterns Described by Clinical Psychologists

Psychologists' behavior classification	Number of pupils with behavior as determined by screening procedure				Number of pupils	Per cent of all pupils
	Teacher and peer evaluations	Teacher and self evaluations	Peer and self evaluations	Teacher, peer, and self evaluations		
Poor interpersonal relations — bizarre, odd	9	0	1	4	14	13
Shy, inhibited, fearful, withdrawn	17	3	3	8	31	28
Primarily aggressive	17	3	3	14	37	33
Socialized delinquent, primarily culture problems, gets along with gang but not others	0	0	0	0	0	0
Organic, marked variability, unpredictable behavior, and instability	3	0	1	1	5	4
Others	9	2	7	6	24	22
TOTAL	55	8	15	33	111	100
Per cent of all pupils	50	7	13	30		

might not, but clues on the kind of extra help which might do the trick. This concept is presented, illustrated, and followed up by Newton and Brown in a study in the Sumter (South Carolina) public schools.[113]

Zax, Cowen, and their associates used two instruments from *A Process for the In-School Screening of Children with Emotional Handicaps*, "Thinking About Yourself" and "A Class Play," in a preventive program in the Rochester (N.Y.) schools.[154] The results of these two instruments were correlated with referrals to nurse, absence, grade point average, intelligence and achievement test scores, an achievement-aptitude discrepancy score, and a teachers' rating of pupil behavior from which was derived a total adjustment score.

The largest number of correlations of any single measure in the two screening instruments was "percentage of negative roles assigned to students by their classmates" in "A Class Play." Only

TABLE VI
Distribution of Clinical Psychologists' Ratings of 30 Pupils (10 from Primary Grades, 20 from Elementary Grades) Randomly Chosen from Emotionally Handicapped Identified by Study Screening Procedure and 30 Randomly Chosen from Pupils Who Were Not Identified as Emotionally Handicapped[1]

Degree of Emotional adjustment	Total rating	Number with rating	
		Emotionally handicapped	Not emotionally handicapped
Good.............	7		
↑	6		1
	5		1
	4		2
Plus | ratings	3		8
	2	1	5
	1	4	4
Neither good nor poor.....	0	1	6
Minus | ratings	1	5	1
	2	5	
	3	3	
	4	6	2
	5	2	
↓	6	2	
Poor.............	7	1	
TOTAL.......		30	30

[1]The ratings were based on the results of psychological tests generally used for such purposes. Each pupil was rated on each test by the psychologists on a scale ranging from —2 to +2. The psychologists were uninformed regarding which, if any, of the pupils were screened as emotionally handicapped.

in "Days Absent" was there a nonsignificant relationship between this measure and any of the other fourteen measures.

This study also suggests other possible uses of data from "A Class Play" for classroom planning. "A Class Play" is composed of twenty hypothetical roles in a play. Each student is instructed to become the director of the play and assign classmates to roles which in his judgment would be most suitable and natural. A second section of "A Class Play" asks each student about roles he would prefer, roles which others would select for him, etc. (see Appendix, "A Class Play"). One can compare how students are seen by others with how they see themselves. In this study, significant negative correlations were found between this discrepancy score and Grade Point and Achievement-Aptitude ratios; significant positive correlation was found with teachers' ratings of adjustment. Children who saw themselves in positive roles but who were not so selected by their classmates tended to earn lower grades and were rated as less well adjusted by their teachers. On the other hand, children who saw themselves more negatively than their classmates achieved at a higher level and were regarded as better adjusted by teachers. Zax, Cowen *et al*, suggests the latter type of school adjustment (intropunitiveness) may be more adaptive in school.

Since boys and girls are different with the differences accentuating in the upper grades it is interesting to note that the discrepancy measure shows the same pattern for both. However, on the "Thinking About Yourself" (see index), the brighter males show the least self-dissatisfaction. The investigators suggest that at least at the third grade level self-esteem may be more rooted in intellectual potency for the male than for the female.

Another investigation using the screening materials was conducted by Stennett in Minnesota.[134] He found the screening materials reliable in that thirty-eight of the forty-six children (83 per cent) were classified in the same way in succeeding years in different class settings; he also found the process equally reliable in identifying nonemotionally handicapped children (82 and 85 per cent respectively). In a follow-up study three years later, the data indicated that 72 per cent of the children were classified as before (correctly?). Again Stennett found that the screening was almost twice as consistent in identifying nonemotionally handicapped children as emotionally handicapped children.

This study was also interested in the educational progress of the emotionally handicapped child and compared the academic progress of the screened versus nonscreened groups over the years. Again the data illustrate dramatically the increasing educational gap between emotionally handicapped children and their classmates. Stennett concludes that (a) about five to ten per cent of children enrolled in elementary school warrant professional attention because of emotional handicaps; (b) the screening devices are generally quite adequate; (c) a significant number of identified children are not likely to resolve their problems and tend to fall progressively behind their classmates.

Lastly, there is Lambert's[97] determined attempt to do as clean a job of validating the screening process as is possible. The first phase consisted of the establishment of two criterion groups of children — one group with few if any problems and another composed of those children who were experiencing some difficulty. These groups were established by clinical teams composed of psychiatrists, clinical psychologists, and social workers who applied their own disciplinary skills in appraising children and then decided collectively if the child could be considered emotionally handicapped or not.

In the second phase, all of the children in the second and fifth grades from which the clinicians drew their sample were screened. The third phase consisted of the analysis of the effectiveness of the screening process in differentiating the children as defined by the clinical team.

This study also developed significant natural history data about the use of psychiatric, psychological, and social work procedures in assessing the mental health and learning potential of students. Mental health clinicians apparently need a clear statement of the location and extent of difficulty before they can begin to use their skills effectively. Most have been trained to work in clinics or agencies where people are motivated to come and present their problems. In this study they were asked to assess children many of whom had no specific complaints and certainly had not come as active seekers of help.

Although teacher and clinician judgments correlated from .36 to .50 indicating a high positive relationship between teachers and the clinical team, it also indicates lots of room for differences between the two groups. Lambert points out that teachers most often see as problems pupils whom they have difficulty teaching or managing. They will often not refer a child with a problem if they feel they understand why (his father is an alcoholic, he has a low IQ, etc.) even though they are able, if questioned, to describe the nature of the problem and the child's need for help. The notion that referrals by teachers are made on the basis of the seriousness of the child's problem fails to take into account that "degree of pathology" is a product of the disturber and the disturbed. The nature of a referral can also vary from a word in passing to the principal to a passionate, overwhelming request by a teacher for an individual study with a sense of impending doom for teacher, parent, child, school, and society if something isn't done immediately. This is one reason why it is often difficult to utilize teacher referrals in screening procedures. In general, Lambert found that 84 per cent of those screened would have achieved criterion scores indicating moderate or serious emotional handicaps. Those pupils not screened who should have been were found to be pupils with passive personalities and low IQ scores. Apparently, these students are not responded to by others and have a difficult time interacting with peers or clinicians.

Chapter 8

REACTIONS TO THE STUDY BY
THE INVESTIGATOR

I T IS NOT WIDELY KNOWN that William of Occam, a philosopher of sorts, circa 1300, devised a blade known as the "spoiler" long before Gillette ever heard of the World Series. Occam's razor was tempered by a few cutting remarks about human functioning which loosely translated and brought up to date could be stated thus: "Don't complicate the hell out of simple things." For those of you who prefer more literal translations, Occam's words were, "Assumptions introduced to explain something should not be multiplied beyond necessity."

It is axiomatic that simple problems are easier to solve than complex ones. One therefore needs to examine the possibilities of finding ways of helping children who are developing serious mental health or delinquency problems early, effectively, and economically. The only institution which can at present administer this kind of program is the school. The focus in this short chapter is on the mythologies and encrustations about mental health and education which have kept this kind of an attempt feeble and ineffective. I am afraid we will need to change blades in Occam's Razor more than once before we get any program of real significance and impact going in this area. Let me state some of the mystique which needs slicing and go on to explain why.

About ten years ago the State of California decided to invest a sizable amount of funds and some of my time to find out if emotionally disturbed children could be identified early in their school life and if so whether something could be done to immobilize, interrupt, or intercept this kind of development. Our research indicated we could identify children with beginning learning and behavior problems effectively and economically using perceptual ratings of students by teachers, peers, and the student himself. Not surprisingly, we found our measures of the state of emotional development of students to be highly reliable, and on the basis of what good sense and little research we had, to be valid. At this point, however, some of our mental health colleagues began to shake their heads. "Remember," they said, "the old Wickman study[152] in which considerable question was raised about the ability of teachers and schools to recognize the symptoms of serious emotional problems. How do we know that the children you have identified are *really and truly* the mental health problems of our society? Are children identified by teachers (and peers and self) really emotionally disturbed? What is more important, how do you know that these are the children who will eventually become mentally ill?" The last question was always posed with the all-knowing scowl of the pipe-smoking scholar searching for the first star in the night sky.

Let me resurrect Wickman's study for those readers too young to have been exposed or too old to remember. What Wickman did was have a group of 511 teachers and a group of thirty mental hygienists rate the seriousness of fifty behavior traits of children. What set the fulminating cap sizzling was his finding that the ratings made by the mental hygienists and those made by the teachers had zero correlation. Wickman himself was not at all dismayed by this result and was most emphatic in pointing out that the directions to each group had been significantly different. The teachers had been asked to rate the behavior as problems in the here and now reality of the classroom, while the mental hygienists were directed to rate the behavior on the basis of its effect on the future life of the child. Teachers were also told to define the seriousness of a problem by the amount of difficulty it produced in the classroom. The mental health group was asked to rate problem behavior in relation to its importance to a child's mental health. When the smoke cleared and the ratings of the two groups were compared, it was obvious that teachers were concerned with behavior which related to classroom disruption, and mental health people were concerned with behavior which was disturbing the child's inner psyche. Each group was looking at the problem pretty much from their own professional biases and job-related firing line.

Although Wickman was careful to point out the limitations of his study, this did not prevent many nonreading professionals from jumping to unwarranted conclusions. Two educators[126] examined twelve texts in psychology and educational psychology which mentioned Wickman's study and found only two which gave a clear and concise statement of the study and its findings. Most discussed the study as indicating that as judges of the mental health status of children, teachers were way off the beam. The basic assumption, of course, was that the mental health experts were right and that teachers were wrong.

The myth still exists that someone, somewhere, somehow, knows how to assess behavior and/or mental health as positive or negative, good or bad, healthy or nonhealthy, independently of the social context in which the individual is living and functioning. I strongly suspect that teachers, by focusing on the child's observable behavior in school, are closer to an operational reality of mental health than one can come up with in a sedentary examination. What a teacher is judging is how a specific behavior affects him, other students, and the student himself in a primary social system. The teacher's major concern when a child behaves in an overly aggressive manner or is unable to learn and cannot be influenced to change is that he is unable to carry out his goal of helping the child to learn.

Similarly, when a child in a play group cannot adhere to the rules of the game, the group will find his behavior a problem in that setting and if he continues, they will not play with him. A child who has little or no emotional responsiveness to a parent will be a problem in a family setting where such responsiveness is one of the expected behaviors of children vis-à-vis parents. Each behavior can only be judged as positive or negative in relation to the social system in which a range of behaviors is expected and prescribed.

It is also necessary to understand that each of the social contexts in which children function have specific goals, rules, and competencies which act as guides for assessing prescribed and expected behavior. A school is a system which demands learning competence; a play group requires rules awareness behavior; a family should provide an opportunity for some interchange of healthy hostility and affection. Life is lived by children within primary humanizing institutions, each of which requires specific functioning skills and behavior appropriate to its goals. Who knows what mental health is in the abstract? One can, however, define it as the kind of competencies and reality testing which allows a child to function effectively in the humanizing institutions in which he is asked to live. Specifically these are the skills he needs to function in the home, peer or play group, and the school.

The fact is that teachers gather enough information about children in their routine operations to make highly accurate professional predictions about the course of a child's school life. However, there is little or no magic in such predictive data unless in the process of gathering such data the key professional person in the system is moved to act. Let us say it another way without changing blades. There is very good evidence that it is possible to detect potential delinquents at an early age using the Social Prediction Scale developed by the Gluecks.[56] Why is it not used as a preventive tool? By and large, I would guess because the process of prediction requires operations not consistent with the goals and processes of the institution itself. In addition, the prediction itself has little curriculum implication or program consequences for the key professional worker in the school, the teacher. Prediction processes must lead to positive action by someone in the system and this is especially critical for problems which have not as yet had full crisis impact on the teacher. How often does one hear a kindergarten or first grade teacher in a teachers' room react to a fifth or sixth grade teacher reciting the gory adventures of a problem child by noting, "Oh, him — he was somewhat of a problem in the first grade. I thought he might get over it." The upper grade teacher shakes her graying hair indicating a sadder, less optimistic state of things.

But can teachers and schools be effective screeners of children with beginning mental health problems? In a 1963 study,[58] teachers were asked to rate children on five steps ranging from (1) Child has no problems and is obviously extremely well adjusted;

there is absolutely no need for referral; to (5) Child has problems of sufficient severity to require referral. Following this, a sample of children were seen by psychiatrists in privately conducted interviews of about fifty minutes each. There was a marked lack of agreement between teachers and psychiatrists in classifying children who had severe adjustment problems and needed referral. The investigator thereupon concluded that teachers cannot adequately serve as casefinders in mental health screening.

In analyzing this research one needs to raise at least two questions: (1) To what extent is a fifty-minute appraisal by a psychiatrist to be considered a more valid assessment of a child's functioning capabilities and liabilities in a school setting than a teacher's day-in and day-out experiences? (2) How exactly do teachers react to the concept and meaning of the term "adjustment" and "referral"?

One teacher explained her meaning of adjustment: "I guess it means how well a student gets along in school and with others. Now I have this one student who gets along pretty well and I guess is well adjusted but can't seem to learn anything." While the concept of adjustment is understood by teachers, its operational implementation is somewhat out of the frame of reference and functioning of teachers. Most feel that in rating "adjustment" they are attempting to fill the role of a psychiatrist and somehow rate the degrees of intrapsychic conflict and chaos in the minds of their students. Whatever adjustment is or means I would suggest that ratings asked of teachers stick to school-related behaviors which can be operationally defined and observed. Does the child get into fights? Can he pay attention when required? Does he learn to read? Is he in a blue funk? Does he get sick? Does he get hurt? Can he express an idea?

To put the shoe on the other foot, a Philadelphia psychiatrist (no relation to a philadelphia lawyer) compared the predictive skill of a teacher, a psychologist, and a child psychiatrist in judging which kindergarten children would learn up to their IQ potential in the first grade.[30] A total of fifty-six kindergarten children were included in the study. Each professional person related to the children as he would have in his normal professional practice. The teacher taught and observed, the psychologist tested, and the child psychiatrist used a standard play situation. All three did a good job of predicting the achievement, but the teacher's was best. The phychiatrist had a tendency to predict more under-achievement than actually occurred. He suggests that the reason may be that some of the clinical anxiety which he picked up in the children and which he expected to lead to underachievement actually produced overachievement. This is, of course, the nub of the problem. It is only the teacher who is able to observe how a child may use different aspects of his personality and self and who can assess the nuances of how the child mediates what he has, be it anxiety, IQ, shyness, or aggressiveness. The investigation confirms Robins' study discussed later that (1) raters in general are better at spotting potential positive achievers than poor achievers; (2) teacher judgments provide the most economical and efficient guide to the prediction of school success.

The Nonmagic of Teacher Referrals

Another wicked slice of Occam's Razor needs to be taken at the notion and concept of the referral. In the past, teachers have been so impressed by their lack of mental health expertise and the expertness of their mental health colleagues that the only significant help which they could conceptualize was the referral. "If we only had adequate referral resources" echoed throughout the land. This process, at least for teachers, has been invested with a penicillin-like magic which unfortunately is dissipated in the realities of limited knowledge and limited manpower. The referral concept for the majority of teachers is one where the child is taken elsewhere, where something magical is done to straighten him out, whereupon he is returned to school a healthy, well-motivated student. This rarely turns out to be the case. Occasionally referrals are consummated to the satisfaction of the teacher. When this happens it is evident that some mental health expert has learned to translate what he knows clinically and psychodynamically into the frame of reference of the teacher and into educational processes and objectives. Unfortunately there are only a few referral agencies that know how to do this. Most teachers have high regard for mental health persons and their professional competence. When the secrets (psychodynamics) of a problem are revealed to a teacher he often stands aghast at the marvels of modern psychiatry, psychology, or casework and is thrilled to be a partner to such mighty revelations. He may reenter the class with a better understanding of the why and what of the student's difficulty but with his major problem still unanswered, "How do I teach this child?"

There is another assumption about teachers and referrals which needs slicing. If, in a hypothetical community, there were available immediate, convenient, and useful referral services (each of these will affect the process significantly) and teachers were encouraged to refer children who needed help, there are still other factors which come into the picture. One psychologist attempting to help teachers in an inner city school wanted to know why he got so few referrals. The teachers laughed when he finally confessed and pointed out that if he were serious they would be happy to send him three fourths of their classes. There is also the phenomenon that when a teacher refers a child she does so because *she* is puzzled or anxious about the behavior. Lambert found that teachers, when asked to refer children, will not refer students with serious problems if they feel they understand some of the background and causes of the problem but will refer less serious problems when the behavior or learning difficulty is puzzling or anxiety provoking.

It is no longer possible in this day and age to think of referral services as desirable or necessary if one is concerned with the basic preventive question, How do you increase the ecological competence of a humanizing institution to serve more children more effectively? I would suggest one way would be to develop mental health workers (clinical behavioral workers) who would not be walled off from the humanizing institutions by having to deal with its casualties but could become an active partner with the teacher, principal, and parents in monitoring and enhancing the behavior of all children in the school.

The Object of Early Identification

It took me quite a while to realize that the notion of early identification meant different things to different professional groups. One of my psychiatric colleagues used to puzzle me by his lack of enthusiasm for research in this field. Once when I confronted him about this, he replied, "I don't see why you get worked up about this early identification of emotionally disturbed children. We've got more cases than we can handle right now without finding some more."

His notion of early discovery had to do with what is known in the trade as "cases." My notion of early discovery has to do with the discovery of a child in a primary institution such as a school who is beginning to have trouble in coping with the demands and processes of that institution. The child's problem may be related specifically to that institution and to the demands of that institution. The nature of the institution is such that left alone a child with a beginning problem either finds a wise, highly competent teacher or the problem continues to grow. In the California studies, children identified as emotionally handicapped fell further behind in reading and arithmetic achievement, were seen increasingly as negative or inadequate students by their peers and after five years were seen in child guidance clinics, appeared in the juvenile index for vehicle code violations and penal code violations, in stark contrast to a randomly selected group of their classmates. This was replicated and amplified by the Minnesota study which illustrates dramatically that children identified as emotionally handicapped get farther and farther behind their classmates in school skills and get stuck on a track which leads to severe educational embarrassment and incompetence.

The humanizing institutions to which children are mandated are unfortunately social systems which tend to reward those who succeed in it and punish whose who fail. Programs of early identification in schools must therefore not only find apathetic and failing children early, but must in the process of finding them provide knowledge for the institutional changes which will make the finding worthwhile. This means that processes of early identification must be carried out by key persons in specific humanizing institutions in the context of the goals and processes of that institution and in such a way that alternative possibilities for action are natural outcomes of the process. Programs of early identification which require teachers to do non-teacherlike jobs will not last and cannot be effective. Early identification processes which do not have educational relevance are research exercises which cannot be implemented. Such processes must lead to and be conceptualized in a school framework and be translatable into valid interventions within the humanizing institution in which the child is living and attempting to function.

The Need for Humanizing Institutions

Nobody believes it is possible for all children to experience our humanly constructed humanizing institutions in a positive and ego-enhancing way. If one can remove one's home-grown complexities and professional blinkers about this sordid world and its people, it is possible to conceptualize humanizing institutions which can carry out their goals and processes for greater ranges of children and eventually for all children. Either we do this or pay the cost in lives and money for remedial or rehabilitative institutions such as prisons, mental hospitals, welfare programs, and alcoholic and drug wards. It is also well to remember that when children can't function in institutions devised for their benefit, they hurt and they bleed. One does not have to ask whether they have broken a leg or cut an artery before administering first aid. One wonders if the children identified as emotionally disturbed in school are really and truly disturbed or if they represent the group who will later become mentally ill. One also wonders how meaningful the question is. I suspect more of them become mentally ill than their classmates. I also suspect more of them become antisocial, inadequate, dependent, alcoholic, drug addicted, and physically ill than a random group of colleagues.

This conclusion is supported by a study of 524 adults who were seen as children in a child guidance clinic and 100 controls of the same age, sex, neighborhood, race, and IQ[120] The purpose of the study was to describe through a longitudinal natural history the kinds of childhood behavior problems which are serious danger signals and those which are not. Robins' study is interesting in that there was an unexpected payoff in the data on the control group.

First, what happened to the 524 adults who had been seen as children in the child guidance clinic? Robins divided them into two gross categories, antisocial and nonantisocial on the basis of behavior which led to referral. He found that antisocial children by and large became antisocial adults. Not only were these adults more often arrested and imprisoned than expected, but they were more mobile, had more marital difficulties, poorer occupational and armed service histories, used alcohol and drugs excessively, and had poorer physical health. "But," Robins adds, "from one point of view . . . what we have found is not so much a pathological patient group as an extraordinarily well adjusted control group" (p. 69). What they did to select control subjects was to set quotas for year of birth, sex, census tract, IQ above 80, no grade repeated, and no record of expulsion or transfer. Microfilm reels were spun and selection made in the Las Vegas tradition. This roulette, however, turned out to be a winner. Using these four not high-standard criteria (IQ over 80, not seen at the municipal psychiatric clinic, no grade repeated, and no expulsion from school), Robins had selected a group of 100 adults of whom only two ever appeared in juvenile court and who as adults had good psychiatric adjustment and social competence. She concludes that while having repeated grades in elementary school certainly does not efficiently predict serious adult problems, *having not had serious school difficulties may be a rather efficient predictor of the absence of gross maladjustment as adults.* Perhaps we have been so concerned with the prediction of deviant behavior that we were not aware how well we could do predicting effective behavior.

In light of our earlier comment about predicting mental illness from school behavior, Robins found no clear connection between type of deviance in childhood and type of problem in adulthood. For example, those adults with antisocial behavior in childhood not only showed antisocial adult behavior, but a greater degree of social alienation, more psychiatric and physical disabilities. As a result, Robbins found that children referred for anti-social behavior have a less promising prediction than children referred for other reasons. This is the group that needs help as do the teachers who try to cope with their behavior and help them to learn.

Chapter 9

HOW TEACHERS CAN USE THE RESULTS
IN SCREENING

With the exception of rate of absence, socioeconomic status, and age-grade relationship, the information selected for study significantly differentiated the emotionally handicapped child from his classmates. In the proposed screening process, however, analysis of differences in IQ and achievement were omitted since the time and effort required by the teacher to manage and utilize the information were found not to be commensurable with the results. However, it should be borne in mind that both IQ and achievement are significant variables and should be considered along with other pertinent information.

For screening purposes, considering economy of teacher time and effort and effectiveness of screening, the "Pupil Behavior Rating Scale," "A Class Play," and "Thinking About Yourself" have proved most useful and sound. They collectively provide a triad of perceptions from the best positions available — teacher, peer, and self. The administration and scoring of each of the instruments has been reduced to simple, light tasks. In addition, the results can be readily synthesized into a composite, understandable picture of each child by most teachers. By and large, teachers find this process of screening interesting and informative; therefore, they tend to see the administration and scoring tasks as rewarding and the subsequent analysis worthy of effort.

The Screening Process

The directions for administration and scoring of each of the instruments are given in the appendix. For screening purposes, the results on the "Pupil Behavior Rating Scale," "A Class Play," and "Thinking About Yourself" are utilized in the following manner:

Step 1—Administration, Scoring, and Ranking of Class on "Pupil Behavior Rating Scale."

Teacher rates all children in class prior to administration of other instruments. After rating, teacher totals ratings for Item 6 through 13. Total score may range from a maximum of 40 to a minimum of 8. The teacher then ranks the class from highest score to lowest.

Step 2—Administration, Scoring, and Ranking of Class on "A Class Play."

Teacher administers and scores the results on "A Class Play." Omitting those who have been selected for a total of less than five parts, the teacher ranks the class from highest percentage in Column C (Teachers Worksheet for "A Class Play" to lowest percentage in Column C. Teacher should also make a sublist of those receiving zero choices.

Step 3—Administration, Scoring, and Ranking of Class on "Thinking About Yourself."

Using the scoring procedures described on page 190, the teacher ranks the boys from highest score to lowest and then ranks the girls from highest to lowest.

Step 4—Determining Eligibility on Each Ranked List.

After the rankings have been completed, the teacher draws a line under the pupils receiving the five highest scores on the "Pupil Behavior Rating Scale"; another line is drawn under the pupils receiving the five highest percentages on "A Class Play," Section I. In the rankings on "Thinking About Yourself," a line is drawn under the third highest boy and the third highest girl. When this is done, the rankings of a sample class might look as follows:

Pupil Behavior Rating	*A Class Play*	*Thinking About Yourself*	
1. Fred A.	1. Norman H.	1. Fred A.	1. Zelda P.
2. Henry B.	2. Maxine I.	2. Grover N.	2. Maxine I.
3. Helen C.	3. Fred A.	3. Bruce O.	3. Kathy Q.
4. Oscar D.	4. Helen C.	4. Henry B.	4. Helen C.
5. Kenneth C.	5. Gilbert J.	5. Kenneth C.	5. Ethel F.
6. James E.	6. Milton K.	6. James E.	6. Esther G.
7. Ethel F.	7. Roy L.	7. Roy L.	7. Janet M.
8. Esther G.	8. Janet M.	8. Milton K.	8. Constance R.
etc.	etc.	etc.	etc.

Step 5—Selection of Screened Group.

Those children who are above the line in two of the three rankings or on all three of the rankings are selected for screening purposes. In the above example, Helen C. is selected on the basis of ranking on the "Pupil Behavior Rating" and "A Class Play." Maxine I. is selected on the basis of ranking on "A Class Play" and "Thinking About Yourself." Fred A. is selected on the basis of high ranking on all three. Some children can be regarded as borderline, i.e. one higher ranking would have placed them in the screened group. Such near misses should be noted for future reference. Studies[77] in which this process has been used indicate that out of every ten children selected, three will be selected on the basis of high rankings on the "Pupil Behavior Rating Scale," "A Class Play" and "Thinking About Yourself"; five will be selected on the basis of high rankings on the "Pupil Behavior Rating Scale" and "A Class Play"; one on the basis of rankings on "A Class Play" and "Thinking About Yourself"; and one on the basis of rankings on the "Pupil Behavior Rating Scale" and "Thinking About Yourself." In an average class of thirty pupils, approximately three pupils will be screened by this method.

It is well to remember that the "Pupil Behavior Rating Scale" and "A Class Play" should not be administered until the class and the teacher have had an opportunity to get to know each other. In most cases, administration should not take place before late October or early November. Although "Thinking About Yourself" can be administered earlier in the school year, it is also well to wait until a good class-teacher relationship has been established before presenting this task to students.

There is little doubt on the basis of these and other studies that the screening procedure outlined above can be successfully employed by teachers and that children who are developing emotional problems can be identified early. As a result of their participation in the process, most teachers felt they were better able to teach and more confident about their referrals. Further, most teachers indicated that if given the opportunity, they would continue to employ the instruments and procedures in subsequent years.

Chapter 10

SOME POSITIVE AND PREVENTIVE OUTCOMES

T HIS STUDY OF A process of screening children who are becoming emotional problems was designed to secure a "psychological thermometer" that might be used by teachers to help them better estimate the mental health of children in their classes. This "thermometer," like a clinical thermometer, was to be one that could be read easily and could indicate with reasonable consistency and accuracy the existence of emotional disturbances in children. Such an objective is described in Howe as follows:

> No longer are we looking for some one definitive measure of mental health comparable to a platinum bar, but rather for indirect indications of the state of being, that is, for indices. What we seem to need is the kind of measuring device that may be compared to a clinical thermometer on which successive readings can be taken in order to chart deviations from and approximations to the norm of 98.6 degrees. Such a thermometer might yield only one limited and partial kind of measurement, to be sure, but this kind of measurement is better than none — at least if proper precautions regarding its interpretation are observed.[75]

Screening and Thermometers

It must be remembered that thermometers provide only one kind of information about an individual's condition and that the information obtained seldom provides a diagnosis of the condition or illness causing the fever. Similarly, the use of the information and process of this study may help a teacher in many ways. It may help him confirm a suspicion about a child or reject a suspicion, or in some cases, to raise a suspicion. The use of the materials and process of this study may provide a teacher with a more accurate and safe base than subjective feelings for communicating his need for help from specialists. It may also provide the interested teacher with a baseline from which individual change can be assessed. For some teachers it can also furnish a standard, helpful procedure for continuous inquiry into the validity of their own judgments about children.

As is true with almost every measuring instrument or process, certain precautions need to be taken. It is important to remember that the significant aspects of human personality do not lend themselves to the precise measurement one employs with confidence in the physical sciences; nor does the use of a number when divorced from its derivation and context have any greater meaning or magic than good qualitative descriptions. Physicians once believed that a fever was the disease itself, the thing to be destroyed. This is only true in part. A direct attack on a fever may not result in quelling the underlying factors which are causing the fever. However, in some cases a reduction of the fever and an increase of self-comfort may enable the person to cope better with the inner difficulty. For example, there is some evidence that certain emotional problems can be reduced by attacking the symptoms directly. Preadolescents whose early emotional problems resulted in poor reading or arithmetic skills can often be helped by attacking the symptoms directly, poor reading or arithmetic. The chances of economically altering the latent emotional maladjustment may be slim. The reduction of the reading or arithmetic inadequacy may yield sufficient ego strength to enable the child to redirect some of the conflicted energy into more positive channels.

Effect on Teacher and Clinician

It has been previously noted that the materials and process of this study might be helpful in increasing the effectiveness of the teacher-clinical staff relationships. An emotionally handicapped child whose behavior is erratic, unpredictable, or disrupting can and often does induce anxiety and despair in a teacher. There is often little in the education of teachers which prepares them to deal with their own anxieties and doubts about personal adequacy which results from teaching one or more emotionally maladjusted children. An excellent discussion of this problem is presented by Berlin.[7]

At times the relationship of the class and teacher to the emotionally handicapped child is such that no solution but separation of the child from the group is acceptable. When this point is reached, the teacher may seek the help of the clinician as a "waver of the magic wand," that is, a person who can solve the problem quickly either by changing the child's personality or by changing his room. Therefore, it may be difficult for the teacher to accept the help of the clinician when the teacher's expectations are unmet and when he is asked to participate in what appears to be a nebulous process of "understanding" the child. Intellectually, he may recognize the limitations of the clinical service, yet feel quite disappointed that nothing happens and that, after all, he is still plagued with the problem. In time, therefore, he may come to feel that the clinical service offers little help. The psychologist or guidance worker, on the other hand, may be so overwhelmed by the numbers and seriousness of the problems that he becomes immersed solely in the clinical nature of his task. As Krugman points out, "Because there is almost never sufficient staff in a school guidance program to do what needs to be done, the tendency is usually to focus on emergencies or immediately annoying problems . . . We still have too great a tendency to throw our full armamentarium of personality appraisal methods into efforts to salvage the problem child."[87]

The anxiety induced in a teacher by one or more emotionally handicapped children is often visited upon all the children in the class. As a result, the teacher may tend to be overly aggressive or negligent with some children whose problems are situational or incipient. A teacher who "knows" the children and the class may be more comfortable about seeking help and more aware of personal anxieties and biases in appraising children. It is also necessary that a teacher accept the fact that some children are seriously disturbed and need the help of community mental health services, such as a clinic, a family caseworker, or a hospital. The number and urgency of serious problems may be greatly reduced, however, if the teacher-clinical team can be helped to make the most of the school's potential for recognizing personality distortions in children early.

Relationship to Working Relationships of Staff

If a society is interested in greater immunization of its population to emotional disorders it might well study ways of making full use of the teacher's unequalled opportunity. What help can be economically given to the teacher's normal judgmental and appraisal processes which he could and would use comfortably and with profit? What self-validating procedures can teachers accept within their own role perception as teachers which can help them be more effective as "suspecticians"? The process of screening as out-lined in Chapter 7 may be seen as one way of providing the teacher with "consensual validation" *a la* Sullivan,[139] confirmation or rejection of a hypothesis *a la* John Dewey, or obtaining a clue to the mystery of a child's behavior *a la* Holmes (Sherlock, not Chief Justice). However, there are many opportunities for such assistance in the processes of educating children which both teachers and mental health workers need to capture.

Although there is evidence to conclude that peers give one a valid and profitable angle of perception, the problem remains of assisting teachers to find meaning in all relevant information so that their perceptions are in turn clarified, modified, or strengthened. For example, in one of the classes being screened, a teacher became actively puzzled by some of the zeros (children who were not chosen for any of the parts) on "A Class Play." He noted, after some deliberation, that he could make better sense out of this data if he related it to the child's intellectual ability. After doing this, he found he could understand why several of his slower students were not perceived by the other students but could not understand why one of his brighter students was relatively invisible to the group. His obvious discomfort at this finding led him to solicit help from the school psychologist on this problem. At this point it is worthy of note that the relationship between the teacher and psychologist relative to the child was not based on an emotionalized emergency, a hostile relationship between teacher and child, a magic perception of the psychologist by the teacher, or a feeling of passivity by the teacher toward the child referred for help. The teacher and clinician were now working on a problem initiated by the teacher's curiosity and were involved in a professional relationship which was mutually reinforcing. Therefore, it can be seen that the results of a process of early identification can be more productive and helpful for both teachers and guidance staff and can act as a lever in initiating more positive and effective working relationships among the school staff.

Relationship to Mental Health Professions

The field of mental health has abounded with much talk at high levels of abstraction about the problem of prevention. A standardized, relatively uncomplicated, nonclinical, actionable procedure for screening children most prone to emotional difficulties is often looked upon with suspicion and doubt, perhaps most often by those in the mental health professions. The more sophisticated one is in this field, the more complexities one can envision; one can to some extent estimate the degree of professional sophistication by a person's ability to see dangers behind any program other than talk. In some cases, one feels that it is of greater value to an individual or a group to find reasons why something simple and productive cannot be done about prevention than to do them.

Another difficulty in implementing preventive programs is that in many instances personnel in the mental health professions have little inclination to leave the boundaries of their discipline for the hazy, uncharted seas of school or community action. In the functions and training of the clinical psychologist, psychiatric social worker, and psychiatrist lies the inherent assumption that they will be treating and managing children and adults who are moderately or severely emotionally disturbed. Primary prevention, however, is concerned with the sniffles and sneezes, the early malaise, as it were, not the high fever and respiratory complexities of pneumonia. Undoubtedly, all degrees of illness require attention; however, reducing sniffles and sneezes may require a somewhat different approach than the treatment of pneumonia.

Problems in Prevention

Agencies which deal with the social results of moderately or severely handicapped personalities often voice the need for early identification. Conferences on delinquency or child welfare also repeatedly note this need as a primary objective of a community. Since early identification is regarded as a highly desired objective, it is puzzling to find little action implementation of this need. One often is led to assume that the accomplishment of such a task is tantamount to scaling Everest in midwinter.

It is not at all surprising, however, to discover as the research facts of this study revealed, that a professional person such as a teacher, who sees a child five days a week for nine months or ten months, in a variety of situations under conditions of stress and ease, with peers and adults, can make a pretty good guess as to the emotional strength, or vulnerability to stress of such a child. The surprise lies more in the inability or reluctance of schools and communities to accept or act on these facts. Part of the problem in such action implementation lies in the multiplicity of roles and tasks which the average school is asked to undertake. Part of the problem, however, lies in the quasi-competitive milieu of the mental health professions. In some cases the concern of teachers and schools with the mental health of their students is seen as inappropriate, unprofessional behavior or an invasion of staked claims. Often, one inadequate or insensitive teacher will convince a professional mental health worker that all would be well if the teacher just plain taught. That there is this covert, competitive relationship, at least on the part of mental health professions, was shown in a study by Rettig and Pasamanick[119] who found the status of the teacher highest among nonpsychiatric physicians and general hospital nurses and lowest among clinical psychologists and private practicing psychiatrists.

Next Steps in Educational Diagnosis

If booby prizes were awarded for significant blunders of the twentieth century, I would give my vote to the early operational notion that children are homunculuslike, shrunken adults and that helping them is a matter of providing adultlike services but with reduced dosage. If therapy is what adults get when they have problems, then therapy is what children get when they have problems. If adults get drugs, children get drugs, in reduced dosage, of course. This miniaturization of children's problems and services from adult problems and services had led many of us down the garden path into the valley of the dead end.[117]

Whereas adults face the task of making a living, adult sexuality, parenthood, etc., children strive to become competent in the skills they consider important to them. They want to walk, to talk, to run, to slide, to put things together, to take things apart, to swim, to read, to understand how and why caterpillars turn into butterflies, and how they themselves grow. Children live by doing, by action, by muscles in motion. If such doing can be channelled into growth, self-satisfactions, and increased competence, this road may be the fastest, most economical route to helping the emotionally handicapped child.

Eventually we will need to conceptualize, describe, and operationalize the specific school tasks and skills required of children to function in school and the specific learning experiences which can be used to help children to master those tasks and skills which they lack for school success. If, for example, a child comes to school disturbed, confused, and unable to learn, the diagnostic workup may conclude that the major lack resulting from all this inner chaos is an inability to pay attention (or control impulses). The child would then be placed into a "how to learn to pay attention" experience where he could learn to manage as much of his impulse life in school as possible as quickly as possible. Whatever might be done about reducing home or other factors which were producing the inner confusion in the child would, of course, be done. But the school will still need to provide ways of helping the child to live and function productively in the school society. It may well be that for some children the reduction or stabilization of problems in the home may be a necessary prerequisite for positive school functioning. It may also be possible to provide the necessary emotional resources for some children to cope with home difficulties through successful ego-enhancing school experiences.

Hewett[72] describes a hierarchy of educational tasks which he has used with hospitalized emotionally handicapped children at the Neuropsychiatric Institute School, UCLA, and in the Santa Monica schools. Such a hierarchy of school-related goals brings into focus the overall strategy which needs to be employed in teaching a difficult child and gives the school and the teacher a starting and striving point. Hewett describes six steps in his hierarchy: acceptance, order, exploration, relationship, mastery, and achievement, with some simple learning exercises or programs to get children to move up the hierarchy.

The future of early identification studies of children in school lies in the development of school programs which can remediate or strengthen functioning deficiencies in children and a psycho-educational system of gathering information about students so that those with learning problems can be helped swiftly and effectively to find their way in the mainstream of the school.

The Vision of Prevention

For the most part, attempts have been made to promote mental health in our society by trying to deal with the consequences of mental illness and its allied manifestations. This, it has been suggested, is about as effective as trying to turn back the Mississippi at New Orleans. Not that we don't need dikes and erosion prevention up and down the line. But, "is it not possible to build dams higher up the stream and to plant more trees on the slopes and hold the water in?"* Certainly there are at present no magic buttons which we can push to insure increased amounts of emotional maturity for our future citizens. It would seem more profitable, however, to attack the problem of enhancing personality growth at definite points with specific programs of action and evaluation.

This research study demonstrated that emotionally handicapped children can be identified early by the use of information

---

*Daniel Blain, M.D., in a speech at the Western Interstate Commission on Mental Health, Salt Lake City, June 2, 1956.

ordinarily available to teachers. The magic of early identification is perhaps more feasible than was thought. Certainly emotionally handicapped children, like any other handicapped group, may need some help in order to profit by school attendance. In the final analysis, the greatest magic in early identification of such children lies in the relative resiliency and elasticity of childhood. "Once we have passed its borders, it will ne're return again."*

---

*From Victor Herbert's song "Toyland" from *Babes in Toyland.*

REFERENCES

1. Andrew, Gwen L., and Lockwood, Hilda: Teachers' evaluations of the mental health status of their pupils. *J Educ Res, 47*:631, 1954.
2. Axline, Virginia M.: Nondirective therapy for poor readers. *J Consult Psychol, 11*:61, 1947.
3. Bedoian, W. H.: Mental health analyses of socially over-accepted, socially under-accepted, over-age and under-age pupils in the sixth grade. *J Educ Psychol, 44*:336, 1953.
4. Bellak, Leopold (Ed.): *Schizophrenia.* New York, Logos Press, 1958.
5. Bendix, R., and Lipset, C.: *Class, Status, and Power.* New York, Basic Books, 1957.
6. Benton, Arthur: Behavioral indices of brain injury in school children. *Child Develop, 33*:199, 1962.
7. Berlin, Irving M.: Teachers' self-expectations: how realistic are they? *School Rev, 46*:134, 1958.
8. Bills, Robert E.: Nondirective play therapy with retarded readers. *J Consult Psychol, 14*:140, 1950.
9. Bills, Robert E., and others: An index of adjustment and values. *J Counsult Psychol, 15*:257, 1951.
10. Bloch, Donald A., and others: *A Study of Children Referred for Residential Treatment in New York State.* Albany, New York State Inter-departmental Health Resources Board, 1959.
11. Block, Jack. The assessment of communication. *J Personality, 21*:272, 1952.
12. Bolman, W. M., and Westman, J. C.: Prevention of mental disorders: an overview of current programs. *Amer J Psychiat, 123*:1058, 1967.
13. Bonney, Merl E.: Social behavior differences between second grade children of high and low sociometric status. *J Educ Res, 48*:481, 1955.
14. Bovet, Lucien: *Psychiatric Aspects of Juvenile Delinquency.* Geneva, Switzerland, World Health Organization, 1951.
15. Bower, Eli M.: A conceptual framework for the development of programs for emotionally disturbed children. In *Guidance in American Education III,* (Edward Landy and Arthur M. Kroll, Eds.) Cambridge, Harvard, 1966.
16. Bower, Eli M.: Evaluating educational experiences for the promotion of mental health. In *The Psychologist in the School,* Eli M. Bower, Ed., Sacramento, Calif. State Dept. of Educ., 1958.
17. Bower, Eli M.; Shellhammer, Thomas A.; Daily, John M., and Bower, Murray: *High School Students Who Later Became Schizophrenic.* Sacramento, Calif. State Dept. of Educ., 1960.

115

18. Bower, Eli M.; Tashnovian, Peter J., and Larson, Carl A.: *A Process for Early Identification of Emotionally Disturbed Children.* Sacramento, Calif. State Dept. of Educ., 1958.

19. Bower, Murray, and Mann, Harold: Problems in referral of children and adults to psychiatrists and mental health clinics. In *The Psychologist in the School,* Eli M. Bower, Ed. Sacramento, Calif. State Dept. of Educ., 1958.

20. Bowman, Paul H., and others: *Mobilizing Community Resources for Youth.* Chicago, U. of Chicago, 1956.

21. Brownell, Samuel M.: The unique position of the school in the prevention and control of delinquency. *Fed Probation, 19:*14, 1955.

22. Buswell, Margaret: The relationship between the social structure of the classroom and the academic success of the pupils. *J Exp Educ, 22:*37, 1953.

23. Butler, Annie: *An Evaluation Scale for Four-and-Five-Year-Old Children.* Bloomington. School of Education, Indiana, 1965.

24. Butterfield, Virginia: School phobia; a study of five cases. *Amer J Orthopsychiat, 24:*350, 1954.

25. Byerly, Carl: A school curriculum for prevention and remediation of deviancy. In *Social Deviancy Among Youth* (65th Yearbook of the NSSE), William Wattenberg, Ed. Chicago, U. of Chicago, 1966.

26. Cannon, Kenneth L.: Stability of sociometric scores of high school students. *J Educ Res, 52:*43, 1958.

27. Cantoni, Louis J.: Study in emotional adjustment: correlation of stu- and adult forms of the Bell Adjustment Inventory over a period of thirteen years. *Educ and Psychol Measurement, 15:*137, 1955.

28. Caplan, Gerald: Mental health consultation in schools. *The Elements of a Community Mental Health Program.* New York, Milbank Memorial Fund, 1956.

29. Child Development Specialists—Hearings Before the General Subcommittee on Education of the Committee on Education and Labor. House of Representatives, 89th Congress, First Session, on H.R. 11322. Held in Washington, D.C., October 19 and 20, 1965, p. 54.

30. Cohen, T. B.: Prediction of underachievement in kindergarten children. *Arch Gen Psychiat, 9:*444, 1963.

31. Conrad, W. G., and Tobiessen, Jon: The development of kindergarten behavior rating scales for the prediction of learning and behavior disorders. *Psychology in the School, 4:*359, 1967.

32. Cooper, Saul; Ryan, William, and Hutcheson, Bellenden R.: Classroom screening for emotional disturbance. *Amer Psychol,* (July), 14, 340, 1959.

33. Clancy, Norah, and Smitter, Faith: A study of emotionally disturbed children in Santa Barbara County Schools. *Calif J Educ Res, 4:*269, 1953.

34. Davids, Anthony, and White, A. A.: Effects of success, failure, and social facilitation on level of aspiration in emotionally disturbed and normal children. *J Personality, 26:*77, 1958.

35. DeHaan, Robert F., and Kough, Jack: *Helping Children with Special Needs.* Chicago, Sci. Res. Assoc., 1958.

36. Domke, Herbert R.: Program of the St. Louis County (Missouri) health department. *Progress and Problems of Community Mental Health Services.* New York, Milbank Memorial Fund, 1959.

37. Driscoll, Gertrude: *How to Study the Behavior of Children.* New York, Teachers College, Columbia, 1954.

38. Dubos, R.: *Mirage of Health.* New York, Harper, 1959, p. 22.

39. Eaton, Merrill; Weather, Garret, and Phillips, Beaman, N.: Some reactions of classroom teachers to problem behavior in school. *Educ Administration and Supervision, 43:*129, 1957.

40. Edwards, A. M.: *Alphabetical Index of Occupations by Industries and Social-economic Groups.* Washington, Bureau of the Census, 1937.

41. Eissler, R.: Scapegoats of society. In *Searchlights on Delinquency,* K. R. Eissler, Ed. New York, Int. Univ., 1955, p. 228.

42. English, H. B., and English, A. C.: *A Comprehensive Dictionary of Psychological and Psychoanalytical Terms.* New York, Longmans, Green, 1958.

43. Felix, Robert H.: Evolution of community mental health concepts. *Amer J Psychiat, 113:*673, 1957.

44. Fenton, Norman: *Mental Hygiene in School Practice.* Stanford, Stanford, 1943.

45. Fine, Harold J.; Fulkerson, Samuel C., and Phillips, Leslie: Maladjustment and social attainment. *J Abnorm Soc Psycho, 50:*33, 1955.

46. FitzSimons, Marian J.: The predictive value of teachers' referrals. In *Orthopsychiatry and the School,* Morris Krugman, Ed. New York, Amer. Orthopsychiatric Assoc., 1958.

47. Fox, T. F.: Priorities. *Steps in the Development of Integrated Psychiatric Services.* New York, Milbank Memorial Fund, 1960, p. 16.

48. Freedman, Lawrence, and Hollingshead, August B.: Neurosis and social class. *Amer J Psychiat, 113:*769, 1957.

49. Frumkin, R. M.: Occupation and major mental disorders. In *Mental Health and Mental Disorder,* A. M. Rose, Ed. New York, Norton, 1955.

50. Gardner, John: *Excellence.* New York, Harper, 1961, p. 115.

51. Gilbert, Gustave M.: A survey of "referral problems" in metropolitan child guidance clinics. *J Clin Psycho, 13:*37, 1958.

52. Gildea, Margaret C. L.: *Community Mental Health: A School Centered Program and a Group Discussion Program.* Springfield, Thomas, 1959.

53. Ginsburg, Sol W.: The mental health movement: its theoretical assumptions. In *Community Programs for Mental Health,* Ruth Kotinsky and Helen L. Witmer, Eds. Cambridge, Harvard, 1955.

54. Glueck, Eleanor T.: Distinguishing delinquents from pseudo-delinquents. *Int J Soc Psychiat, 13:*174-183, 1967.

55. Glueck, Eleanor T.: Identifying juvenile delinquents and neurotics. *Ment Hyg, 40:*24, 1956.

56. Glueck, Sheldon, and Glueck, Eleanor: *Unraveling Juvenile Delinquency.* New York, The Commonwealth Fund, 1950.

57. Glueck, Sheldon, and Glueck, Eleanor: Early detection of future delinquents. *J Criminal Law, Criminology and Police Sci, 47:*174, 1956.

58. Goldfarb, Allan: Teacher ratings in psychiatric case-findings. *Amer J Public Health, 53:*1919, 1963.

59. Goldfarb, William: Variations in adolescent adjustment of institutionally reared children. *Amer J Orthopsychiatry, 17:*449, 1947.

60. Goodlad, John I.: Some effects of promotion and nonpromotion upon the social and personal adjustment of children. *J Exp Educ, 22:*301, 1954.

61. Gough, Harrison G.: The relationship of socioeconomic status to personality inventory and achievement test scores. *J Educ Psychol, 37:* 527, 1946.

62. Grambs, J. D.: *Group Processes in Intergroup Education.* New York, Nat. Council of Chrstians and Jews, 1953.

63. Great Britain, Ministry of Education: *Report of the Committee on Maladjusted Children.* London, England, Her Majesty's Stationery Office, 1955.

64. Gronlund, Norman E.: Personality characteristics of socially accepted, socially neglected, and socially rejected junior high school pupils. *Educ Administration and Supervision, 43:*329, 1957.

65. Gronlund, Norman E.: Generality of teachers' sociometric perceptions: relative judgment accuracy on several sociometric criteria. *J Educ Psychol, 47:*25, 1956.

66. Gronlund, Norman E.: *The Accuracy of Teachers' Judgments Concerning the Sociometric Status of Sixth Grade Pupils.* New York, Beacon House, 1951.

67. Gronlund, Norman E., and Holmlund, Walter S.: The value of elementary school sociometric status scores for predicting pupils' adjustment in high school. *Educ Administration and Supervision, 44:* 225, 1958.

68. Gronlund, Norman E., and Whitney, Algard P.: Relation between pupils' social acceptability in the classroom, in the school, and in the neighborhood. *School Rev, 64:*267, 1956.

69. Group for the Advancement of Psychiatry: *The Psychiatrist in Mental Health Education.* New York, Group for the advancement of Psychiatry (1770 Broadway), Report no. 35, 1954.

70. Hanlon, Thomas E., and others: Congruence of self and ideal self in relation to personality adjustment. *J Consult Psychol, 18:*215, 1954.
71. Heffernan, Helen: The role of the teacher in guidance. *Nat Elementary Principal, 34:*60, 1954.
72. Hewett, Frank: A hierarchy of educational tasks for children with learning disorders. *Except Child, 31:*207, 1964.
73. Hofstadter, R.: *Social Darwinism in American Thought.* Boston, Beacon, 1955.
74. Hollingshead, A. B., and Redlich, F. C.: Social stratification and psychiatric disorders. In *Mental Health and Mental Disorder,* A. M. Rose, Ed. New York, Norton, 1955.
75. Howe, Louisa P.: Problems in the evaluation of mental health programs. In Community Programs for Mental Health, Ruth Kotinsky and Helen L. Witmer, Eds. Cambridge, Harvard, 1955.
76. Hunter, Elwood C.: Changes in teachers' attitudes toward children's behavior over the last thirty years. *Ment Hyg, 41:*3, 1957.
77. Inge, William: *Bus Stop. New York,* Random, 1955.
78. Jahoda, Marie: *Current Concepts of Positive Mental Health.* New York, Basic Books, 1958.
79. Jastak, Joseph: *Wide Range Achievement Test.* Wilmington, Delaware, Charles Story, 1946.
80. Jennings, Helen: Sociometry in group relations. In *Intergroup Education in Cooperating Schools.* Washington. A. C. E., 1955.
81. Kagan, Jerome, and others: Personality and IQ change. *J Abnorm Soc Psychol, 56:*261, 1958.
82. Kahn, Alfred J.: The case of the premature claims—public policy and delinquency prediction. *Crime and Delinquency, 11:*217, 1965.
83. Kaplan, Louis: *Mental Health and Human Relations in Education.* New York, Harper, 1959.
84. Klein, Donald, and Lindemann, Elizabeth: Approaches to pre-school screening. *J School Health, 34:*365, 1964.
85. Klein, Donald C., and Ross, Ann: Kindergarten entry: a study of role transition. In *Orthopsychiatry and the School.* Morris Krugman, Ed. New York, Amer. Orthopsychiatric Assoc., 1958.
86. Klopfer, Bruno: Personality diagnosis in childhood. In *Modern Trends in Child Psychiatry,* D. C. Lewis and B. L. Pacella, Eds. New York, Int. Univs., 1945.
87. Krugman, Morris: Appraisal and treatment of personality problems in a guidance program. In *Education in a Free World.* Washington, A. C. E., 1954.
88. Krugman, Morris (Ed.): *Orthopsychiatry and the School.* New York, Amer. Orthopsychiatric Assoc., 1958.
89. Kubie, Lawrence S.: Social forces and the neurotic process. In *Explorations in Social Psychiatry,* Alexander H. Leighton, John A. Clausen, and Robert Wilson, Eds. New York, Basic Books, 1957.

90. Kuhlen, Raymond G., and Colister, E. G.: Sociometric status of sixth and ninth graders who failed to finish high school. *Educ Psychol Measurement, 12:*632, 1952.
91. Kvaraceus, William: Programs of early identification and prevention of delinquency. *Social Deviancy Among Youth.* (65th Yearbook of the NSSE), William Wattenberg, Ed.) Chicago, U. of Chicago, 1966.
92. Kvaraceus, William, and others: *Delinquent Behavior.* Washington, N. E. A. Project on Delinquency, 1959, vols. 1 and 2.
93. Lambert, Nadine: A study of the "Pupil Behavior Rating Scale" in the identification of emotionally handicapped children. Sacramento, Calif. State Dept. of Educ., 1959. Unpublished study.
94. Lambert, Nadine: A study of the test re-test reliability of "A Class Play." Sacramento, Calif. State Dept. of Educ., 1959, Unpublished study.
95. Lambert, Nadine: A study of the test re-test reliability of "Thinking About Yourself." Sacramento, Calif. State Dept. of Educ., 1959, Unpublished study.
96. Lambert, Nadine: Correlation of "A Class Play" with "Thinking About Yourself" and "Pupil Behavior Rating Scale." Sacramento, Calif. State Dept. of Educ., 1959, Unpublished study.
97. Lambert, Nadine: The development and validation of a process for screening emotionally handicapped children in school. Cooperative Research Project 1186, U. S. Office of Education, 1963.
98. Leacock, Eleanor: Three social variables and the occurrence of mental disorder. In *Explorations in Social Psychiatry,* Alexander H. Leighton, John A. Clausen, and Robert Wilson, Eds. New York, Basic Books, 1957.
99. Lehrman, Louis J., and others: *Success and Failure of Treatment of Children in the Child Guidance Clinics of the Jewish Board of Guardians. New York, Jewish Board of Guardians* (228 E. 19th Street), 1949.
100. Lindemann, Erich: *The Wellesley Project for the Study of Certain Problems in Community Health, New York, Milbank Memorial Fund,* 1953.
101. Long, Nicholas; Morse, William, and Newman, Ruth: *Conflict in the Classroom: The Education of Emotionally Disturbed Children.* Belmont, California, Wadsworth, 1965.
102. Maddy, Nancy: Comparison of children's personality, traits, attitudes, and intelligence with parental occupation. *Genet Psychol Monog, vol. 27;* 1943.
103. Maes, Wayne R.: The identification of emotionally disturbed elementary school children. *Exceptional Child, 33:*607, 1966.
104. McCord, William; McCord, Joan, and Zola, I. K.: *Origins of Crime: A New Evaluation of the Cambridge-Somerville Youth Study.* New York, Columbia, 1959.

105. McGinnis, Manon: The Wellesley project program of preschool emotional assessment. *J Psychiat Soc Work, 23*:135, 1954.
106. *The Mental Health Survey of Los Angeles County, 1957-59.* Sacramento, Calif. State Dept. of Ment. Hyg., 1960.
107. Miller, Alan D.: The role of the school system in a mental health program. In *Orthopsychiatry and the School,* Morris Krugman, Ed. New York, Amer. Orthopsychiatric Assoc., 1958.
108. Mitchell, J. A.: A study of teachers' and mental hygienists' ratings of certain behavior problems of children. *J Educ Res, 36*:292, 1942.
109. Mullen, Margaret M.: Personal and situational factors associated with perfect attendance. *Personnel Guid J, 33*:438, 1955.
110. Murphy, G.: The prevention of mental disorder: some research suggestions. *J Hillside Hosp, 9*:146, 1960.
111. National Education Association: *Teacher Opinion on Pupil Behavior, Research Bulletin, 34*:51, 1956.
112. Neubauer, Peter B., and Beller, Emanuel K.: Differential contributions of the educator and clinician in diagnosis. *Orthopsychiatry and the School,* Morris Krugman, Ed. New York, Amer. Orthopsychiatric Asso., 1958.
113. Newton, M. Robert, and Brown, Racine D.: A preventive approach to developmental problems in school children. *Behavioral Science Frontiers in Education,* Eli M. Bower, and William G. Hollister, Eds. New York, Wiley, 1967.
114. Olson, Willard C.: *Problem Tendencies in Children: A Method for Their Measurement and Description.* Minneapolis, U. of Minn., 1930.
115. Phillips, Beeman N., and DeVault, M. Vere: Relation of positive and negative sociometric valuations to social and personal adjustment of school children. *J App Psychol, 39*:409, 1955.
116. Powers, Edwin, and Witmer, Helen: *An Experiment in the Prevention of Delinquency.* New York, Columbia, 1951.
117. Rae-Grant, Quentin; Gladwin, Thomas, and Bower, Eli M.: Mental health, social competence and the war on poverty. *Amer J Orthopsychiat, 36*:652, 1966.
118. *Reducing Juvenile Delinquency: What New York Schools Can Do.* Albany, N. Y. State Youth Commission, 1952.
119. Rettig, S., and Pasamanick, B.: Status and job satisfaction of public school teachers. *School and Society, 87*:113, 1959.
120. Robins, Lee. *Deviant Children Grown Up.* Baltimore, Williams and Wilkins, 1966.
121. Rogers, Carl A.: Mental health findings in three elementary schools. *Educ Res Bull* (Ohio State University), *21*:No. 3, 1942.
122. Rogers, Carl A., and others: The role of self-understanding in the prediction of behavior. *J Consult Psychol, 3*:174, 1948.

123. Ross, Ann, and Lindemann, Elizabeth B.: A follow-up study of a predictive test of social adaptation in pre-school children. In *Emotional Problems of Early Childhood,* Gerald Caplan, Ed. New York, Basic Books, 1956.

124. Sanford, R. N.: The development of the healthy personality in the society of today. In *Modern Mental Health Concepts and their Application in Public Health Education.* Berkeley, Calif. State Dept. of Public Health, 1959.

125. Satterlee, Robert: Sociometric analysis and personality adjustment. *Calif J Educ Res, 6:*181, 1955.

126. Schrupp, Manfred H., and Gjerde, Clayton M.: Teacher growth in attitudes toward behavioral problems in children. *J Edu Psychol, 44:*203, 1953.

127. Sears, Pauline: Levels of aspiration in academically successful and unsuccessful children. *J Abnorm Soc Psychol, 35:*498, 1940.

128. Sheerer, Elizabeth: An analysis of the relationship between acceptance of self and respect for others in ten counseling cases. *J Consult Psychol, 13:*169, 1949.

129. Skodak, Marie: Intellectual growth of children in foster homes. In *Child Behavior and Development,* Robert C. Barker, and others, Eds. New York, McGraw, 1943.

130. Smith, H. L., and Hightower, N. C.: Incidence of functional disease (neurosis) among patients of various occupations. *Occup Med, 5:* 182, 1948.

131. Smith, Louis M.: The concurrent validity of six personality and adjustment tests for children. *Psychol Monogr, Vol. 72,* 1958.

132. Sontag, L. W., and Baker, Charles T.: Personality as a determinant of performance. *Amer J Orthopsychiat, 25:*557, 1955.

133. Southard, Curtis G.: A view of local community mental health programs. *Progress and Problems of Community Mental Health Services.* New York, Milbank Memorial Fund, 1959.

134. Stennett, R. G.: Emotional handicap in the elementary years: phase or disease. *Amer J Orthopsychiat, 36:*444, 1966.

135. Stevenson, Ian: Dirct instigation of behavioral changes in psychotherapy. *Arch Gen. Psychiat, 1:*99, 1959.

136. Stevenson, Ian: Is the human personality more plastic in infancy and and childhood? *Amer J Psychiat, 114:*151, 1957.

137. Stock, Dorothy: An investigation into the interrelationships between the self-concept and feelings directed toward other persons and groups. *J Consult Psychol, 13:*176, 1949.

138. Stouffer, George A. W.: Behavior problems of children as identified by today's teachers and compared with those reported by E. K. Wickman. *J Educ Res, 48:*321, 1955.

139. Sullivan, H. S.: *Conceptions of Modern Psychiatry.* Washington, William A. White Psychiatric Foundation, 1947.

140. Suttenfield, Virginia: School phobia: a study of five cases. *Amer J Orthpsychiat, 24*:368, 1954.
141. Taba, Hilda: *With Perspective on Human Relations.* Washington, A.C.E., 1955.
142. Tindall, Ralph H.: Relationships among indices of adjustment status. *15*:152, 1955. ..
143. Ullmann, Charles A.: Teachers, peers and tests as predictors of adjustment. *J Educ Psychol, 48*:257, 1957.
144. Ullmann, Charles A.: *Identification of Maladjusted School Children.* Monograph No. 7. Washington, U. S. Public Health Service, 1952.
145. von Bertalanffy, L.: The mind-body problem: a new view. *Psychosom Med, 24*:29, 1964
146. Waldfogel, Samuel; Coolidge, John C., and Hahn, Pauline B.: The development, meaning and management of school phobia. Workshop, 1956. *Amer J Orthopsychiat, 27*:754, 1957.
147. Wall, William D.: *Education and Mental Health.* New York, Columbia, 1955.
148. Warner, Lloyd, and others: *Social Class in America.* Chicago, Sci. Res. Asso., 1949.
149. Wechsler, David: Cognitive, conative, and nonintellective intelligence. *Amer Psychol, 5*:78, 1950.
150. White, Mary A., and Charry, June (Eds.) : *School Disorder, Intelligence and Social Class.* New York, Teachers College, 1966.
151. Whyte, William H.: *The Organization Man.* New York, Random, 1956.
152. Wickman, E. K.: *Children's Behavior and Teachers' Attitudes.* New York, Commonwealth Fund, 1928.
153. Witmer, Helen, and Tufts, Edith: *The Effectiveness of Delinquency Prevention Programs.* Children's Bureau publication no. 350. U. S. Dept. HEW, 1954.
154. Zax, Melvin; Cowen, Emory; Izzo, Louis, and Trost, Mary: Identifying emotional disturbance in the school setting. *Amer J Orthopsychiat, 34*:447, 1964.

APPENDIX

INTRODUCTION

THE MATERIAL that follows is part of the kit, *A Process for In-School Screening of Children with Emotional Handicaps,* and has been selected to illustrate the basic rationale and procedure of the screening process, the screening materials themselves, instructions to the teacher on the administration of the materials, and how to use the results. With the exception of the screening instruments, the rest of the material is excerpted from *The Manual for School Administrators and Teachers* (42 pages) and *Technical Report for School Administrators and Teachers* (72 pages).

As with many things in life, a great deal of any success in the use of this process and materials rests on the enthusiasm and competence of the professional school staff. Of major importance in any program of this kind is an open, positive and non-jargon-like interpretation of the process to parents and community personnel including other professional groups.

Nothing in this process or in these materials is intended to bypass professional know-how or plain old common sense. There will be instances when screening results will seem to fly against everything else known or suspected. Investigate before coming to any conclusions.

It must also be remembered that almost all screening measures are group measures, and assume a normal heterogeneity of students in classes of a particular grade level. The application of these procedures in special classes or special groupings except for selected research is not good practice.

Remember these are screening procedures. Nothing can be or should be said about any child on the basis of results which pin any diagnostic label on him.

As you may have already noted, the materials contained herein are copyrighted by the California State Department of Education and are distributed for research uses by Educational Testing Service, Princeton, N. J. Reproductions of any of the materials or instruments are prohibited without permission.

A PROCESS FOR IN-SCHOOL SCREENING OF CHILDREN WITH EMOTIONAL HANDICAPS

Manual for School Administrators and Teachers

Table of Contents

129

TO TEACHERS AND SCHOOL ADMINISTRATORS

Before you begin a program of this kind it is important that
parents and community personnel understand what you are doing
and why. It is important to know enough about the rationale and
procedures so that one can interpret what the screening program
is and what it is not. It is aimed at (1) helping children, (2) by
finding early those who are developing learning and behavior
problems, (3) helping the school to find adequate school-related
resources, (4) so that the child can realize his full educational
development. The program is not aimed at discovering the mentally ill, labelling children, making therapists out of teachers or
vice versa, turning classrooms into group psychotherapy, or doing
anything other than helping to plan successful educational experiences for more children.

Either one of the following two letters to parents can be
adapted and used as a starter. Each school and school district
should use its own style in communicating with the parents and
community. However it is planned and done, the program must
be understood and supported by the parents and community if
it is to be of any lasting and meaningful help to children.

SAMPLE LETTER TO PARENTS (NO. 1)

Dear Parent:

This school district has as its major aim the best education for each child. We are aware that children differ in interest and learning potential and that almost all children see success in school as a satisfying and rewarding experience.

One of our concerns is the prevention of learning or behavior problems in our students. One specific preventive approach has been our regular screening programs to find vision, hearing, and speech problems as early as possible and work with the home in correcting the difficulty. We are now planning to add to our regular screening program procedures to help us find children with beginning learning, attitudes or emotional problems which might interfere with their school work.

This year we plan to test —— grade children to discover which students if any may need extra help, special resources in or out of school or other services. The purpose of this additional screening program is to find such students early so that remedial or special services if needed can be successful in helping the child.

Many of the classes in this school will be participating in this program. When the screening has been completed we will of course be happy to discuss with you any relevant findings.

Sincerely,

SAMPLE LETTER TO PARENTS (NO. 2)

Dear Parent:

As you may know, this district administers school screening procedures to detect physical handicaps such as vision or hearing problems or beginning illnesses when these show up in school. The purpose of these programs is to find children with handicaps which affect their school performance and correct them where possible. One of the best examples of this type of preventive approach is our vision and hearing screening program which we feel has been instrumental in many cases in preventing a sight or hearing loss from becoming a learning handicap.

This year we are planning to include an additional screening procedure to assist us in recognizing as early as possible children with learning, attitude, or emotional difficulties which hamper their school functioning. As in the case of vision and hearing screening, we feel this new program can be very useful to parents and teachers in helping children before they develop serious learning or behavior problems in school.

The class in which your child is enrolled will be participating in this program. This will entail taking some simple group tests. When the screening process has been completed we will of course be happy to discuss any significant findings with you.

Sincerely,

133

PREFACE — SCREENING MATERIALS

THE SCREENING INSTRUMENTS you are about to use are research instruments — with a difference. The word "instruments" connotes devices for precise measurement, diagnosis, prediction. But our devices are not so precise, and we are not measuring wind velocity, atmospheric pressure, wave lengths, the strength of materials or any other purely physical phenomenon. Our devices are designed to be used as part of a screening process which, like many other screening processes, is not intended to make fine, precise discriminations, but to identify those who should be studied and observed further. It is well to remember, also, that this screening process will be taking place *within* a process — the process of living, learning, reacting within a classroom and the community of the school — which we call education.

As a teacher, you are obviously an important part of the process of education. You contribute to it, participate in it, are yourself affected by it. Your part in the screening process — and in the larger research process — is therefore extremely important and ought to prove stimulating and satisfying.

For what you are being asked to do is to take readings on the "emotional climate" of a class, a group of boys and girls who are with you *now,* this month, this term, this year. And just as the weather man must take many readings — of air pressure, humidity, wind velocity and direction, and so on — before he can describe what are called the *weather systems* developing within the area in which we live, so we must take many readings of the emotional climate of the class and of the individual emotional "systems" within it.

And again — just as there may be many weather observers sending their observations into a central clearing office without making predictions themselves, leaving that to the one who collects all the data and is trained to read them, so the individual teacher will be reporting his findings carefully and accurately without making diagnoses or predictions. It will be the function of specialists in the field of mental health to diagnose, to predict, and to recommend necessary measures. Your principal can also be of some help in interpreting and defining the limits of your data, and, of course, he will play a large part in planning action to be taken.

We have said that our instruments are not so precise as those of physical scientists. We are, however, confident that they can become, through careful use, far more refined and accurate than they are at present. They have worked well within one state; *your* help, and the help of thousands of teachers, is needed to make them valid and reliable everywhere, under almost any school-room conditions.

You will be contributing to research in a difficult area, but one in which you are, by profession, temperament, and choice, deeply interested: human behavior, specifically those modes of behavior among children which give us clues to developing emotional health and developing emotional handicaps. How carefully you do your part will determine *how* effective these instruments can become. Very few instruments are proof against inept handling, of course, but instruments such as these screening instruments, which must be used in the classroom with living, growing children, require particular care and interest on the part of the teachers administering them. Care, conscientiousness, and a firm willingness to suspend all preconceptions and wishful thinking about the behavior of children are essential.

Your success in achieving this scientific point-of-view will determine, in large measure, the success of this investigation into the practicability of screening or identifying, *in school,* children who are beginning to develop emotional handicaps. The results of this investigation, once made firm and usable by all investigators, promise great benefits to school children everywhere and to their teachers, their principals, and their parents.

The children in your class are very much alive and, like all living creatures, they are living in a particular place, among twenty-five or thirty other individuals, with you as their teacher. This is their world for a large part of their days. This is the climate in which they must grow — in knowledge, in inner strength, in emotional and social maturity. All of us would like to know more surely how sound that growth is, but for the most part we have had to rely on hunches, intuition, and experience, and the comforting assurance of statistics that most children "make it."

We do have instruments to help us chart some aspects of growth: diagnostic and achievement tests to check progress in subject matter, TB tests, screening programs to check for deficiencies in hearing and vision, IQ tests to give us an estimate of what levels of achievement we may expect of students. There may be others, depending upon the nature and scope of such programs in your school.

But we have, too often, left inquiries into the mental and emotional health of our students to chance, to guesswork — or, in emergency situations, to the services of a psychologist or a psychiatrist. Emergencies are not our concern here, however. The child who is disruptive, the child who cannot read, the child who is a persistent truant — these are all too painfully visible to everyone concerned.

But what of the youngster who is only beginning to have trouble with his classmates? What of the youngster who is only beginning to resist learning? — Who is only beginning to build unhealthful defenses against stresses which he cannot understand or manage? Just as we cannot detect incipient eye disorders by looking into the faces of children, so we cannot detect incipient emotional disorders by simple observation.

We are not all of us trained psychologists or psychiatrists, and even the trained professional would not accept the evidence of casual, empiric observation as the basis for judgment or diagnosis. Further, he knows that symptoms of emotional disorder can be as misleading as physical symptoms. A rash is not necessarily the sign of an allergy. A high fever is not in itself an indication of pneumonia or any other specific illness. Behavioral differences among children, even difficulties, may indicate nothing but emerging personality differences; they may indicate growing personality strength *or* growing weakness. Finally, they may indicate one thing in the context of *this* place and time, and something else in another place and at another time.

All growth is a process; *healthful* growth takes place when the stresses of life are mediated and managed in a positive and healthful manner by the organism. Some children, however, because of a combination of factors, find themselves unable to manage stress positively and are therefore unable to work or function up to their abilities. As a result, a consistent number of children develop in the course of their lives emotional handicaps which interfere moderately or markedly with their educational progress. These are the children we hope to screen early in the course of their difficulty.

Evaluating growth is also a process — a process in which the teacher plays a vital role. The process involves many people with different training and responsibilities. Indeed, the process of evaluating growth involves many sub-processes, of which screening for potential emotional handicaps is only one. To contend over whether one part or sub-process is more important than another would be idle and un-becoming to educators. The whole is what is important, and all contributions to the whole are equally important, equally vital. It is in this spirit that we welcome your assistance in our effort to make our schools of even greater service to the community and to its children.

NOTE TO TEACHERS

Wʜᴇɴ ʏᴏᴜ ʀᴇᴄᴇɪᴠᴇ your screening materials, read all the instructions which apply to the grade level you will be screening. You should then arrange your administration of the instruments to suit your own convenience (within, of course, the plan worked out in your school or school district). And always do the teacher rating before administering the peer ratings and the self ratings.

However, do not begin until at least two months after school has started. (Some schools even prefer to wait until the beginning of the second half of the school year. If this plan accords with administration policy, and if it seems to promise a truer evaluation by all involved in the screening process, you, too, may wish to delay administration of the instruments.)

Note:

White pages — introductory and concluding material, of interest to all teachers and school personnel concerned with the screening process.

Blue pages — instructions for administering and scoring, Grades K-3.

Pink pages — instructions for administering and scoring, Grades 3-7.

Yellow pages — instructions for administering and scoring, Grades 7-12.

Materials Needed by Each Teacher for Screening Emotionally Handicapped Children

Primary Grades—Each teacher will need:

One *Manual for In-School Screening of Children With Emotional Handicaps*
One "Screening Summary"
One *Behavior Rating of Pupils*

One "Class Record Sheet for *A Picture Game*"
One pink box of pink *Picture Game* cards (re-usable) for every
    girl in class
One blue box of blue *Picture Game* cards (re-usable) for every
    boy in class
One set *Class Pictures* (re-usable)
One "Teacher's Worksheet for Scoring Peer Ratings"
"Recording Forms for *Class Pictures*" — one for every pupil in
    class
"Pupil Record Folders" — one for every pupil in class

Elementary Grades—Each teacher will need:
One *Manual for In-School Screening of Children With Emotional
    Handicaps*
One "Screening Summary"
One *Behavior Rating of Pupils*
Thinking About Yourself — one for every pupil in class
    "Form A — For Boys" (blue paper)
    "Form B — For Girls" (pink paper)
    "Class Record for *Thinking About Yourself*" — one for each
        class
    "Score Sheet for *Thinking About Yourself*" — one for every
        pupil in class
A Class Play — one for every pupil in class
One "Teacher's Worksheet for Scoring Peer Ratings"
"Pupil Record Folders" — one for every pupil in class

Secondary Grades—Each teacher will need:
One *Manual for In-School Screening of Children With Emotional
    Handicaps*
One "Screening Summary"
One *Behavior Rating of Pupils*
A Self Test — one for every pupil in class
"Score Sheet for *A Self Test*" — one for every pupil in class
One "Class Record for *A Self Test*"
Student Survey — one for every pupil in class
One "Teacher's Worksheet for Scoring Peer Ratings"

"Pupil Record Folders" — one for every pupil in class

Steps in Planning Use of the In-School Screening Process

The following are suggested steps in the procedure for screening emotionally handicapped children. The screening procedure will involve, in most cases, designation of a principal, guidance specialist, or counselor as administratively responsible for the screening, and of the teacher or teachers who will be using the screening materials.

Steps	Administrator's role	Teacher's role
1.	Review screening materials and the *Manual,* and plan which school groups are to be screened.	
2.	Inform parents of children who will be involved of the nature and purpose of the screening, using letters suggested in the *Technical Report (Appendix A)* or other acceptable means of communication.	
3.	Plan for meeting with teachers who will be involved in screening. Introduce them to the materials; go over the instructions in the *Manual* for administration and the procedures for combining scores for screening.	Attend initial planning meeting.
4.	If desired, have teachers list children in their classes who seem to them to have an uncomfortable number of emotional problems before screening. These names can be compared with screened children later.	List names of children in class who have a large number of emotional problems and describe briefly.
5.	Distribute screening materials to each teacher. See page IX of	Check to see that the screening materials

Manual for the list of materials needed.

sent you agree with list in *Manual,* page IX.

6. Be available for help or for answering questions.

Administer the screening materials as indicated in *Manual.*

7. Be available for help or for answering questions.

Score all materials and combine scores for screening as explained in *Manual.* Complete "Screening Summary" for each class.

8. After teachers have completed screening, call a meeting to discuss results. Prepare the list of children who were named by the teachers before screening for comparison with those screened. Discuss those missed by teacher and those possibly missed by screening.
Make notes indicating why screening instruments might have missed a particular child. These notes should be sent in with your summary data.

T e a c h e r s   b r i n g "Screening Summary" to meeting. Out of general knowledge of child behavior and knowledge of the behavior of specific children, be prepared to discuss the children who have been screened.

9. Prepare list of all children who are screened for follow-up diagnostic work.

Teachers prepare case materials on children screened for diagnostic follow-up.

10. Screening phase is completed. All children who are screened are referred to clinical specialist in school or in clinic for diagnosis and placement. The diagnostician will determine the nature of the

emotional difficulty and the degree of the handicap. He and the administrator and the teacher will plan for education of the child after the diagnostic work is completed.

BEHAVIOR RATINGS OF PUPILS

District _____ School _____ Grade _____

Teacher's Name _____ Date _____ Subject and period _____

Note to the Teacher

ONE OF THE MOST IMPORTANT and useful kinds of information obtained by the school is the teacher's professional judgment of children's behavior. Teachers see children over a period of time in a variety of situations, in stress situations, in work, and in play. The teacher's observation and judgment have been sharpened by his professional training and day-to-day experience with the normal behavior of children. Often the teacher's rating can be the single most useful index of a pupil's growth and development.

Few professional persons, no matter how well trained, can make ratings of others with absolute certainty and complete comfort. Don't spend too much time worrying about whether your rating for a particular child is "right" or "wrong." Make your best judgment of each student and go on to the next.

As you will see, these ratings are made in a way somewhat different from any you might have done before. The instructions on the inside of this folder will explain how to proceed.

Instructions

1. Copy the names of all your pupils in the appropriate spaces on the right-hand edge of the inside back cover so that all names will be visible to you when you make your ratings.

2. There are eight pages, each with a pyramid grid and a one-sentence description of behavior. Your rating job on each of these eight pages is to locate every pupil in your class on a scale that runs from "**most like**" the pupil described to "**least like**" him.

    Let us use the first page as an example. The statement below the pyramid (Statement **A**) reads: **This pupil gets into fights or quarrels with other pupils.** Look at your list of pupils and identify those who you think are **most like** the pupil referred to in the statement. You will note there are only two boxes at the extreme right of the pyramid (Column 7) on the page. Choose the two pupils who are **most like** the pupil in the statement and write their name in the boxes in Column 7 of the pyramid, one name to a box.

    Now, look at your list of students and identify those who are **least like** the pupil in Statement **A** below the pyramid. Choose the two pupils who are **least like** the pupil in the statement and write their names in the boxes in Column 1 of the pyramid, one name to a box.

3. Now, return to your list of students and again identify from the remaining students those who are **most like** the pupil mentioned in the statement. These will be pupils who show this behavior to a great degree but not to the extreme found in the two pupils listed in Column 7. Write their names in the boxes of Column 6 of the pyramid.

4. Again, return to your list of pupils and identify other pupils who are **least like** the pupil mentioned in the statement on the bottom of the page. These will be pupils who show this behavior to a very slight degree but somewhat more than the two in Column 1. Place their names in the boxes of Column 2 of the pyramid. Continue in this manner until all names have been used.

5. When you have completed the ratings, you should have on the right pupils **most like** the pupil in the statement, and on the left those who are **least like** the pupil in the statement. For example, for the first statement, pupils who seldom, if ever, fight or quarrel will be in columns on the left side of the paper and pupils who fight or quarrel quite a lot (or at least enough to be noticed by you) will be on the right side. The pupils who are average or "not extreme in either direction" with respect to the described behavior will fall into the larger middle categories.

6. Use the boxes shown with dotted lines only if you have a large class and find you do not have enough spaces for all your students. Be sure that each pupil's name is placed in only one box. Some teachers check off names on the class list with light pencil marks to keep track of names used.

7. Try your best to complete the boxes in Columns 1 and 7 first, Columns 2 and 6 second, and in Columns 3 and 5 last. If you cannot completely fill these columns, use dashes to indicate that the boxes have not been overlooked or omitted. Some teachers who have small classes or insufficient contact with some children may find it necessary to omit names in several of of the boxes. If you feel uncertain about placing a child near either extreme of the rating scale, place his name in the middle column, Column 4. When you have completed the ratings, the name of every child in your class should be found in one of the boxes in one of the seven columns of the pyramid. Unused boxes should have dashes in them.

8. When you finish with your rating on the first statement of behavior, go on to the others, repeating the procedure just described. Complete your ratings on all eight statements of behavior — rating every pupil in your class on every statement — before you undertake the scoring.

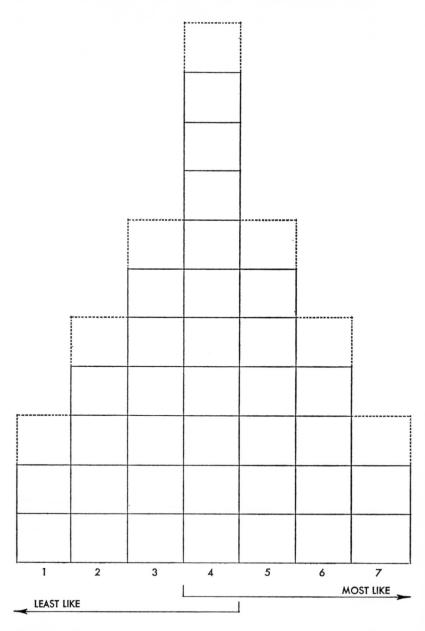

A. This pupil gets into fights or quarrels with other pupils more often than others.

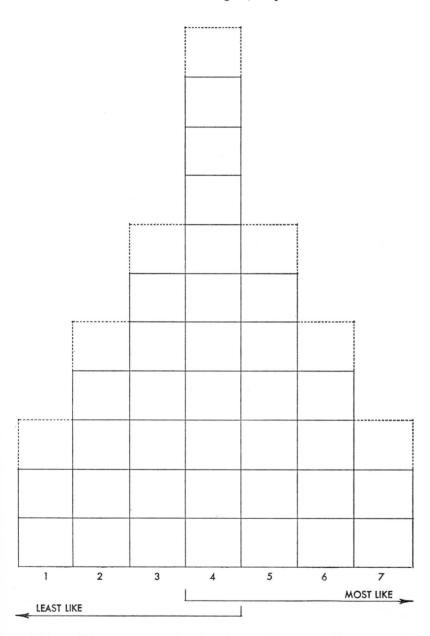

B. This pupil has to be coaxed or forced to work or play with other pupils. He or she will actively avoid having any contact with classmates.

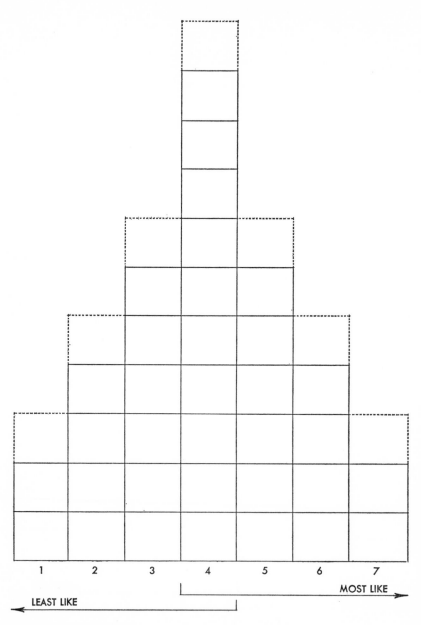

C. This pupil has difficulty in learning school subjects.

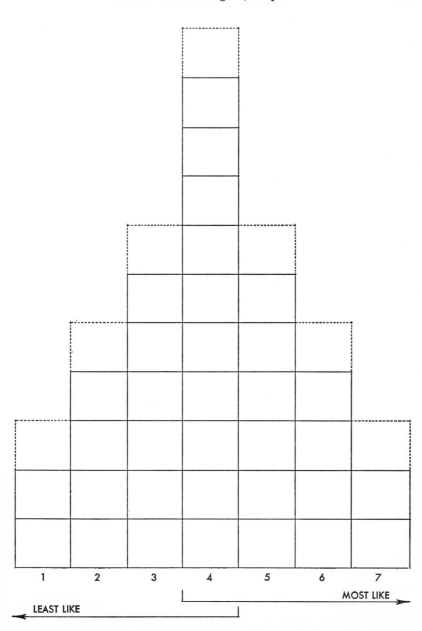

D. This pupil makes unusual or inappropriate responses during normal school activities. His behavior is unpredictable.

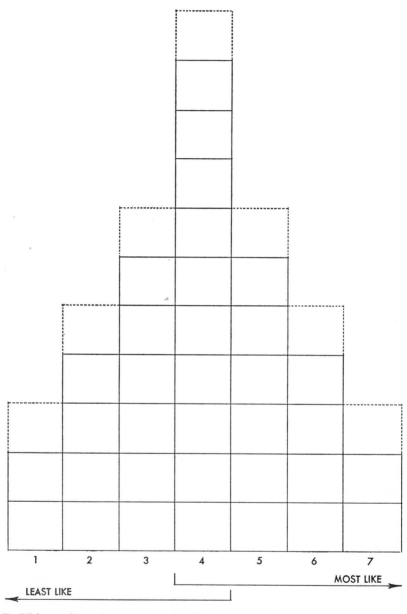

E. This pupil works extremely hard in learning school subjects to the exclusion of any other interests or activities. This pupil pours all his energies into school work.

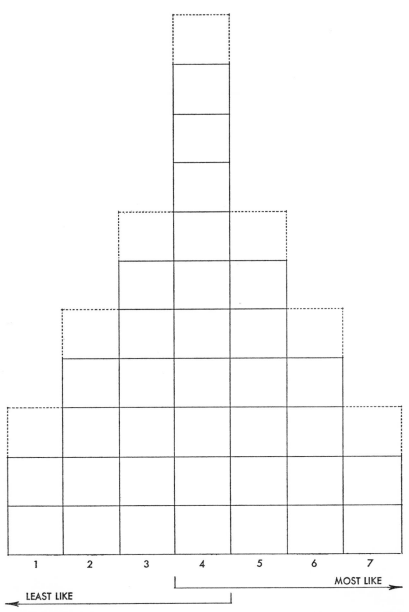

F. This pupil behaves in ways which are dangerous to self or others. This pupil will get into situations in which he or she may be hurt or frightened.

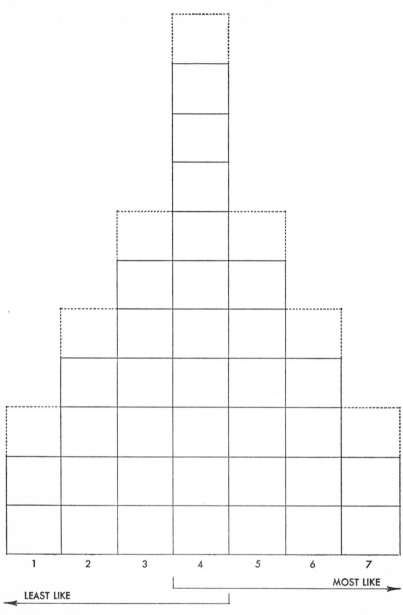

G. This pupil is unhappy or depressed. He or she may cry easily, be inattentive, or daydream.

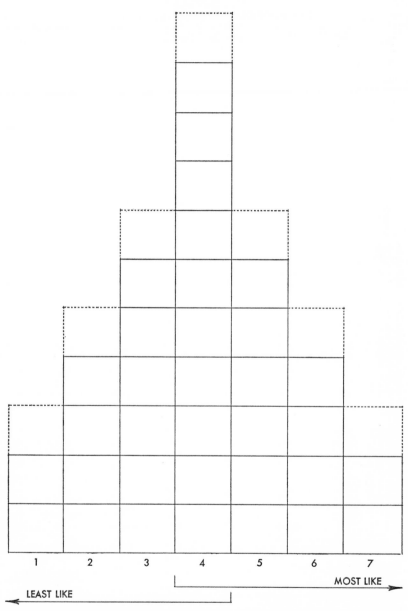

LEAST LIKE · MOST LIKE

1 2 3 4 5 6 7

H. This pupil becomes upset or sick often, especially when faced with a difficult school problem or situation.

STATEMENTS OF BEHAVIOR

	H Total 16	STATE-MENT A	STATE-MENT B	STATE-MENT C	STATE-MENT D	STATE-MENT E	STATE-MENT F	STATE-MENT G	STATE-MENT H	Total	Name of Pupil	Sex
H 1												
G 2												
F 3												
E 1												
D 1												
C 2												
B 3												
A 3												
EXAMPLE												

After you have completed each of the behavior ratings, enter under the correct letter the *number* of the column in which you placed each pupil's name. When you have finished entering the numbers (and have checked them to be sure), add the eight numbers for each pupil and enter the total.

THE CLASS PICTURES

Peer Rating—Kindergarten to Grade 3

Description

AFTER YOU HAVE completed the *Behavior Rating of Pupils,* your next step in screening is to plan for administration of the peer ratings. The peer rating instrument for kindergarten and primary grades, *The Class Pictures,* must be given to each child in your class individually, following the instructions given. This may take fifteen to twenty minutes of time for each child. Administration of *The Class Pictures* to the entire class, however, may be spread over a period of time — up to, but not exceeding, one month.

Administer the instrument to children one at a time when the rest of the class is engaged in seat work of some kind or occupied in other activities which do not require constant supervision. Such a schedule will require a minimum of interruption in your regular teaching program. Read the instructions for administering and scoring *The Class Pictures* before you start.

The Class Pictures are composed of twelve picture cards with a total of twenty scoring items (one or two items on a card). Five of the items are pictures of boys in situations related to emotionally maladjusted behavior; five are pictures of girls in situations related to emotionally maladjusted behavior; five are pictures of boys in situations related to positive or neutral types of behavior; and five are pictures of girls in situations related to positive or neutral types of behavior.

The Class Pictures have been developed as a means of analyzing, in a systematic and measurable way, how children are perceived or "seen" by their peers. The responses of most pupils to the pictures will not surprise you. Some responses, however, may seem unrealistic and inappropriate. *Accept each child's responses*

155

without comment unless the child obviously misunderstands directions. Your role during the administration of *The Class Pictures* is one of test proctor and recorder of responses.

The Class Pictures are used with children who have not yet learned to read or write well. Therefore, the responses of each child will need to be recorded individually by you. You will, of course, have to make special provision for the rest of the class while you are administering *Class Pictures* to individual children. If an additional school person is available, he may work with the class while you administer *Class Pictures*. The actual administration should always be done by you. If you are able to organize the class into working groups, *Class Pictures* may be administered to a few individuals daily during such work periods — but you will decide for yourself how best to accomplish this task.

On the test each child is asked to consider which of his classmates is most like the child in everyone of the twenty situations. Some children will pick twenty different names. Others may name one or two peers for several or many different items. Still others may make no response for one or more items (within the 15-second time limit set in the instructions for administering. *Do not expect any fixed pattern of responses.*

When the responses for every child in the class are collected, the teacher can tally the number of times a particular child is chosen for each of the twenty pictures. The total number of times a child is chosen for *all* of the pictures indicates how clearly or how vividly he is "seen," or perceived, by his peers.

The number of times a pupil is picked for the ten *negative* pictures indicates the degree to which he or she is *negatively* perceived by his peers. By dividing the number of times a child is picked for the ten negative pictures by the total number of times he is picked for all twenty of the pictures, a per cent, indicating the ratio of negative perception by peers, is obtained and used in screening.

The mean or average number of negative selections of emotionally handicapped boys and girls has been found to be significantly different from the mean number of negative selections in the general school population of that grade and sex. Consequently, the per cent of negative perception has been found to be a reliable indicator of those children whose behavior, as observed by peers, indicates some degree of emotional difficulty. The higher the per cent, the greater the possibility that the child has emotional problems. The per cent of negative selections on *The Class Pictures,* when combined with teacher ratings and self ratings, has been found effective in primary grades for screening children with emotional handicaps.

Administration

In the administration of *The Class Pictures,* you should proceed in the following manner:

Announce to the class that they will be playing a game with some pictures in the next few days, and, since many boys and girls cannot as yet write very well, you will be playing the game with each child individually. Use a table other than your own desk and set it apart somewhat from the rest of the class. On the table or desk place a set of *The Class Pictures* and a pad of "Recording Forms for *The Class Pictures.*" While the pictures are administered, the child should have his back toward the class so that the other children are not directly visible to him.

When the child is seated and ready to begin,

SAY: "I am going to show you pictures about school. In each picture you will see arrows pointing to children who will be acting as some children do in this class. I want you to look at each picture and tell me who in this class might act like the boy or girl in the picture. Use your imagination and try to think of someone in your class who might be acting like the boys and girls in these pictures. Now, let's try this one."

As the pupil gives you his choice, write the names of the children selected, in the spaces provided, making certain you write each name on the correct numbered line (line 1 for Arrow 1, and so on). If there is no response for a picture in an interval of 15 seconds, draw a line in that space and go on to the next arrow.

Pick up the first card (Arrow 1) and point to Arrow 1.

1. SAY: "Who could this be, sitting at his desk listening to the teacher?" Enter the name suggested, on line 1 of the recording sheet. Place the first card face down and turn over the second card.

    Point to Arrow 2 and

2. SAY: "Who could this be talking to her friend while the teacher is explaining something to the class?" Record response. Place the second card face down and pick up the third card.

    With the third card in hand, point to Arrow 3 and

3. SAY: "Who could this be having fun on the swings?" Record response. Place the third card face down and pick up the fourth card.

    Point to Arrow 4 and

4. SAY: "Who could this be chasing this boy and trying to hit him?"

    Place the fourth card face down and continue in this way with the rest of the cards.

5. "Who could this be, playing ball with the other children?"
6. "Who could this be, fighting with this other boy?"
7. "Who could this be, playing kick-ball with other children?"
8. "Who could this be, this unhappy child watching other children play?"
9. "Who could this be, carrying milk back to the class?"
10. "Who could this sick child be, in the nurse's office?"
11. "Who could this happy child be?"
12. "Who could this child be who is being brought to school by her mother?"
13. "Who could this be, playing on the bars?"
14. "Who could this child be who seems to have a stomach-ache?"
15. "Who could this be, walking along with her friends?"
16. "Who could this be, fighting with another child?"
17. "Who could this be, working quietly at the table?"

18. "Who could this be, playing with toys while the rest of the class is working?"
19. "Who could this be, playing tether-ball?"
20. "Who could this be, being told by the teacher not to do something?"

Scoring

To score *The Class Pictures,* you will need the recording forms on which you wrote each student's responses and a "Teacher's Worksheet for Scoring Peer Ratings." First, write the names of all the pupils in your class (last name first) in alphabetical order in the spaces provided on the "Worksheet."

The scoring process is essentially one of noting the frequency of perception of each child by his peers (Column **A**), the frequency of negative perception of each child by his peers (Column **B**), and quantifying the relationship between these two perceptions (Column **C**). Section II of the "Worksheet" is not used for *The Class Pictures,* so you may ignore that part.

Begin with any student's recording form and note the name of the pupil chosen for the first picture or item.* Put a tally mark in the column for Item 1 opposite the pupil's name. Note the name of the pupil chosen for the second item. Put a tally mark in the column for Item 2 opposite that pupil's name. Do this for all the remaining items and repeat the process with all the recording forms from the class. Make your tally marks small, because some pupils are chosen many times by their peers for the same item.

After all the selections of each student in the class have been tallied, count up all the tally marks in each little rectangle on the worksheet and, using a colored pencil, place a large figure indicating the total number of tally marks in each rectangle. Then, add each of these subtotals across the line for each pupil and write the total in Column **A**.

Next, add up the number of times each student was picked for

---

*"Item" is the term commonly used for "questions" on a test, regardless of whether they are phrased as interrogatives, or whether they refer to text matter, pictures, diagrams, charts, or any other type of material. We shall hereafter refer to "items," therefore, rather than to "pictures" or "questions."

the even-numbered items (shaded columns) and place that total number in Column **B**. Do this for every pupil.

To find the percent of negative selections (Column **C**), use the "Computation of Percentage for Peer Rating" on the cover of the "Teacher's Worksheet for Peer Ratings." (See also Appendix 1, where the "Computation" is reproduced for reference use.) Read the percentage at the point on the chart where the total number of selections (vertical columns) and the total *even-numbered selections* (horizontal columns) intersect. Write the percentage of negative selections for each pupil in Column **C**.

High percentages indicate a high degree of negative perception of a pupil by his peers. Low percentages indicate that a student is generally perceived in a positive way.

In order for a high percentage to be used in screening, a child has to be selected by at least one-fifth of the class. That is, the number in Column **A** for a particular child has to be at least one-fifth of the total class enrollment. For example: if, in a class of twenty-five, a student is picked four times and has 100% negative selection by peers, his percentage should nevertheless *not* be used.

If, however, a student is picked a total of five or six times, this is one-fifth or more of a class of twenty-five. If this student also has one of the five highest percentages in the class, mark his score (in Column **C**), with an asterisk or a check, as one of the five highest in your group.

Make your mark clear and distinct, because later, in combining scores for screening, you will be picking out these five highest percentages and the names of the students who received them.

A PICTURE GAME

(Self Rating—Kindergarten to Grade 3)

Description

A *Picture Game* is designed to give a measure of young children's perception of *self*. It is used along with the *Behavior Rating of Pupils* (teacher rating) and *The Class Pictures* (peer rating) to identify pupils who are vulnerable to, or handicapped by, emotional problems.

A Picture Game consists of 66 pictures, including two sample pictures. Each picture is illustrative of normal home and school relationships and events. With the exception of the two sample cards and the first ten pictures, each picture is emotionally neutral in the portrayal of the relationship or event. The child is asked to sort each picture into one of two categories: "This is a happy picture" or "This is a sad picture." The sorting is done by placing each picture in the "happy" or "sad" side of a two-compartment box which has a happy face shown on one compartment and a sad face on the other. The child categorizes each picture in accordance with his perception of it.

The first ten pictures the child sorts are stereotypes: obviously happy or obviously sad situations. The purpose of including them in the test items is to check on each pupil's understanding of the task. If a child sorts the first ten pictures correctly, you can be fairly sure that he has understood the process well enough for you to use his score in screening. If, on the other hand, he does not sort the first ten pictures correctly, you will need to meet with him individually and ask him to sort the pictures again for you, making certain that he understands the process. Some children *choose* to place pictures differently from others. If you find that such children understand the process but continue, on re-administration, to sort the pictures in an independent fashion, make a note of it on the "Class Record Sheet," and use the child's score in screening.

161

A Picture Game can be administered to your class as a group by providing each child with the special two-compartment box and a set of pictures. There are separate forms of *A Picture Game* for boys and girls. The boys' form is printed on blue cards, contained in a blue box. The girls' form is on pink cards, contained in a pink box.

It should take about one half hour to administer *A Picture Game* to your class, including time for distribution and collection.

Pictures in *A Picture Game* (Boys)

a. boy, smiling
b. boy, sullen
1. boy with Christmas presents
2. boy crying
3. boy happy
4. boy in father's clothes
5. boy being scolded
6. boy having bad dream
7. boy being spanked
8. boy being read to in mother's lap
9. boy being carried on dad's shoulders
10. boy with dropped glass in kitchen
11. boy being given book by teacher
12. boys running
13. boy eating alone
14. boy playing baseball
15. boy eating meal with parents
16. boy sitting in principal's office
17. boy in bed
18. boy opening door, looking at adult woman
19. boy handing paper to teacher
20. boy alone with teacher
21. boy awaiting arrival of father
22. (halloween) costumed children at door
23. two boys whispering on school playground
24. boy with dog
25. boy in car
26. boy on slide with waiting friends
27. boy observing parents' discussion
28. boy observing other children ready to play
29. boy sitting in classroom
30. boy talking to teacher
31. boy riding bicycle
32. teacher handing paper to boy
33. boy observing other children about to play
34. boy watching rain
35. boy watching other children play
36. teacher and boy sitting in empty classroom
37. boy watching television
38. boy sitting alone watching clock
39. boy alone walking down corridor
40. boy walking from classroom
41. boy with bicycle
42. boys and girls sitting around campfire
43. boy entering closet
44. boy with hand in fishtank
45. boy watching woman talk on phone
46. woman observing boy painting
47. boy playing in mud
48. bathroom
49. boy observing parent and teacher talking
50. boy with model trains
51. boy in discussion with father
52. woman opening door for boy
53. man pointing at boy
54. boy opening mother's purse
55. boy entering classroom
56. boy dressing with father observing
57. boy watching father at handiwork
58. boy on bike approaching rock
59. boy about to cross intersection
60. boy approaching father
61. boy approaching dog
62. boy dreaming of others
63. boy undressing with adult in room
64. boy having dream of fantasy

Administration

You should have enough pink boxes and sets of pink cards for each girl in your class and enough blue boxes and sets of blue cards for each boy. Distribute a box and a set of cards to each boy and girl along with small pieces of scratch paper on which they will write their names to put into their boxes when they have finished the game. You may, if you wish, distribute papers with the names already written on them. When all the children are ready, **say to the class:**

"We are going to play a picture game. Open your boxes. Notice that on the inside of the box cover there are two pictures. On the left is a picture of a sad boy or a sad girl. On the right, there is a picture of a happy boy or a happy girl. Each of you also has a set of picture cards. Girls have pink picture cards and pink boxes and boys have blue cards and blue boxes. Some of the pictures will seem sad to you and some of them will seem happy. You are to decide which are the sad pictures and which are the happy ones.

"Look at picture **A**. Is that a happy picture or a sad picture? (*Wait for class response.*) Yes, that is a happy picture. Put it in the compartment under the happy face—at your *right* hand.

"Look at Picture **B**. Is that a happy picture or a sad picture? (*Wait for class response.*) Yes, that is a sad picture. Put it in the compartment under the sad face—at your *left* hand.

"The game is for you to look at all the pictures in your set and decide which ones are *happy* pictures and which are *sad* pictures.

"Place the sad pictures in the compartment under the picture of the sad boy or girl. Place the happy pictures in the compartment under the picture of the happy boy or girl. You will probably all choose different pictures as happy or sad. I expect that. Play the game by yourself and don't work with your neighbor.

"When you are finished with all the pictures, place the slip of paper with your name on it in one of the compartments; it does not matter which. Then close your box and wait for me to pick it up."

Collect the boxes one by one, as the children complete the task, and place them out of sight until class is dismissed for the day. When you are ready to score them, take your "Class Record Sheet for *A Picture Game*," and turn to the instructions for "Scoring."

Scoring

To score *A Picture Game* you will need "Class Record Sheet— *A Picture Game*" and all the boxes, into which the students sorted the picture cards. Complete the identifying information at the top of the "Class Record Sheet" and write the names of the boys and girls in the spaces provided. Note that boys and girls are listed separately. Next, count the number of cards in the "happy" compartment of the first pupil's box and record that number in the column headed "Total No. of Happy Pictures" on your "Class Record Sheet," opposite the pupil's name.

The first ten columns of the "Class Record Sheet" provide a check to see if a pupil has understood the instructions. When you have finished counting and recording the number of pictures the pupil has placed in the "happy" compartment, note where he placed each picture numbered one through ten (1-10). A child's placement of each of these ten pictures should correspond with the "H" (happy) or "S" (sad) at the top of the column on the "Class Record Sheet." "H" indicates that most children see the picture as happy; "S" indicates that most children see the picture as sad. Where a child's placement does not correspond with the "H" or "S" at the top of the column, place an "X" in that square. Put an "X" in every square where the pupil's choice disagrees with the selection indicated at the top of the column.

If a pupil has three or more "X's," there is a strong possibility that the child misunderstood the directions or cannot grasp the concepts of "happy" or "sad." In any case, the test should be re-administered with the instructions explained individually to the child. The fact that you have administered the test a second time should then be noted in the column under "Comments" and the number in the "Total No. of Happy Pictures" column should be that counted in the second administration.

The two sample cards, **A** and **B**, and the first ten cards, unlike the other cards, are supposed to be what an average child sees as "happy" or "sad." If a pupil sorts out cards **A** and **B** and the first ten pictures as most children do, you can be fairly confident that he understood how to take the test. But if he has three or more choices which disagree with the average choices indicated on the "Class Record Sheet," you should suspect that he has not sorted the rest of the pictures according to the instructions and you will need to give him individual help in a re-administration of *A Picture Game.*

Now, in giving such help, you may find that the pupil *does* understand the instructions but still wishes to sort the cards in his own way. You should recognize that some children will react to the pictures in a manner quite different from, even opposite to, what you expect. Immature or retarded pupils, especially, have trouble understanding the instructions at first, and they, too, may sort pictures 1-10 differently. However, with a little individual help in a second administration, they should be able to make their choices and place the cards in the appropriate side of the box.

Research during the development of these instruments has shown that pupils with very high scores (many happy pictures) often have as many emotional problems as pupils with very low scores (few happy pictures). The importance of these extreme scores comes to light *only* when they occur in addition to a negative rating from either the teacher or peers or both.

Even though boys and girls have slightly different average scores, a rule of thumb can be used to designate the scores that should be considered very high or very low: On the "Class Record Sheet," mark with an asterisk the name of every pupil who has earned a score of 37 *or higher,* or 20 *or lower.* These marked scores—37 and higher, and 20 and lower—will be used in the screening summary. Scores of 21 - 36 inclusive will be ignored in the screening process.

To summarize the scoring procedure: take a pupil's box and, first, count and record the number of pictures from 1 to 64 he placed in the "happy" compartment. Then, check to see how he sorted pictures 1-10. Put an "X" in every space on the "Class

Record Sheet" where his choice disagrees with the expected choice.

When you have finished all the boxes for your class, put the sets of cards back in numerical order (1 through 64) with **A** and **B** on top, and place a set in each of the boxes (in either compartment; it does not matter), so that all will be ready for use by the next teacher. If you find that a card is missing, report it to your principal so that he can get a replacement.

Make plans to re-administer the test individually to every pupil who has three or more disagreements on pictures 1-10. If one of these pupils continues to sort the pictures in the same way during individual administration as he did during group administration, and you are sure that he understands the instructions, you can use his score for screening purposes. If the pupil cannot understand the instructions even in an additional setting, do not use his score for screening purposes.

Combining Scores in Screening (Kindergarten—Grade 3)

After you have completed the administration and scoring of the *Behavior Rating of Pupils, The Class Pictures,* and *A Picture Game,* the next step is to combine the scores on these three instruments to determine which pupils in your class should be screened as emotionally handicapped.

After screening, a child from your class can be seen by a school guidance person or a mental health specialist to determine the extent and nature of his emotional disability. You may be interested in checking on each of your pupils who is screened by looking over his previous school history, by talking to other teachers who have had him in class, and perhaps by seeking additional information about conditions in his home. The specific course of action taken after screening will depend upon the school programs for handling emotional disability and upon procedures planned by your school administration.

The completed records you will need to draw from for this screening process are: a) *Behavior Rating of Pupils,* b) "Teacher's Worksheet for Scoring Peer Ratings," c) "Class Record Sheet for *A Picture Game.*"

Follow each step explained below to combine scores and to complete the screening process:

1. Complete the identifying information at the top of the "Screening Summary" form, supplied with your materials. In the space at the top of the columns for peer rating and self rating, identify the instruments you used by writing *Class Pictures* under peer rating, and *Picture Game* under self rating.

2. Find the five pupils who received the five highest scores on the *Behavior Rating of Pupils* (teacher rating) and write their names at the left side of the page. After each name, enter the score from *Behavior Rating of Pupils* in the column provided.

3. Enter the names of the students who received the five highest percentages on *The Class Pictures* (marked with asterisks or checks on the "Teacher's Worksheet for Scoring Peer Ratings," Column **C**), writing their three percentages in the columns for peer ratings. If a pupil is already listed because he had one of the five highest teacher ratings, simply add his peer rating percentages in the columns after his name. If these pupils are not already listed, write in their names and record their peer rating percentages.

4. Use your "Class Record Sheet for *A Picture Game*" to find those pupils who have been noted as having extreme scores on self rating (names marked with asterisks during scoring process). If any of these names has already been written in the column for pupils' names, simply add the *Picture Game* score in the space provided. For any name not written in that column, write in the name and record the score in the self rating column.

5. Your "Screening Summary" will now have the name of every pupil in your class who has a high negative score on the teacher rating, the peer rating, or the self rating—and you will be able to see quickly which students have negative scores on more than one instrument. In the last column of the "Screening Summary"—"How Screened"—use the following notations:

168 *Early Identification of Emotionally Handicapped Children*

"T" if the pupil has a score noted on *Behavior Rating of Pupils* only.

"P" if the pupil has a score noted on *Class Pictures* only.

"S" if the pupil has a score noted on *Picture Game* only.

"TP" if the pupil has scores noted on *Behavior Rating of Pupils* and *Class Pictures*.

"TS" if the pupil has scores noted on *Behavior Rating of Pupils* and an extreme score on *Picture Game*.

"PS" if the pupil has scores noted on *Class Pictures* and on *Picture Game*.

"TPS" if the pupil has a critical score on all three instruments.

"T" stands for negative teacher rating; "P" stands for negative peer rating; "S" stands for negative self rating. A pupil should be considered as "screened" for special attention when he has *two or more negative* scores. Some pupils may have one negative rating and borderline scores on one or both of the other two ratings. You may want to make a notation of these pupils on your "Summary," especially if they are individuals who appear to you to have a significant number of debilitating, or handicapping, emotional problems.

Place an asterisk beside the name of every pupil with two or more negative scores on the "Screening Summary." These, then, are the pupils in your class who are screened as vulnerable to, or handicapped by, moderate to serious emotional problems, and their names are to be referred for further action under the plan or procedures adopted by your school or school district.

A sample "Screening Summary" is shown on page 169.

Pupil Record Folder (All Students—All Grades)

As their teacher, you will be interested in the performance of every pupil in your class whether or not he is identified as emotionally handicapped. There is a "Pupil Record Folder of Teacher, Peer, and Self Perceptions" on which you can record the scores on the three ratings for each pupil in the class. When completed, the "Pupil Record Folder" can be placed with a child's cumulative record. There are spaces for additional scores on these same ratings if the screening process is repeated at a later time or in future grades.

The instructions for completing the "Pupil Record Folder" are provided on the folder itself. The information which you record may become a helpful indicator of such aspects of children's growth as progress or change in relationships to teachers and peers, and modifications in self perception. In this way the school can keep track of each child's emotional growth and personality development over a period of time.

SCREENING SUMMARY

Teacher _E. Wilcox_ School _Horace Mann_ District _Crescent Bend_

Grade _2_ Class____ Period____ Date of Screening _December 1960_ Number of pupils in class _32_

Name of Pupil	TEACHER RATING Behavior Rating of Pupils	PEER RATING Class Pictures COLUMN A	B	C	SELF RATING Picture Game	How Screened
*Bean, Linda	51				46	(TS)
*Carroll, John	52	42	42	100		(TP)
*Perkins, Teddy	47				41	(TS)
Heard, Peter	45	18	13	72 borderline		T borderline
*Shaffner, Elizabeth	40	27	22	85	15	(TPS)
*Stanger, Bill		7	7	100	11	(P.S)
Richards, Shelley		18	15	83		P
Parker, Bobby		39	37	97		P.
Foster, Danny					37	S
Ravel, Connie					19	S
Vasquez, Guillermo					20	S

A CLASS PLAY

(Peer Rating—Grades 3-7)

Description

A *Class Play* is a peer rating instrument with greatest applicability in grades 4, 5, and 6, though it has been used with success in grades 3 and 7. It should be administered reasonably soon after you have completed the *Behavior Rating of Pupils*. It should take no more than 35 to 45 minutes.

Section I of the instrument contains descriptions of twenty hypothetical roles in a play, with instructions directing each pupil to choose a classmate who would be most suitable and natural in each of the roles. A second section of the *Play* (Section II) elicits from each pupil an indication of the roles he would prefer, or which he thinks other people would select for him. This section has thirty different quartets of the twenty roles, with a question aimed at finding out how the child sees himself in relation to each role.

The scoring of *A Class Play* is very much like the scoring of *The Class Pictures*. Each pupil names a classmate for each of the roles in the play. By counting the number of times a pupil is picked for each of the roles in the play, and then counting the number of times each pupil is picked for the *even numbered* (negative) roles, a percentage is obtained indicative of the positive or negative perception of each pupil by his classmates. This score is used in the screening.

Administration

In almost every class there will be children who will have some difficulty reading the material. You should plan a special administration of *A Class Play* for this group of pupils. Children who need special help with reading the materials can be engaged in an independent classroom activity while the rest of the class completes *A Class Play*. The slow readers can then take *A Class Play* during a reading-group period.

Standard testing procedures for administering this instrument should be followed to insure validity of the results. Some care should be taken to see that pupils do not compare answers. Provisions such as those made during the administration of a group test will be sufficient.

Distribute a copy of *A Class Play* to every pupil who will be taking it during the administration period. Be sure that each pupil has a pencil with an eraser. When each student has a booklet and a pencil, and is ready to begin,

SAY: "At the top of the cover of your booklet there are spaces for your school, your name, grade, your teacher's name, and to-day's date. Fill in these spaces now." Wait until students have completed filling in the identifying data and then,

"Just suppose our class is going to have a play. Would you like to pretend you are going to direct the play? The director of a play has to do many things, but the most important job is to select the right people to act in the play.

"When you turn the page you will find a list of characters or 'parts' in this make-believe play. As director, you must try to think of the boy or girl in the class who can play each part best.

"You may want to choose a boy or a girl in your class for more than one part. That is all right so long as you think carefully about your choices and are sure that boy or that girl fits both parts.

"Do not choose yourself for any of the parts. You will have a chance to do this later.

"If you are not sure of what you are to do, or if you do not understand all of the words, ask your teacher.

"Are there any questions, class? *(Wait for and answer any questions.)* If not, turn the page and write in the first names of the classmates you choose for each of the twenty parts described on the page. Stop when you have finished the page."

(When there are two Johns or two Marys, instruct the class to enter "the first name and first initial of the last name." If someone other than yourself will be doing the scoring, you will have to ask the children to write in the first initial of the last name on all their choices. It should be noted here that the instruction to "write in the first names" is given (1) to save time, and (2) because often children in the elementary grades are not thoroughly familiar with the last names of all their classmates. You may adjust the instructions to suit your own situation and needs — so long as you avoid writing out all names on the blackboard or any other procedure which *suggests* names to the children.)

If you administer *A Class Play* to a slow reading group, turn the page with the class, read the number of each statement and then the description of the role. Wait a few minutes until every pupil finishes writing in a name before continuing to the next role, or item.

When every pupil has finished Section I,

SAY: "Stop. Put your pencil down and turn your booklet to Section II. Read to yourselves the instructions for Section II while I read them aloud.

"Most children find it is fun to choose parts they would like to play and parts they would not like to play. It might also be fun to guess the parts which your classmates or your teacher would choose you to play.

"On the following pages you will be asked questions like these:

Which one of these parts would your *classmates* pick you to play?
Which one of these parts would you *not* be picked for?
Which one of these parts do you think your *teacher* might pick you to play?
Which one of these parts would your teacher *not* pick you for?

"And finally:
Which one of these parts would you *not* pick for yourself?

"For each question there will be four parts or characters to choose from. Choose only one part for each question and mark an X on the line next to the number of that part.

"Choose the part that best answers the question for you. Be sure to mark a choice for every question."

NOW SAY: "When you finish the first page, go on to the next pages and answer all of the questions. Then close your booklet and wait for me to collect it."

If you are administering the test to a slow reading group, turn the page with the pupils and read each item and each of the item choices, and wait for each pupil to mark his answer. Go on to the next item, and the next, until you have read all the items.

When all the pupils have finished, make certain that every pupil has written his name on his booklet, collect the booklets, and put them in your desk until you are ready to score them. For scoring, use your "Teacher's Worksheet for Scoring Peer Ratings." Follow the instructions for scoring *A Class Play*, page 184.

School _____ Name _____

Grade _____ Date _____ Teacher _____

A CLASS PLAY

Section I

J UST SUPPOSE our class is going to have a play. Would you like to pretend you are going to direct the play? The director of a play has to do many things, but the most important job is to select the right people to act in the play.

When you turn the page you will find a list of characters or "parts" in this make-believe play. As director, you must try to think of the boy or girl in the class who can play each part best.

You may want to choose a boy or a girl in your class for more than one part. That is all right so long as you think carefully about your choices and are sure a boy or girl fits both parts.

Do not choose yourself for any of the parts. You will have a chance to do this later.

If you are not sure of what you are to do, or if you do not understand all of the words, ask your teacher.

On the line next to each part, write the name of either a boy or girl who you think could best play the part.

_____ 1. A true friend.

_____ 2. Somebody who is often afraid and who acts like a little boy or girl.

_____ 3. A class president.

_____ 4. Somebody who is stuck-up and thinks he's better than everyone else.

_____ 5. A girl to act the part of a teacher of small children.

_____ 6. A mean, cruel boss.

_____ 7. A boy to act the part of a team captain, someone good in sports and liked by all.

_____ 8. A mean, bossy sister.

_____ 9. Someone who is smart and usually knows the answer.

_____10. A person who often gets angry over nothing and gets into lots of arguments.

_____11. Someone who is jolly and doesn't cause any trouble in class.

_____12. A bully who picks on smaller boys and girls.

_____13. Someone who is liked by everybody and who tries to help everybody.

_____14. A very lazy person.

_____15. A very fair person who plays games fairly.

_____16. A nice pest — someone who often gets into trouble, but is really nice.

_____17. Someone else, besides yourself, who could direct the play.

_____18. A smaller, younger child who is always falling down and getting hurt.

_____19. A school nurse or a doctor.

_____20. Somebody who seems always to be late for

Section II

Most children find it is fun to choose parts that they would like to play and parts that they would not like to play. It might also be fun to guess the parts which your classmates or your teacher would choose you to play.

On the following pages you will be asked questions like these:

Which one of these parts would your classmates pick you to play?

Which one of these parts would you **not** be picked for?

Which one of these parts do you think your teacher might pick you for?

Which one of these parts would your teacher **not** pick you for?

And finally:

Which of these parts would you **not** pick for yourself?

For each question there will be four parts or characters to choose from. Choose only **one** part for each question and mark an X on the line next to the number of that part.

Choose the part that best answers the question for you. Be sure to mark a choice for every question.

Which one of these four parts would your classmates NOT pick you to play?

_____1. Somebody who seems always to be late for school.

_____2. Someone who is smart and usually knows the answer.

_____3. A nice pest — someone who often gets into trouble, but is really nice.

_____4. A true friend.

Which one of these four parts would your classmates pick you to play?

_____1. The person who would be good as the director of the play.

_____2. A very lazy person.

_____3. A school nurse or a doctor.

_____4. Somebody who seems always to be late for school.

Which one of these four parts would a teacher NOT pick you to play?

_____1. The part of a mean, bossy sister or brother.

_____2. The part of a teacher of small children.

_____3. Somebody who is stuck-up and thinks he's better than everyone else.

_____4. Someone who is smart and usually knows the answer.

Which one of these four parts would a teacher pick you to play?

_____1. A class president.

_____2. A smaller, younger child who is always falling down and getting hurt.

_____3. The captain of the team — someone good in sports and liked by all.

_____4. Somebody who seems always to be late for school.

Which one of these four parts would you LEAST like to play?

_____1. Somebody who is stuck-up and thinks he's better than everyone else.

_____2. The person who would be good as the director of the play.

_____3. A smaller, younger child who is always falling down and getting hurt.

_____4. The captain of the team — someone good in sports and liked by all.

Which one of these four parts would you MOST like to play?

_____1. Someone who is jolly and doesn't cause any trouble in class.

_____2. A smaller, younger child who is always falling down and getting hurt.

_____3. A true friend.

_____4. Somebody who is stuck-up and thinks he's better than everyone else.

Which one of these four parts would your classmates NOT pick you to play?

_____1. A person who often gets angry over nothing and gets into lots of arguments.

_____2. A class president.

_____3. A smaller, younger child who is always falling down and getting hurt.

_____4. The captain of the team — someone good in sports and liked by all.

Which one of these four parts would you MOST like to play?

_____1. The part of a teacher of small children.

_____2. The part of a mean, bossy sister or brother.

_____3. A very fair person who plays games fairly.

_____4. Somebody who seems always to be late for school.

Which one of these four parts would you LEAST like to play?

_____1. A very lazy person.

_____2. The part of a teacher of small children.

_____3. A nice pest — someone who often gets into trouble, but is really nice.

_____4. A class president.

Which one of these four parts would your classmates pick you to play?

_____1. A very fair person who plays games fairly.

_____2. A bully who picks on smaller boys and girls.

_____3. Someone who is smart and usually knows the answer.

_____4. A mean, cruel boss.

Which one of these four parts would a teacher NOT pick you to play?

_____1. Somebody who seems always to be late for school.

_____2. A class president.

_____3. Somebody who is often afraid and who acts like a little boy or girl.

_____4. A very fair person who plays games fairly.

Which one of these four parts would a teacher pick you to play?

_____1. A school nurse or a doctor.

_____2. A bully who picks on smaller boys and girls.

_____3. Someone who is smart and usually knows the answer.

_____4. A mean, cruel boss.

Which one of these four parts would a teacher pick you to play?

_____1. Someone who is a jolly and doesn't cause any trouble in class.

_____2. Somebody who is stuck-up and thinks he's better than everyone else.

_____3. A very fair person who plays games fairly.

_____4. A nice pest — someone who often gets into trouble, but is really nice.

Which one of these four parts would a teacher NOT pick you to play?

_____1. A person who often gets angry over nothing and gets into lots of arguments.

_____2. Someone who is liked by everybody and who tries to help everybody.

_____3. A very lazy person.

_____4. Someone who is jolly and doesn't cause any trouble in class.

Which one of these four parts would you MOST like to play?

_____1. A school nurse or a doctor.

_____2. A mean, cruel boss.

_____3. The person who would be good as the director of the play.

_____4. Somebody who is often afraid and who acts like a little boy or girl.

Which one of these four parts would your classmates pick you to play?

_____1. Someone who is liked by everybody and tries to help everybody.

_____2. Somebody who is often afraid and who acts like a little boy or girl.

_____3. The captain of the team — someone good in sports and liked by all.

_____4. A smaller, younger child who is always falling down and getting hurt.

Which one of these four parts would your classmates NOT pick you to play?

_____1. A bully who picks on smaller boys and girls.

_____2. Someone who is liked by everybody and who tries to help everybody.

_____3. A very lazy person.

_____4. The part of a teacher of small children.

Which one of these four parts would you LEAST like to play?

_____1. Somebody who is often afraid and who acts like a little boy or girl.

_____2. Someone who is smart and usually knows the answer.

_____3. Somebody who seems always to be late for school.

_____4. Someone who is jolly and doesn't cause any trouble in class.

Which one of these four parts would your classmates pick you to play?

_____1. A true friend.

_____2. Somebody who is stuck-up and thinks he's better than everyone else.

_____3. Someone who is jolly and doesn't cause any trouble in class.

_____4. A nice pest — someone who often gets into trouble, but is really nice.

Which one of these four parts would a teacher pick you to play?

_____1. The part of a teacher of small children.

_____2. A person who often gets angry over nothing and gets into lots of arguments.

_____3. Someone who is liked by everybody and who tries to help everybody.

_____4. The part of a mean, bossy sister or brother.

Which one of these four parts would a teacher NOT pick you to play?

_____1. A nice pest — someone who often gets into trouble, but is really nice.

_____2. A true friend.

_____3. A mean, cruel boss.

_____4. The person who would be good as the director of the play.

Which one of these four parts would you MOST like to play?

_____1. A class president.

_____2. A very lazy person.

_____3. The captain of the team — someone good in sports and liked by all.

_____4. A bully who picks on smaller boys and girls.

Which one of these four parts would you LEAST like to play?

_____1. The part of a mean, bossy sister or brother.

_____2. Someone who is liked by everybody and who tries to help everybody.

_____3. A bully who picks on smaller boys and girls.

_____4. A very fair person who plays games fairly.

Which one of these four parts would your classmates NOT pick you to play?

_____1. The part of a mean, bossy sister or brother.

_____2. Someone who is jolly and doesn't cause any trouble in class.

_____3. Somebody who is stuck-up and thinks he's better than everyone else.

_____4. A very fair person who plays games fairly.

Which one of these four parts would your classmates NOT pick you to play?

_____1. A mean, cruel boss.

_____2. A school nurse or a doctor.

_____3. Somebody who is often afraid and who acts like a little boy or girl.

_____4. The person who would be good as the director of the play.

Which one of these four parts would your classmates pick you to play?

_____1. A class president.

_____2. A person who often gets angry over nothing and gets into lots of arguments.

_____3. The part of a teacher of small children.

_____4. The part of a mean, bossy sister or brother.

Which one of these four parts would a teacher pick you to play?

_____1. A true friend.

_____2. A very lazy person.

_____3. The person who would be good as the director of the play.

_____4. Somebody who is often afraid and who acts like a little boy or girl.

Which one of these four parts would you LEAST like to play?

_____1. A mean, cruel boss.

_____2. A true friend.

_____3. A person who often gets angry over nothing and gets into lots of arguments.

_____4. A school nurse or a doctor.

Which one of these four parts would you MOST like to play?

_____1. Someone who is smart and usually knows the answer.

_____2. A nice pest — someone who often gets into trouble, but is really nice.

_____3. Someone who is liked by everybody and who tries to help everybody.

_____4. A person who often gets angry over nothing and gets into lots of arguments.

Which one of these four parts would a teacher NOT pick you to play?

_____1. A smaller, younger child who is always falling down and getting hurt.

_____2. The captain of the team — someone good in sports and liked by all.

_____3. A bully who picks on smaller boys and girls.

_____4. A school nurse or a doctor.

Scoring

To score *A Class Play,* you will need booklets, marked by the pupils, and a copy of the "Teacher's Worksheet for Scoring Peer Ratings." First, write in the names of all pupils in your class (last name first) in alphabetical order in the spaces provided on the "Worksheet." List at the bottom of the page those pupils who were absent during the administration.

Section I of *A Class Play* contains each student's peer selections. The scoring process is essentially one of computing the total perception of each child by his peers (Column **A**) and the negative perception of each child by his peers (Column **B**), then quantifying the relationship between the two perceptions (Column **C**).

In Section II the objective of the scoring is similar. Here you can find out how the pupil sees himself. Column **F** indicates the proportion of negative roles selected by each pupil for himself. A comparison of Column **C** and Column **F** will indicate the congruence or incongruence between a student's perception of himself and the way he is perceived by others. To put it another way, it will indicate to what extent a student's image of himself matches the image his classmates have of him.

Computing Peer Ratings (Section I)

Begin with any pupil's marked booklet and note the name of the pupil he chose for the first item. On the "Worksheet," put a tally mark in the column for Item 1 opposite that pupil's name. Note the name of the pupil chosen by the same child for the second item. Put a tally mark in the column for Item 2 opposite that pupil's name. Do this for all the remaining items in Section I of the marked booklet and repeat the process with all the marked booklets for the class. Make your tally marks small, because some pupils are chosen many times by their peers for the same role.

After all the role-selections of each pupil in the class have been tallied, count up all the tally-marks in each little rectangle on the "Worksheet" and, using a colored pencil, print a large figure in each rectangle indicating the total number of tally-marks in that rectangle. Now, add each of these sub-totals across the line for each pupil and write the total in Column **A**.

Next, add up the number of times each student was picked for even-numbered roles (in the shaded columns) and place the total number in Column **B**.

To find the per cent of total selections to even-numbered selections (Column **C**), use the "Computation of Percentage for Peer Rating," page 1 of the "Teacher's Worksheet for Scoring Peer Ratings." (See also Appendix 1 of this *Manual*, where the "Computation" is reproduced for reference use.) Read the percentage at the point on the chart where the total number of selections (vertical columns) and the total of even-numbered selections (horizontal columns) intersect. Write the percentage of negative selections for each pupil in Column **C**.

High percentages indicate a high degree of negative perception of a pupil by his peers. Low percentages indicate that a student is generally perceived in a positive way.

In order for a high percentage to be used in screening, a child has to be selected by at least one-fifth of the class. That is, the number in Column **A** for a particular child has to be at least one-fifth of the total class enrollment. For example: if, in a class of twenty-five, a student is picked four times and has 100% negative selection by peers, his percentage should nevertheless *not* be used.

If, however, a student is picked a total of five or six times, this is one-fifth or more of a class of twenty-five. If this student also has one of the five highest percentages in the class, mark his score (in Column **C**), with an asterisk or a check, as one of the five highest in your group.

Make your mark clear and distinct, because later, in combining scores for screening, you will be picking out these five highest percentages and the names of the students who received them.

Computing Self Scores (Section II)

To score Section II of *A Class Play,* count the number of checks each student has made on the questions for Section II and record that number in Column **D**. Most students will choose only one answer for each question, and will answer every question. Since there are 30 questions, the number that you are most likely to record in Column **D** is 30. If a student has answered some questions, the number will be more or less than 30. Whatever the number is, write it in Column **D**.

Next, total the number of checks on all answers numbered either 2 or 4. Write this number in Column **E**. To find the per cent of negative *self* ratings, use the percentage chart just as you did for Section I.

High percentages indicate that a student identifies with negative roles and also that the student perceives teachers and classmates selecting him for negative roles. Further discussion of peer-self comparisons can be found in the section on "Interpreting the Results of the Screening Process," page 233.

THINKING ABOUT YOURSELF
(Self Rating—Grades 3-7)

Description

THE PURPOSE of *Thinking About Yourself* is to elicit from the pupil himself an *intra-self* measure of the relationship between a pupil's perception of his environment and his conception of what it ought to be. What is looked for is the degree of discrepancy between a pupil's self perception and an ideal self, between his perception of himself as he *is* and as he would like to be.

Many pupils with serious emotional problems cannot bring themselves to disclose their difficulties in writing, or are uncomfortable about disclosing them. Their responses will therefore very much resemble those of other children in the class. These youngsters are most likely to be screened by teachers and peers.

There are other pupils, however, who do not manifest their difficulties to teachers or peers, but who rise to the opportunity to express inner discomfort and *can* communicate their disturbance on a self rating instrument. Since the average discrepancy between self and *ideal* self has been found to discriminate between pupils with emotional problems and those with normal behavior adjustment, *Thinking About Yourself* provides a meaningful and useful screening dimension not available from teacher or peer ratings.

This instrument should be administered after you have completed the *Behavior Ratings of Pupils* and *A Class Play*, the teacher and peer ratings.

Note: Some teachers prefer to administer *A Class Play* and *Thinking About Yourself* in the same period or on the same day. Decide what is best for your pupils, and administer the tests to suit your schedule.

Administration

In every class there may be children who will have difficulty reading the material. You should plan a special administration of *Thinking About Yourself* for this group. Children who need special help in reading the materials can be engaged in independent classroom activity while the rest of the class completes *Thinking About Yourself*. The slow readers then can take *Thinking About Yourself* during a reading-group period.

Standard testing procedures for administering this instrument should be followed to insure validity of the results. Some care should be taken to see that pupils do not compare answers. Provisions such as those made during the administration of any group test will be sufficient.

Distribute pink forms of *Thinking About Yourself* to the girls and blue forms to the boys. Be sure each pupil has a pencil with an eraser. When each student has a booklet and a pencil, and is ready to begin,

SAY: "Fill in the spaces at the top of the cover of your booklet. Today's date is _____. *(Give them the date and wait until all have filled in the spaces.)*

"Read to yourselves the instructions for Section I, on the cover of your booklet, while I read them aloud.

"All of us at one time or another would like to be someone else. Often we play at being other persons during games or parties. We also think about what it would be like to be someone in a book, in the movies, or on a television program. On the next two pages, are descriptions of many different girls or boys. Use your imagination to decide if you would want to be like the girl or boy described in each sentence.

"If you would *like very much* to be the girl or boy described in the sentence, circle the big 'YES.'
"If you *perhaps would like* to be the girl or boy described in the sentence, circle the small 'yes.'
"If you think you *would not like* to be the girl or boy described in the sentence, circle the small 'no.'
"If you would *very much not want* to be like the girl or boy described in the sentence, circle the big 'NO.'

"Now, try these examples **A** through **D**."

Wait for the class to try items **A** through **D**, then
SAY: "Are there any questions, class? *(Wait for hands to be raised, and answer any questions.)*

"There are no right or wrong answers. Each of you will *want* to be like some of the girls or boys and *not* want to be like others. Read each sentence carefully before deciding how you will answer. If you do not understand how to answer some of the questions, ask your teacher. Answer questions 1 through 40 and then close your booklet and wait for further instructions.

"Now, turn your page and begin."

When the class has finished Section I,

SAY: "Now turn to Section II. Read the instructions silently while I read them aloud.
"All of us think about ourselves, at times. We think about what we like, what we don't like, what we do, and what we don't do. To some extent we are able to see ourselves as others see us. Each of us, however, has his own ideas about himself. Decide what you are like and then decide whether or not you are like the girl or boy described in each of the following sentences.

"If you see yourself as *very much like* the girl or boy described in the sentence, circle the big 'YES.'
"If you think you are *somewhat* or *sometimes* like the girl or boy described in the sentence, circle the small 'yes.'
"If you believe you are *not* much like the girl or boy described in the sentence, circle the small 'no.'
"If you believe you are *not at all like* the boy or girl described in the sentence, circle the big 'NO.'
"Now try the examples from **A** through **D**."

Wait for the class to try items **A** through **D**, then

SAY: "Are there any questions, class? *(Wait for and answer any questions.)* Remember that this time you are to answer each question on the basis of whether you think you are or are not like the boy or girl in the sentence.

"There are no right or wrong answers. You will probably decide that you are *somewhat* like or *very much* like some of the girls or boys described in the sentences, and *not* much like or *not at all* like other girls or boys described.

"Read each sentence carefully before deciding how you will answer. If you do not understand how to answer some of the questions, ask your teacher."

When the class has finished Section II, collect the booklets and put them out of sight in your desk. When you are ready to score them, turn to the instructions for "Scoring."

Scoring

When you are ready to begin scoring *Thinking About Yourself,* gather all the booklets and the transparent "Score Sheets" supplied with your kit of materials. You should have one of these "Score Sheets" for every student in your class.

The first step is to complete the identifying data on the fold at the top of the score sheet for each pupil. (The "Score Sheet" is folded for your convenience. The fold provides a "hanger" to hold the guide in place as you score each page of *Thinking About Yourself.*)

Next, place the fold of the transparent score sheet over the top of the A-page of a student's test, matching the horizontal sequences of 1, 2, 3, 4 under **A** on the "Score Sheet" with the horizontal rows of "**YES yes no NO**" under **A** on the page of the test booklet. (The vertical figures, item numbers 1-20, should align also.)

Next, using a crayon or soft pencil, start circling the numbers on the score sheet corresponding to the words "**YES yes no NO**" marked by the pupil for each item in his test booklet. When you have finished marking **A**, you will have circles around a 1 or a 2 or a 3 or a 4 for every item.

When you have finished page **A**, go on to page **B** (the next page), and do the same thing. Notice that Column B on your score sheet is the third column, not the second. You will have to skip one column on your score sheet in order to put the correct marks on the score sheet for Column **B**. Match up the sequences of **1, 2, 3, 4** under **B** as you did with Column **A** and put circles around the numbers corresponding to the marks in the student's booklet.

For Section II, put Column **C** of your score sheet over Column **C** in the test booklet, match the horizontal sequences of **1, 2, 3, 4,** under **C** on the "Score Sheet" with the horizontal rows of "**YES** **yes no NO**" on page **C** of the test booklet, and mark the answers in a similar fashion. (Note that Column **C** on your score sheet is the second column.) Then mark page **D** by placing the last column of the score sheet over the **D** column of the booklet. Mark the answers as you did for the other columns.

By this time you are probably curious to know how the answers on Section I correspond to the answers on Section II. If you look at a booklet, you will see that the items under **A** (Section I) are exactly the same as the items under **C** (Section II). Similarly, the items under **B** (Section I) are the same as those under **D** (Section II) . In short, the items for both Sections I and II are the same. The student marks Section I as he would like to be, and he marks Section II as he sees himself. This system for scoring the test enables you to note easily how the student's *present* self concept corresponds with his *ideal* self concept.

When you have completed marking the answers on the score sheet for each pupil, you will be able to translate these answers into a total score. Alongside Column **C** is a vertical column of short lines headed score. There is also a score column alongside Column **D**.

To score item 1, compare the number circled in Column **A** with the number circled in Column **C**. Subtract the smaller number from the larger and write the difference in the score column on the line provided for item 1. For example: Assume you have circled a "3" for item 1 in Column **A** and a "1" in Column **C**. Simply subtract 1 from 3 and enter 2 on the first line under score. Do this for all 40 items.

When you finish entering the score for each item, make a subtotal at the bottom of each score column, add the scores for the two score columns, and enter the grand total in the box after the student's name. The grand total is the pupil's score on *Thinking About Yourself*. A low total score indicates that a pupil's ideal self and perceived self are very much the same. A high score indicates that a pupil sees himself quite differently from what he would like to be. The discrepancy or lack of discrepancy between ideal self and perceived self has been found to be helpful in identifying pupils with serious emotional problems. You will be comparing this self rating, secured from *Thinking About Yourself*, with teacher and peer ratings in order to locate those pupils who should be screened as vulnerable to, or handicapped by, serious emotional problems.

Finally, transfer the scores for all students to the "Class Record Sheet for *Thinking About Yourself*," listing boys and girls separately.

Combining Scores for Screening (Grades 3-7)

When you have completed the administration and scoring of the *Behavior Rating of Pupils, A Class Play*, and *Thinking About Yourself*, you can combine scores for certain pupils to determine those in your class who should be identified as having possibly moderate to severe emotional problems. The children who are screened should then be evaluated by a school guidance person or referred to a mental health specialist outside the school to determine the extent and nature of their problems.

You yourself may be interested in following up on these pupils by looking over their previous school histories, talking to their other teachers, and perhaps gaining additional information about conditions in their homes. At times, the use of the screening process can help to deepen your understanding of some individual pupils in your class and thus help you in planning effective educational experiences for others. The information you collect, including observations and other testing results, will be of great value to a mental health specialist in studying, diagnosing, and helping the student. The specific course of action taken after you and other teachers in your school have completed the screening process will depend on the school program for mental health and the follow-up plans established by your school administration.

Follow the steps listed below to combine scores and to complete the screening process:
1. Complete the identifying information at the top of the "Screening Summary" form. In the space at the top of the columns for peer rating and self rating, write in the names of the ratings you used: *A Class Play* (peer rating), *Thinking About Yourself* (self rating).
2. Find the five students who received the five highest scores on the *Behavior Rating of Pupils*. Write their names at the left side of the page and their scores on the *Behavior Rating of Pupils* after each name. Check the sample "Summary Sheet" on page 22 to clarify this and the subsequent procedures.
3. Write the names of the students whe received the five highest percentages on Section I of *A Class Play*. ("Teacher's Worksheet for Scoring Peer Ratings," Column **C**). Note that some of these names may be the same as those already entered in Step 2.

When you have located the pupils with the five highest (most negative) percentages, enter their names on the "Summary Sheet" and record their percentages in the column for peer ratings. If a pupil's name is already listed with one of the five highest teacher ratings, simply add his peer rating percentage in the appropriate column after his name.
4. Use your "Class Record Sheet for *Thinking About Yourself*" to find those pupils who should be noted as having a negative self rating. On the "Class Record Sheet," put a mark beside the names of the boys with the *three* highest scores among the boys, and the names of the girls with the *three* highest scores among the girls (Since boys and girls have different averages, it is best to consider them separately.) Next, record in the self rating column of the "Screening Summary" the score on *Thinking About Yourself* for each of the three boys and three girls whose names you have marked. If a pupil's name has already been written in the column for pupils' names on the "Screening Summary," simply add the *Thinking About Yourself* score in the space provided.

5. Your "Screening Summary" will now have the name of any pupil who had a high negative score on a teacher rating, on a peer rating, or on a self rating, and you will be able to see quickly which students have negative scores on more than one instrument. In the last column, "How Screened," place the following notations:

"T" if the pupil has a recorded score on the *Behavior Rating of Pupils* only.

"P" if the pupil has a recorded per cent on *A Class Play* only.

"S" if the pupil has a recorded score on *Thinking About Yourself* only.

"TP" if the pupil has recorded scores on the *Behavior Rating of Pupils* and *A Class Play*.

"TS" if the pupil has recorded scores on the *Behavior Rating of Pupils* and *Thinking About Yourself*.

"PS" if the pupil has recorded scores on *A Class Play* and *Thinking About Yourself*.

"TPS" if the pupil has a critical score on all three instruments.

"T" stands for negative teacher rating; "P" stands for negative peer rating; "S" stands for negative self rating. A pupil will be identified for screening when he has two or more negative scores. Some pupils have one negative rating and borderline scores on one or more of the other, two ratings. If so, you may want to make a notation of these pupils on your "Summary," especially if they are ones who appear to you to have a significant number of debilitating, or handicapped, emotional problems.

Place an asterisk beside the name of any pupil with two or more negative scores on the "Screening Summary." These, then, are the pupils in your class who are screened as being vulnerable to, or handicapped by, moderate to serious emotional problems and their names are to be referred for further action under the plan or procedures adopted by your school or school district.

A sample "Screening Summary" sheet is shown on the next page.

Name_____Grade_____

School_____Date_____

THINKING ABOUT YOURSELF

Form A
BOYS

Section I

All of us at one time or another would like to be someone else. Often we play at being other persons during games or parties. We also think about what it would be like to be someone in a book, in the movies, or on a television program. On the next two pages, are descriptions of many different boys. Use your imagination to decide if you would want to be like the boy described in each sentence.

If you would **like very much** to be the boy described in the sentence, circle the big "**YES**," this way———————→ (YES)   yes   no   NO

If you **perhaps would like** to be the boy described in the sentence, circle the small "**yes**," this way——————→ YES   (yes)   no   NO

If you think you **would not like** to be the boy described in the sentence, circle the small "**no**," this way——————→ YES   yes   (no)   NO

If you would **very much not want** to be like the boy described in the sentence, circle the big "**NO**," this way——————→ YES   yes   no   (NO)

Now, try these examples from **A** through **D**.

		"Oh, very much!"	"Well, yes."	"I don't think so."	"No, no, a thousand times, no!"
A. This boy owns a pony.	Would you like to be him?	YES	yes	no	NO
B. This boy hits little children.	Would you like to be him?	YES	yes	no	NO
C. This boy gets good grades.	Would you like to be him?	YES	yes	no	NO
D. This boy gets sick.	Would you like to be him?	YES	yes	no	NO

There are no right or wrong answers. Each of you will **want** to be like some of the boys and **not** want to be like others. Read each sentence carefully before deciding how you will answer. If you do not understand how to answer some of the questions, ask your teacher. Answer questions 1 through 40 and then close your booklet and wait for further instructions.

	A				**A**

1. This boy has many dreams.

	Do you want to be like him?	YES	yes	no	NO	1.

2. This boy enjoys teasing girls.

	Do you want to be like him?	YES	yes	no	NO	2.

3. This boy does not have to go to school.

	Do you want to be like him?	YES	yes	no	NO	3.

4. When he grows up, this boy will be a teacher.

	Do you want to be like him?	YES	yes	no	NO	4.

5. This boy studies hard at home.

	Do you want to be like him?	YES	yes	no	NO	5.

6. This boy plays games whenever possible.

	Do you want to be like him?	YES	yes	no	NO	6.

7. This boy goes to the dentist.

	Do you want to be like him?	YES	yes	no	NO	7.

8. This boy has a light in his room all night.

	Do you want to be like him?	YES	yes	no	NO	8.

9. This boy plays with many different children.

	Do you want to be like him?	YES	yes	no	NO	9.

10. This boy goes to bed without being told.

	Do you want to be like him?	YES	yes	no	NO	10.

11. This boy daydreams a lot.

	Do you want to be like him?	YES	yes	no	NO	11.

12. This boy will be rich and famous.

	Do you want to be like him?	YES	yes	no	NO	12.

13. This boy gets to school on time.

	Do you want to be like him?	YES	yes	no	NO	13.

14. This boy plays by himself a lot.

	Do you want to be like him?	YES	yes	no	NO	14.

15. This boy is asked to take charge when the teacher leaves the room.

	Do you want to be like him?	YES	yes	no	NO	15.

16. Getting good grades is very important to this boy.

	Do you want to be like him?	YES	yes	no	NO	16.

17. This boy cries sometimes.

	Do you want to be like him?	YES	yes	no	NO	17.

18. This boy fights a great deal.

	Do you want to be like him?	YES	yes	no	NO	18.

19. This boy is going to quit school as soon as possible.

	Do you want to be like him?	YES	yes	no	NO	19.

20. This boy gets angry sometimes.

	Do you want to be like him?	YES	yes	no	NO	20.

| | **B** | | | | **B** | |

		YES	yes	no	NO	
21. This boy keeps his friends a long time.						
	Do you want to be like him?	YES	yes	no	NO	21.
22. This boy gets his clothes dirty.						
	Do you want to be like him?	YES	yes	no	NO	22.
23. This boy is a very good baseball player.						
	Do you want to be like him?	YES	yes	no	NO	23.
24. This boy is often picked as the captain of a team.						
	Do you want to be like him?	YES	yes	no	NO	24.
25. This boy talks to his parents about his problems.						
	Do you want to be like him?	YES	yes	no	NO	25.
26. This boy sometimes hits smaller children.						
	Do you want to be like him?	YES	yes	no	NO	26.
27. Sometimes this boy is punished.						
	Do you want to be like him?	YES	yes	no	NO	27.
28. This boy is likely to be chosen class president.						
	Do you want to be like him?	YES	yes	no	NO	28.
29. This boy watches television.						
	Do you want to be like him?	YES	yes	no	NO	29.
30. This boy is very smart.						
	Do you want to be like him?	YES	yes	no	NO	30.
31. This boy sings in the shower or tub.						
	Do you want to be like him?	YES	yes	no	NO	31.
32. This boy does funny things in school.						
	Do you want to be like him?	YES	yes	no	NO	32.
33. This boy reads a lot of books.						
	Do you want to be like him?	YES	yes	no	NO	33.
34. This boy worries about getting hurt when he plays games.						
	Do you want to be like him?	YES	yes	no	NO	34.
35. Sometimes this boy is teased by other children.						
	Do you want to be like him?	YES	yes	no	NO	35.
36. This boy plays when he should be studying.						
	Do you want to be like him?	YES	yes	no	NO	36.
37. This boy is very good in arithmetic.						
	Do you want to be like him?	YES	yes	no	NO	37.
38. Being president of the class is important to this boy.						
	Do you want to be like him?	YES	yes	no	NO	38.
39. This boy sleeps late on school holidays.						
	Do you want to be like him?	YES	yes	no	NO	39.
40. This boy eats lots of different foods.						
	Do you want to be like him?	YES	yes	no	NO	40.

Section II

All of us think about ourselves, at times. We think about what we like, what we don't like, what we do, and what we don't do. To some extent we are able to see ourselves as others see us. Each of us, however, has his own ideas about himself. Decide what you are like and then decide whether or not you are like the boy described in each of the following sentences.

If you see yourself as **very much like** the boy described in the sentence, circle the big "**YES**," this way⎯⎯⎯⎯⎯⎯⎯⎯→ (YES) yes no **NO**

If you think you are **somewhat or sometimes like** the boy described in the sentence, circle the small "**yes**," this way⎯⎯⎯ YES (yes) no **NO**

If you believe you are **not much like** the boy described in the sentence, circle the small "**no**," this way⎯⎯⎯⎯⎯⎯⎯→ YES yes (no) **NO**

If you believe you are **not at all like** the boy described in the sentence, circle the big "**NO**," this way⎯⎯⎯⎯⎯⎯⎯→ YES yes no (**NO**)

Now, try the examples from **A** through **D**.

	"Oh, very much!"	"Well, yes."	"I don't think so."	"No, no, a thousand times, no!"
A. This boy owns a pony. Are you like him?	YES	yes	no	NO
B. This boy hits little children. Are you like him?	YES	yes	no	NO
C. This boy gets good grades. Are you like him?	YES	yes	no	NO
D. This boy gets sick. Are you like him?	YES	yes	no	NO

There are no right or wrong answers. You will probably decide that you are **somewhat like** or **very much like** some of the boys described in the sentences, and **not much like** or **not at all like** other boys described. Read each sentence carefully before deciding how you will answer. If you do not understand how to answer some of the questions, ask your teacher.

	C			C		

1. This boy has many dreams.						
Are you like him?	YES	yes	no	NO	1.

| 2. This boy enjoys teasing girls. |
| Are you like him? | YES | yes | no | NO | 2. |

| 3. This boy does not have to go to school. |
| Are you like him? | YES | yes | no | NO | 3. |

| 4. When he grows up, this boy will be a teacher. |
| Are you like him? | YES | yes | no | NO | 4. |

| 5. This boy studies hard at home. |
| Are you like him? | YES | yes | no | NO | 5. |

| 6. This boy plays games whenever possible. |
| Are you like him? | YES | yes | no | NO | 6. |

| 7. This boy goes to the dentist. |
| Are you like him? | YES | yes | no | NO | 7. |

| 8. This boy has a light in his room all night. |
| Are you like him? | YES | yes | no | NO | 8. |

| 9. This boy plays with many different children. |
| Are you like him? | YES | yes | no | NO | 9. |

| 10. This boy goes to bed without being told. |
| Are you like him? | YES | yes | no | NO | 10. |

| 11. This boy daydreams a lot. |
| Are you like him? | YES | yes | no | NO | 11. |

| 12. This boy will be rich and famous. |
| Are you like him? | YES | yes | no | NO | 12. |

| 13. This boy gets to school on time. |
| Are you like him? | YES | yes | no | NO | 13. |

| 14. This boy plays by himself a lot. |
| Are you like him? | YES | yes | no | NO | 14. |

| 15. This boy is asked to take charge when the teacher leaves the room. |
| Are you like him? | YES | yes | no | NO | 15. |

| 16. Getting good grades is very important to this boy. |
| Are you like him? | YES | yes | no | NO | 16. |

| 17. This boy cries sometimes. |
| Are you like him? | YES | yes | no | NO | 17. |

| 18. This boy fights a great deal. |
| Are you like him? | YES | yes | no | NO | 18. |

| 19. This boy is going to quit school as soon as possible. |
| Are you like him? | YES | yes | no | NO | 19. |

| 20. This boy gets angry sometimes. |
| Are you like him? | YES | yes | no | NO | 20. |

	D			**D**	
21. This boy keeps his friends a long time.					
Are you like him?	YES	yes	no	NO	21.
22. This boy gets his clothes dirty.					
Are you like him?	YES	yes	no	NO	22.
23. This boy is a very good baseball player.					
Are you like him?	YES	yes	no	NO	23.
24. This boy is often picked as the captain of a team.					
Are you like him?	YES	yes	no	NO	24.
25. This boy talks to his parents about his problems.					
Are you like him?	YES	yes	no	NO	25.
26. This boy sometimes hits smaller children.					
Are you like him?	YES	yes	no	NO	26.
27. Sometimes this boy is punished.					
Are you like him?	YES	yes	no	NO	27.
28. This boy is likely to be chosen class president.					
Are you like him?	YES	yes	no	NO	28.
29. This boy watches television.					
Are you like him?	YES	yes	no	NO	29.
30. This boy is very smart.					
Are you like him?	YES	yes	no	NO	30.
31. This boy sings in the shower or tub.					
Are you like him?	YES	yes	no	NO	31.
32. This boy does funny things in school.					
Are you like him?	YES	yes	no	NO	32.
33. This boy reads a lot of books.					
Are you like him?	YES	yes	no	NO	33.
34. This boy worries about getting hurt when he plays games.					
Are you like him?	YES	yes	no	NO	34.
35. Sometimes this boy is teased by other children.					
Are you like him?	YES	yes	no	NO	35.
36. This boy plays when he should be studying.					
Are you like him?	YES	yes	no	NO	36.
37. This boy is very good in arithmetic.					
Are you like him?	YES	yes	no	NO	37.
38. Being president of the class is important to this boy.					
Are you like him?	YES	yes	no	NO	38.
39. This boy sleeps late on school holidays.					
Are you like him?	YES	yes	no	NO	39.
40. This boy eats lots of different foods.					
Are you like him?	YES	yes	no	NO	40.

SCREENING SUMMARY

Teacher _Miss Betsy Morris_   School _J. P. Jones_   District _Jefferson_

Grade _5_ Class____ Period____   Date of Screening _November 1960_   Number of pupils in class _32_

Name of Pupil	TEACHER RATING Behavior Rating of Pupils	PEER RATING A Class Play COLUMN A	B	C	SELF RATING Thinking about Yourself	How Screened
*Faunt, Richard	48	45	44	98%	45	(T P S)
Morse, Linda	46	22	19	86%		T Pborderline
Jones, Kimball	42					T
*Kibbe, Dennis	40	43	43	100%		(T P)
*Owen, Regina	39				43	(T S)
*Clayton, Orlando		14	14	100%	39	(P S)
Mathews, Melinda		19	17	89%		P
Bass, Mark		12	12	100%		P
Lewis, Barbara					45	S
Gray, Marsha					44	S
Pemberton, Robert					38	S

STUDENT SURVEY

(Peer Rating—Grades 7-12)

Description

THE *Student Survey* is the peer rating instrument for use in the junior and senior high schools. In order for this test to have validity, it is necessary to administer it to a class in which the students have had an opportunity for some social and intellectual interaction, as well as for observation of one another in a variety of classroom situations. Previous work with this test has shown that social studies or English classes are usually best for this purpose.

Some students in the junior and senior high school may be sensitive to the kinds of questions asked on the *Student Survey*. It is important, therefore, that you anticipate the possibility of such sensitivity and take steps to allay any suspicion or resentment. For example, some teachers have found it helpful to have ready an envelope into which all the tests can be placed when the students are finished. This helps to reassure the class that the test results are confidential and reinforces statements made in the instructions that the results will not be discussed with others.

Section I of the *Student Survey* consists of twenty items. Ten are illustrative of maladjusted or emotionally disturbed behavior and ten are illustrative of neutral or positive behavior. For each statement of behavior, the students are asked to list the name of a classmate who is most like the student described in the item.

Section II of the *Student Survey* contains the same twenty behavior statements randomly arranged in thirty groups of four statements each. The student is asked to select one of the four statements in each group as the one which he thinks others in the class might apply to him, or which he thinks would apply to himself. The responses to Section II can be used to compare the peer ratings of a student with his self rating. The value of providing two sections in the *Student Survey,* a peer rating and a self rating on the same items, is, that after scoring both sections, the teacher is able to measure and analyze how a student sees himself in relation to how he is seen by others.

Complete the *Behavior Rating of Pupils* and then plan to administer the *Student Survey* and *A Self Test.* Many teachers have administered both of these tests during the same period. You may do the same, or you may wish to use two different days for administration.

Administration

Distribute copies of the *Student Survey* to all pupils in the class. Be sure that each pupil has a pencil with an eraser. When each student has a booklet and a pencil, and is ready to begin,

SAY: "At the top of the cover of your booklet are spaces for you to write in your name, grade, school, subject, period, and today's date. Fill in these spaces now." Wait until the students have finished filling in the identifying data, then

SAY: "Read to yourselves the instructions for Section I on the cover of your booklet while I read them aloud.
"Education means learning about different subjects, about other places, other people, other ideas. But education also means learning about ourselves, about our own ideas and attitudes.

"The purpose of this survey is to help you find out, and to help your teachers understand, how students your age see yourselves and others your age—your classmates particularly. Your individual answers will *not* be discussed in class. However, the results of this survey, for the class as a whole, may be presented by your teacher at a later time.

"On the following page, there are twenty statements which describe different kinds of students. Think of someone in your class who is *most like* or *often like* the student described in each statement. Then, write his name on the line to the left of the statement. Only students in your present class or class period can be named in completing the twenty statements. You may, if you wish, use the same student for more than one statement. Students who are noted as absent by the teacher may also be used in completing the statements. Remember, select students who are in your present class only.

"To save time, use only the initial of the first name and the full last name.

"If you have any questions about the meaning of a word or statement, ask your teacher.

"Do you have any questions, class (*Wait for, and answer any questions.*) If not, turn the page and write in a name for each of the twenty statements on the first page. When you have finished, stop, put your pencil down, and wait for further instructions."

When all have completed Section I of *Student Survey,*

SAY: "Turn to the instructions for Section II. Read to yourselves the instructions for Section II while I read them aloud.

"Students have found it fun to guess which of the twenty statements teachers, classmates, and friends think are most typical of them. It has also been interesting to discover which of the twenty statements each student thinks is most typical of himself.

"On the following pages you will find these statements, often repeated, in groups of four under questions like these:

Which one of these four students is *most* like you?

Which one of these four students would your *classmates* think is *least* like you?

Which one of these four students would your *teachers* think is *most* like you?

"In other words, how do you see yourself? And, for better or worse, how do you think your classmates and your teachers see you?

"There are no 'right' or 'wrong' answers; there is no 'grade' or 'mark' for filling out this form. Nor is this a popularity contest. Your answers are confidential and have meaning only as they represent a clear-eyed effort on your part to see yourself as you think others see you, and as you—in a moment without false pride or vanity—see yourself.

"Make only *one* choice for each question. Read each question carefully. Indicate your choice by placing an X on the line next to the number of your choice.

"When you finish the first page, go on to the next pages and answer all of the questions. Then close your booklet and wait for me to collect it."

When all the students have finished, collect the booklets, place them in an envelope, and fasten the clasp or seal the envelope. Do not leave the booklets loose on your desk. Let the class observe the care with which you handle these confidential materials so that all may be assured that inquisitive classmates will not have an opportunity, or the temptation, to see what other students have written.

To score the results of the *Student Survey,* follow the directions on page 215.

School _____   Name _____

Grade _____ Date _____ Teacher _____

STUDENT SURVEY

Section I

Education means learning about different subjects, about other places, other people, other ideas. But education also means learning about ourselves, about our own ideas and attitudes.

The purpose of this survey is to help you find out, and to help your teachers understand, how students your age see yourselves—and others your age, your classmates particularly. Your individual answers will **not** be discussed in class. However, the results of this survey, for the class as a whole, may be presented by your teacher at a later time.

On the following page there are 20 statements which describe different kinds of students. Think of someone in your class who is **most like** or **often like** the described student in each statement. Then, write his name on the line to the left of the statement. Only students in your present class or class period can be named in completing the statements. You may, if you wish, use the same student for more than one statement. Students who are noted as absent by the teacher may also be used in completing the statements. Remember, select students who are in your present class only.

To save time, use only the initial of the first name and the full last name.

If you have any questions about the meaning of a word or a statement, ask your teacher.

Think of the name of a student in your present class who is MOST LIKE or OFTEN LIKE the student described. Write his or her name in the space provided to the left of each statement.

_____ 1. A student who is good in school work.

_____ 2. A student who gets into fights or quarrels with other students.

_____ 3. One who can accept responsibilities.

_____ 4. One who has to be coaxed or forced to work with other students.

_____ 5. A student who is well liked.

_____ 6. One who has difficulty learning.

_____ 7. Someone who is helpful to others.

_____ 8. Someone who is interested in things he can do alone.

_____ 9. A person upon whom you can depend.

_____10. One who makes unusual or odd remarks in class.

_____11. One who is respected by other students.

_____12. One who sometimes behaves in ways which are dangerous to self or others.

_____13. Someone who will probably be a success in life.

_____14. A student who is often unhappy or "blue."

_____15. One who has lots of common sense.

_____16. A student who has more problems than other students.

_____17. Someone who has lots of self-confidence.

_____18. One who gets upset when faced with a difficult school problem.

_____19. A person who is seldom sick.

_____20. A person who is moody.

Section II

Students have found it fun to guess which of the twenty statements teachers, classmates, and friends think are most typical of them. It has also been interesting to discover which of the twenty statements each student thinks is most typical of himself.

On the following pages you will find these statements, often repeated, in groups of four under questions like these:

Which one of these four students is **most** like you?

Which one of these four students would your **classmates** think is **least** like you?

Which one of these four students would your **teachers** think is **most** like you?

In other words, how do you see yourself? And, for better or worse, how do you think your classmates and your teachers see you?

There are no right or wrong answers; there is no grade or mark for filling out this form. Nor is this a popularity contest. Your answers are confidential and have meaning only as they represent a clear-eyed effort on your part to see yourself as you think others see you, and as you—in a moment without false pride or vanity—see yourself.

Make only **one** choice for each question. Read each question carefully. Indicate your choice by placing an X on the line next to the number of your choice.

Which one of these four students would your classmates think is LEAST like you?

_____1. One who sometimes behaves in ways which are dangerous to self or others.

_____2. One who has difficulty learning.

_____3. One who gets upset when faced with a difficult school problem.

_____4. One who has lots of common sense.

Which one of these four students would your classmates think is MOST like you?

_____1. A student who is good in school work.

_____2. One who has diffiiculty learning.

_____3. Someone who will probably be a success in life.

_____4. One who makes unusual or odd remarks in class.

Which one of these four students would your teachers think is LEAST like you?

_____1. One who gets upset when faced with a difficult school problem.

_____2. Someone who has lots of self-confidence.

_____3. A student who is often unhappy or "blue."

_____4. A student who is good in school work.

Which one of these four students would your teachers think is MOST like you?

_____1. One who is respected by other students.

_____2. One who makes unusual or odd remarks in class.

_____3. Someone who will probably be a success in life.

_____4. One who has difficulty learning.

Which one of these four students is LEAST like you?

_____1. One who makes unusual or odd remarks in class.

_____2. A student who is good in school work.

_____3. Someone who is interested in things he can do alone.

_____4. Someone who will probably be a success in life.

Which one of these four students is MOST like you?

_____1. Someone who will probably be a success in life.

_____2. One who gets upset when faced with a difficult school problem.

_____3. Someone who has lots of self-confidence.

_____4. A student who has more problems than other students.

Which one of these four students would your classmates think is LEAST like you?

_____1. A student who has more problems than other students.

_____2. Someone who is helpful to others.

_____3. Someone who is interested in things which he can do alone.

_____4. A student who is good in school work.

Which one of these four students is MOST like you?

_____1. One who is respected by other students.

_____2. One who sometimes behaves in ways which are dangerous to self or others.

_____3. A person upon whom you can depend.

_____4. Someone who is interested in things which he can do alone.

Which one of these four students is LEAST like you?

_____1. One who has to be coaxed or forced to work with other students.

_____2. Someone who is helpful to others.

_____3. One who sometimes behaves in ways which are dangerous to self or others.

_____4. A student who is well liked.

Which one of these four students would your classmates think is MOST like you?

_____1. Someone who has lots of common sense.

_____2. A person who is moody.

_____3. Someone who has lots of self-confidence.

_____4. A student who has more problems than other students.

Which one of these four students would your teachers think is LEAST like you?

_____1. A student who has more problems than other students.

_____2. A person who is seldom sick.

_____3. Someone who is interested in things he can do alone.

_____4. Someone who is helpful to others.

Which one of these four students would your teachers think is MOST like you?

_____1. A student who is well liked.

_____2. A person who is moody.

_____3. Someone who has lots of self-confidence.

_____4. One who sometimes behaves in ways which are dangerous to self or others.

Which one of these four students would your teachers think is MOST like you?

_____1. Someone who has lots of common sense.

_____2. Someone who is interested in things he can do alone.

_____3. A person who is seldom sick.

_____4. One who has to be coaxed or forced to work with other students.

Which one of these four students would your teachers think is LEAST like you?

_____1. A person who is moody.

_____2. Someone who has lots of common sense.

_____3. One who has to be coaxed or forced to work with other students.

_____4. One who is respected by other students.

Which one of these four students is MOST like you?

_____1. One who can accept responsibilities.

_____2. A student who is often unhappy or "blue."

_____3. Someone who is helpful to others.

_____4. A student who gets into fights or quarrels with other students.

Which one of these four students would your classmates think is MOST like you?

———1. One who can accept responsibilities.

———2. One who gets upset when faced with a difficult school problem.

———3. A person upon whom you can depend.

———4. Someone who is interested in things he can do alone.

Which one of these four students would your classmates think is LEAST like you?

———1. One who has difficulty learning.

———2. A student who is well liked.

———3. A person who is moody.

———4. A person who is seldom sick.

Which one of these four students is LEAST like you?

———1. A person who is moody.

———2. One who has lots of common sense.

———3. A student who gets into fights or quarrels with other students.

———4. A person upon whom you can depend.

Which one of these four students would your classmates think is MOST LIKE you?

———1. A person who is seldom sick.

———2. One who sometimes behaves in ways which are dangerous to self or others.

———3. One who is respected by other students.

———4. One who has to be coaxed or forced to work with other students.

Which one of these four students would your teachers think is MOST LIKE you?

———1. One who can accept responsibilities.

———2. A student who gets into fights or quarrels with other students.

———3. A person upon whom you can depend.

———4. One who gets upset when faced with a difficult school problem.

Which one of these four students would your teachers think is LEAST like you?

_____1. A student who gets into fights or quarrels with other students.

_____2. One who can accept responsibilities.

_____3. One who has difficulty learning.

_____4. A student who is well liked.

Which one of these four students is MOST like you?

_____1. A student who is well liked.

_____2. One who makes unusual or odd remarks in class.

_____3. Someone who has lots of common sense.

_____4. One who has to be coaxed or forced to work with other students.

Which one of these four students is LEAST like you?

_____1. One who has difficulty learning.

_____2. Someone who has lots of self-confidence.

_____3. One who gets upset when faced with a difficult school problem.

_____4. A person who is seldom sick.

Which one of these four students would your classmates think is LEAST like you?

_____1. One who makes unusual or odd remarks in class.

_____2. One who is respected by other students.

_____3. A student who gets into fights or quarrels with other students.

_____4. Someone who will probably be a success in life.

Which one of these four students would your classmates think is LEAST like you?

_____1. One who has to be coaxed or forced to work with other students.

_____2. Someone who has lots of self-confidence.

_____3. A student who is often unhappy or "blue."

_____4. A person upon whom you can depend.

Which one of these four students would your classmates think is MOST like you?

_____1. Someone who is helpful to others.
_____2. A student who is often unhappy or "blue."
_____3. A student who is well liked.
_____4. A student who gets into fights or quarrels with other students.

Which one of these four students is MOST like you?

_____1. A student who is good in school work.
_____2. One who has difficulty learning.
_____3. A person who is seldom sick.
_____4. A person who is moody.

Which one of these four students is LEAST like you?

_____1. A student who has more problems than other students.
_____2. One who can accept responsibilities.
_____3. A student who is often unhappy or "blue."
_____4. One who is respected by other students.

Which one of these four students would your teachers think is MOST like you?

_____1. A student who is good in school work.
_____2. A student who is often unhappy or "blue."
_____3. Someone who is helpful to others.
_____4. A student who has more problems than other students.

Which one of these four students would your teachers think is LEAST like you?

_____1. One who makes unusual or odd remarks in class.
_____2. A person upon whom you can depend.
_____3. One who sometimes behaves in ways which are dangerous to self or others.
_____4. Someone who will probably be a success in life.

Scoring

To score the *Student Survey,* you will use the marked booklets and a "Teacher's Worksheet for Scoring Peer Ratings." First, write the name of all pupils in your class (last names first) in alphabetical order in the spaces provided on the "Worksheet." List at the bottom of the page those pupils who were absent during the administration. Be sure that each pupil has written his name on the booklet.

Section I of the *Student Survey* contains each student's peer selections. The scoring process is essentially one of computing the frequency of the perception of each child by his peers (Column **A**), the frequency of negative perception of each child by his peers (Column **B**), and then quantifying the relationship between these two perceptions (Column **C**).

In Section II the objective of the scoring, although similar, is related to the self perception of each pupil. Column **F** indicates the proportion of negative roles selected by each pupil for himself. A comparison of Column **C** and Column **F** will indicate the discrepancy or lack of discrepancy between a student's perception of himself and the way he is perceived by others.

Begin with any student's responses and note the name of the pupil he chose for the first item. Put a tally mark in the column for Item 1 (one the "Worksheet") opposite the pupil's name. Note the name of the pupil he chose for the second item. Put a tally mark in the column for Item 2 opposite that pupil's name. Do this for all the remaining items and repeat the process through the marked booklets of all the students in the class. Make your tally marks small, because some pupils are chosen many times by their peers for the same item.

After all the selections of each student in the class have been tallied, count up all the tally marks in each little rectangle on the worksheet and, using a colored pencil, place a large figure indicating the total number of tally marks in each rectangle. Then, add each of these sub-totals across the line for each pupil and write the total in Column **A**.

Next, add the number of times each student was picked for

the even-numbered items (shaded columns) and place that total number in Column **B**. Do this for every pupil.

To find the per cent of negative selections (Column **C**), use the "Computation of Percentage for Peer Ratings," page one, "Teacher's Worksheet for Scoring Peer Ratings." (Or see Appendix 1.) Read the percentage at the point on the chart where the total number of selections (vertical columns), and the total *even-numbered* selections (horizontal columns) intersect. Write the percentage of negative selections for each pupil in Column **C**.

High percentages indicate a high degree of negative perception of a pupil by his peers. Low percentages indicate that a student is generally perceived in a positive way.

In order for a high percentage to be used in screening, a child has to be selected by at least one-fifth of the class. That is, the number in Column **A** for a particular child has to be at least one-fifth of the total class enrollment. For example: if, in a class of twenty-five, a student is picked four times and has 100% negative selection by peers, his percentage should nevertheless *not* be used.

If, however, a student is picked a total of five or six times, this is one-fifth or more of a class of twenty-five. If this student also has one of the five highest percentages in the class, mark his score (in Column **C**), with an asterisk or a check, as one of the five highest in your group.

Make your mark clear and distinct, because later, in combining scores for screening, you will be picking out these five highest percentages and the names of the students who received them.

Computing Self Scores for the Student Survey

To score Section II of the *Student Survey,* count the number of checks each student has made on the questions for Section II and record that number in Column **D**. Most students will choose only one answer for each question, and will answer every question. Since there are 30 questions, the number that you are most likely to record in Column **D** is 30. If a student has answered some questions more than one or not answered some questions, the number will be more or less than 30. Whatever the number is, write it in Column **D**.

Next, total the number of checks on all answers numbered 2 or 4. Write this number in Column **E**. To find the per cent of negative *self* ratings, use the percentage chart just as you did for Section I.

High percentages indicate that a student identifies with negative roles. High percentages also indicate that the student believes that teachers and classmates would select him for negative roles.

A SELF TEST

(Self Rating—Grades 7-12)

Description

A *Self Test* is INTENDED to obtain a measure of the difference between the way a pupil sees himself and the way he would like to be—in other words, a measure of the difference between self and ideal self. To the extent that a student is able to disclose the differences or similarities between these two aspects of self, the instrument is useful in screening. However, some pupils with moderate or serious emotional problems cannot bring themselves to disclose the discomfort or dissatisfaction which this instrument invites them to disclose. Their responses, therefore, will very much resemble those of other students in the class. These youngsters are more likely to be identified by teachers and peers in the screening process.

There are other pupils, however, who do not manifest their difficulties to teachers or peers, but who rise to the opportunity to express inner discomfort and *can* communicate their disturbance on a self rating. For these students, the *Self Test* provides the opportunity. Since the average discrepancy between self and *ideal* self has been found to discriminate between pupils with emotional problems and those with normal behavior adjustment, *A Self Test* provides a meaningful screening dimension not available from teacher or peer ratings.

A Self Test contains forty statements describing people behaving in a number of different ways. In Section I, the student is asked to indicate how strongly he *would like* to be or *would not like* to be the person described. In Section II, the items are repeated and the student is asked to indicate how strongly he feels he *is* like or *is not* like the person described. The two responses by the student (i.e., whether or not he *wants* to be like and whether or not he *is* like) are then compared in the scoring process, after which the amount of discrepancy between the two "selves" is compared.

A Self Test should be administered in the social studies class or in an English class in which the *Student Survey* has been given. It may be given during the same period as the *Student Survey,* or administered on a different day. You must take care that the booklets are placed in a safe place so that each student's answers will be treated with professional confidence.

Administration

Standard testing procedures for administering this test should be followed to insure validity of the results. Some care should be taken to see that pupils do not compare answers. Provisions like those made during the administration of a group achievement test will be sufficient.

Distribute a copy of *A Self Test* to each student in the class. Be sure that each pupil has a pencil with an eraser. When each student has a booklet and a pencil, and is ready to begin,

SAY: "In the spaces on the cover of your booklet, print your name and grade, the name of the school, and today's date. Read to yourselves the instructions for Section I on the cover of your booklet, while I read them aloud.

"All of us at one time or another would like to be someone else. Often, during games or parties, or while daydreaming, we imagine what it might be like to be someone else. We also think about what it would be like to be someone in a book, in a TV play, or in a movie. On the next two pages, you will find descriptions of many different young people. Use your imagination to decide if you would want to be like the person described in each sentence.

"If you would *like very much* to be the person described in the sentence, circle the large 'YES.'

"If you *perhaps would like* to be the person described in the sentence, circle the small 'yes.'

"If you think you *would not like* to be the person described in the sentence, circle the small 'no.'

"If you would *very much not want* to be like the person described in the sentence, circle the large 'NO.'

"Now try the examples from **A** through **D**."
   Wait for the class to finish the examples, then

SAY: "Are there any questions, class? (*Wait for and answer any questions.*)

"There are no right or wrong answers. Each of you will *want* to be like some of the people and *not* want to be like others. Read each sentence carefully before deciding how you will answer. If you do not understand how to answer some of the questions, ask your teacher. Answer questions 1 through 40 and then stop."

   When the class has finished Section I,

SAY: "Now turn to Section II. Read the instructions silently while I read them aloud.

"All of us think about ourselves at times. We think about what we like, what we don't like, what we do, and what we don't do. To some extent we are able to see ourselves as others see us. Each of us, however, has his own ideas about himself. Decide what you are like and then decide whether or not you are like the person described in each of the following sentences.

"If you see yourself as *very much like* the person described in the sentence, circle the large 'Yes.'

"If you thing you are *somewhat or sometimes* like the person described in the sentence, circle the small 'yes.'

"If you think you are *not much like* the person described in the sentence, circle the small 'no.'

"If you believe you are *not at all like* the person described in the sentence, circle the large 'NO.'

"Now try the examples from **A** through **D**."
   Wait until the class has finished the examples, then

SAY: "Are there any questions, class? (*Wait for and answer any questions.*)

"Again, there are no 'right' or 'wrong' answers. You will probably decide that you are *somewhat like* or *very much like* some of the people described, and *not much like* or *not at all like* others. Your answers, which will *not* be seen by any classmate, have meaning only as they represent the person you think *you are now,* in a moment of clear-eyed and level-headed frankness or candor—not the person you want to be or hope to become.

"Read each sentence carefully before deciding how you will answer. If you do not understand some of the questions, consult your teacher.

"Answer questions 1 through 40 on Section II. When you are finished, close your booklet and wait for further instructions."

When the class has finished Section II, collect the booklets and put them out of sight in your desk, preferably in a special envelope. In this way the students will be certain that their answers are confidential and you will have reduced the possibility that curious students may examine the papers.

Scoring

When you are ready to begin scoring *A Self Test,* gather all the booklets and the transparent "Score Sheets" supplied with your kit of materials. You should have one "Score Sheet" for every student in class.

The first step is to complete the identifying data on the fold at the top of the score sheet for each pupil. (The "Score Sheet" is folded for your convenience. The fold provides a "hanger" to help hold the guide in place as you score each page of *A Self Test.*)

Next, place the fold of the transparent score sheet over the top of page **A** of a student's test, matching the horizontal sequences of **1, 2, 3, 4** under **A** on the "Score Sheet" with the horizontal rows of "**YES yes no NO**" under **A** on the page of the test booklet. (The vertical figures, item numbers 1-20, should align also.)

Next, using a crayon or soft pencil, start circling the numbers on the score sheet corresponding to the words "**YES yes no NO**" marked by the pupil for each item in his test booklet. When you have finished marking **A**, you will have circles around a 1 or a 2 or a 3 or a 4 for every item.

When you have finished page **A**, go on to page **B** (the next page), and do the same thing. Notice that Column **B** on your score sheet is the third column, not the second. You will have to skip one column on your score sheet in order to put the correct marks on the score sheet for Column **B**. Match up the sequences of 1, 2, 3, 4 under **B** as you did with Column **A** and put circles around the numbers corresponding to the marks in the student's booklet.

For Section II, put Column **C** of your score sheet over Column **C** in the test booklet, match the horizontal sequences of 1, 2, 3, 4, under **C** on the "Score Sheet" with the horizontal rows of "YES yes no NO" on page **C** of the test booklet, and mark the answers in a similar fashion. (Note that Column **C** on your score sheet is the second column.) Then mark page **D** by placing the last column of the score sheet over the **D** column of the booklet. Mark the answers as you did for the other columns.

By this time you are probably curious to know how the answers on Section I correspond to the answers on Section II. If you look at a booklet, you will see that the items under **A** (Section I) are exactly the same as the items under **C** (Section II). Similarly, the items under **B** (Section I) are the same as those under **D** (Section II). In short, the items for both parts are the same. The student marks Section I as he would like to be, and he marks Section II as he sees himself. This system for scoring the test enables you to note easily how the student's *present* self concept corresponds with his ideal self concept.

When you have completed marking the answers on the score sheet for each pupil, you will be able to translate these answers into a total score. Alongside Column **C** is a vertical column of short lines headed SCORE. There is also a SCORE column alongside Column **D**.

To score item 1, compare the number circled in Column **A** with the number circled in Column **C**. Subtract the smaller number from the larger and write the difference in the SCORE column on the line provided for item 1. For example: Assume you have circled a "3" for item 1 in Column **A** and a "1" in Column **C**. Simply subtract 1 from 3 and enter 2 on the first line under SCORE. Do this for all 40 items.

When you finish entering the score for each item, make a subtotal at the bottom of each SCORE column, add the scores for the two SCORE columns, and enter the grand total in the box after the student's name. The grand total is the pupil's score on *A Self Test*. A low total score indicates that a pupil's ideal self and perceived self are very much the same. A high score indicates that a pupil sees himself quite differently from what he would like to be. The discrepancy or lack of discrepancy between ideal self and perceived self has been found to be helpful in identifying pupils with serious emotional problems. You will be comparing this self rating, secured from *A Self Test,* with teacher and peer ratings in order to locate those pupils who should be screened as vulnerable to, or handicapped by, serious emotional problems.

Transfer the "Grand Total" scores for all pupils to the "Class Record Sheet for *A Self Test,*" listing boys and girls separately.

Combining Scores for Screening (Grades 7-12)

When you have completed the administration and scoring of the *Behavior Rating of Pupils,* the *Student Survey,* and *A Self Test,* you can combine scores for certain pupils to determine those in your class who should be identified as having possibly moderate to severe emotional problems. The children who are screened should then be evaluated by a school guidance person or referred to a mental health specialist outside the school to determine the extent and nature of their problems.

You yourself may be interested in following up on these pupils by looking over their previous school histories, talking to their other teachers, and perhaps gaining additional information about conditions in their homes. At times, the use of the screening process can help to deepen your understanding of some individual pupils in your class and thus help you in planning effective educational experiences for others. The information you collect, including observations and other testing results, will be of great value to a mental health specialist in studying, diagnosing, and helping the student. The specific course of action taken after you and other teachers in your school have completed the screening process will depend on the school program for mental health and the follow-up plans established by your school administration.

Follow the steps listed below to combine scores and to complete the screening process:

1. Complete the identifying information at the top of the "Screening Summary" form. In the space at the top of the columns for peer rating and self rating, write in the names of the ratings you used: *Student Survey* (peer rating), *A Self Test* (self rating).

2. Find the five students who received the five highest scores on the *Behavior Rating of Pupils*. Write their names at the left side of the page and their scores on the *Behavior Rating of Pupils* after each name. Check the sample "Summary Sheet" on page 201 to clarify this and the subsequent procedures.

3. Write the names of the students who received the five highest percentages on Section I of the *Student Survey*. ("Teacher's Worksheet for Scoring Peer Ratings," Column C.)

    When you have located the pupils with the five highest (most negative) percentages, enter their names on the "Summary Sheet" and record their percentages in the column for peer ratings. If a pupil's name is already listed with one of the five highest teacher ratings, simply add his peer rating percentage in the appropriate column.

4. Use your "Class Record Sheet for *A Self Test*" to find those pupils who should be noted as having a negative self rating. On the "Class Record Sheet," put a mark beside the names of the boys with the *three* highest scores among the boys and the names of the girls with the *three* highest scores among the girls. (Since boys and girls have different averages, it is best to consider them separately.) Next, record in the self rating column of the "Screening Summary" the score on *A Self Test* for each of the three boys and three girls whose names you have marked. If a pupil's name has already been written in the column for pupils' names on the "Screening Summary," simply add the score for *A Self Test* in the space provided.

5. Your "Screening Summary" will now have the name of any pupil who had a high negative score on a teacher rating, on a peer rating, or on a self rating—and you will be able to see quickly which students have negative scores on more than one instrument. In the last column, "How Screened," place the following notations:

"T" if the pupil has a recorded score on the *Behavior Rating of Pupils* only.

"P" if the pupil has a recorded per cent on the *Student Survey* only.

"S" if the pupil has a recorded score on *A Self Test* only.

"TP" if the pupil has recorded scores on the *Behavior Rating of Pupils* and the *Student Survey*.

"TS" if the pupil has recorded scores on the *Behavior Rating of Pupils* and *A Self Test* .

"PS" if the pupil has recorded scores on the *Student Survey* and *A Self Test*.

"TPS" if the pupil has a critical score on all three instruments.

"T" stands for negative teacher rating; "P" stands for negative peer rating; "S" stands for negative self rating. A pupil will be identified for screening when he has two or more negative scores. Some pupils have one negative rating and borderline scores on one or more of the other two ratings. If so, you may want to note these pupils on your "Summary," especially if they appear to you to have a significant number of debilitating, or handicapping, emotional problems.

Place an asterisk beside the name of any pupil with two or more negative scores on the "Screening Summary." These, then, are the pupils in your class who are screened as being vulnerable to, or handicapped by, moderate to serious emotional problems and their names are to be referred for further action under the plan or procedures adopted by your school or school district.

A sample "Screening Summary" appears on page 232.

Name_____Grade_____

School_____Date_____

A SELF TEST

Section I

All of us at one time or another would like to be someone else. Often, during games or parties, or while daydreaming, we imagine what it might be like to be someone else. We also think about what it would be like to be someone in a book, in a TV play, or in a movie. On the next two pages, you will find descriptions of many different young people. Use your imagination to decide if you would want to be like the person described in each sentence.

If you would **like very much** to be the person described in the sentence, circle the large "**YES**," this way———————→ (YES)   yes   no   NO

If you **perhaps would like** to be the person described in the sentence, circle the small "**yes**," this way———————→ YES   (yes)   no   NO

If you think you **would not like** to be the person described in the sentence, circle the small "**no**," this way———————→ YES   yes   (no)   NO

If you would **very much not want** to be like the person described in the sentence, circle the large "**NO**," this way———————→ YES   yes   no   (NO)

Now, try the examples from **A** through **D**.

	"Yes, indeed!"	"Well, yes."	"I don't think so."	"No, no, a thousand times, no!"
A. This person owns a horse. Would you want to be this person?	YES	yes	no	NO
B. This person hits smaller children. Would you want to be this person?	YES	yes	no	NO
C. This person gets good grades. Would you want to be this person?	YES	yes	no	NO
D. This person gets sick. Would you want to be this person?	YES	yes	no	NO

There are no right or wrong answers. Each of you will **want** to be like some of the people and **not** want to be like others. Read each sentence carefully before deciding how you will answer. If you do not understand how to answer some of the questions, ask your teacher. Answer questions 1 through 40 and then stop.

			YES	yes	no	NO	
1. This person has many dreams.							
	Do you want to be like this person?		YES	yes	no	NO	1.
2. This person dates a lot.							
	Do you want to be like this person?		YES	yes	no	NO	2.
3. This person does not have to go to school.							
	Do you want to be like this person?		YES	yes	no	NO	3.
4. This person will become a teacher.							
	Do you want to be like this person?		YES	yes	no	NO	4.
5. This person studies hard at home.							
	Do you want to be like this person?		YES	yes	no	NO	5.
6. This person takes part in athletics.							
	Do you want to be like this person?		YES	yes	no	NO	6.
7. This person goes to the dentist.							
	Do you want to be like this person?		YES	yes	no	NO	7.
8. This person stays awake till late at night.							
	Do you want to be like this person?		YES	yes	no	NO	8.
9. This person goes around with lots of different people.							
	Do you want to be like this person?		YES	yes	no	NO	9.
10. This person has a regular time for going to bed.							
	Do you want to be like this person?		YES	yes	no	NO	10.
11. This person daydreams a lot.							
	Do you want to be like this person?		YES	yes	no	NO	11.
12. This person will be rich and famous.							
	Do you want to be like this person?		YES	yes	no	NO	12.
13. This person is on time for classes.							
	Do you want to be like this person?		YES	yes	no	NO	13.
14. This person works alone a lot of the time.							
	Do you want to be like this person?		YES	yes	no	NO	14.
15. The teacher often picks this person to be in charge of the class.							
	Do you want to be like this person?		YES	yes	no	NO	15.
16. Getting good grades is very important to this person.							
	Do you want to be like this person?		YES	yes	no	NO	16.
17. This person sometimes cries.							
	Do you want to be like this person?		YES	yes	no	NO	17.
18. This person fights or argues a great deal.							
	Do you want to be like this person?		YES	yes	no	NO	18.
19. This person is going to quit school as soon as possible.							
	Do you want to be like this person?		YES	yes	no	NO	19.
20. This person gets angry sometimes.							
	Do you want to be like this person?		YES	yes	no	NO	20.

B					**B**	

	YES	yes	no	NO	
21. This person keeps his friends a long time.					
Do you want to be like this person?	YES	yes	no	NO	21.
22. This person is neat and clean.					
Do you want to be like this person?	YES	yes	no	NO	22.
23. This person is a good athlete.					
Do you want to be like this person?	YES	ves	no	NO	23.
24. This person is often picked as captain of a team.					
Do you want to be like this person?	YES	yes	no	NO	24.
25. This person talks to his or her parents about problems.					
Do you want to be like this person?	YES	yes	no	NO	25.
26. This person is sometimes mean to smaller boys or girls.					
Do you want to be like this person?	YES	yes	no	NO	26.
27. This person is punished at times.					
Do you want to be like this person?	YES	yes	no	NO	27.
28. This person is likely to be chosen class president.					
Do you want to be like this person?	YES	yes	no	NO	28.
29. This person has little to do after school.					
Do you want to be like this person?	YES	yes	no	NO	29.
30. This person is very smart.					
Do you want to be like this person?	YES	yes	no	NO	30.
31. This person sings in the shower or tub.					
Do you want to be like this person?	YES	yes	no	NO	31.
32. This person does funny things in school.					
Do you want to be like this person?	YES	yes	no	NO	32.
33. This person reads a lot of books.					
Do you want to be like this person?	YES	yes	no	NO	33.
34. This person worries about getting hurt when he plays games.					
Do you want to be like this person?	YES	yes	no	NO	34.
35. This person is teased by others.					
Do you want to be like this person?	YES	yes	no	NO	35.
36. This person fools around when he should be studying.					
Do you want to be like this person?	YES	yes	no	NO	36.
37. This person is very good in arithmetic.					
Do you want to be like this person?	YES	yes	no	NO	37.
38. Becoming class president is important to this person.					
Do you want to be like this person?	YES	yes	no	NO	38.
39. This person sleeps late on school holidays.					
Do you want to be like this person?	YES	yes	no	NO	39.
40. This person eats a variety of foods.					
Do you want to be like this person?	YES	yes	no	NO	40.

Section II

All of us think about ourselves at times. We think about what we like, what we don't like, what we do, and what we don't do. To some extent we are able to see ourselves as others see us. Each of us, however, has his own ideas about himself. Decide what you are like and then decide whether or not you are like the person described in each of the following sentences.

If you see yourself as **very much like** the person described in the sentence, circle the large "YES," this way————→ (YES)   yes   no   NO

If you think you are **somewhat or sometimes like** the person described in the sentence, circle the small "yes," this way——→ YES   (yes)   no   NO

If you think you are **not much like** the person described in the sentence, circle the small "no," this way————————→ YES   yes   (no)   NO

If you believe you are **not at all like** the person described in the sentence, circle the large "NO," this way————→ YES   yes   no   (NO)

Now, try the examples from **A** through **D.**

		"Yes, indeed!"	"Well, yes."	"I don't think so."	"No, no, a thousand times, no!"
A. This person owns a horse.	Are you like this person?	YES	yes	no	NO
B. This person hits smaller children.	Are you like this person?	YES	yes	no	NO
C. This person gets good grades.	Are you like this person?	YES	yes	no	NO
D. This person gets sick.	Are you like this person?	YES	yes	no	NO

Again, there are no right or wrong answers. You will probably decide that you are **somewhat like** or **very much like** some of the people described, and **not much like** or **not at all like** others. Your answers, which will **not** be seen by any classmate, have meaning only as they represent the person you think **you are now**, in a moment of clear-eyed and level-headed frankness or candor—not the person you want to be or hope to become.

Read each sentence carefully before deciding how you will answer. If you do not understand some of the questions, consult your teacher.

		C			C		

1. This person has many dreams.

Are you like this person?	YES	yes	no	NO	1.

2. This person dates a lot.

Are you like this person?	YES	yes	no	NO	2.

3. This person does not have to go to school.

Are you like this person?	YES	yes	no	NO	3.

4. This person will become a teacher.

Are you like this person?	YES	yes	no	NO	4.

5. This person studies hard at home.

Are you like this person?	YES	yes	no	NO	5.

6. This person takes part in athletics.

Are you like this person?	YES	yes	no	NO	6.

7. This person goes to the dentist.

Are you like this person?	YES	yes	no	NO	7.

8. This person stays awake till late at night.

Are you like this person?	YES	yes	no	NO	8.

9. This person goes around with lots of different people.

Are you like this person?	YES	yes	no	NO	9.

10. This person has a regular time for going to bed.

Are you like this person?	YES	yes	no	NO	10.

11. This person daydreams a lot.

Are you like this person?	YES	yes	no	NO	11.

12. This person will be rich and famous.

Are you like this person?	YES	yes	no	NO	12.

13. This person is on time for classes.

Are you like this person?	YES	yes	no	NO	13.

14. This person works alone a lot of the time.

Are you like this person?	YES	yes	no	NO	14.

15. The teacher often picks this person to be in charge of the class.

Are you like this person?	YES	yes	no	NO	15.

16. Getting good grades is very important to this person.

Are you like this person?	YES	yes	no	NO	16.

17. This person sometimes cries.

Are you like this person?	YES	yes	no	NO	17.

18. This person fights or argues a great deal.

Are you like this person?	YES	yes	no	NO	18.

19. This person is going to quit school as soon as possible.

Are you like this person?	YES	yes	no	NO	19.

20. This person gets angry sometimes.

Are you like this person?	YES	yes	no	NO	20.

		D				**D**	
21.	This person keeps his friends a long time.						
	Are you like this person?	YES	yes	no	NO	21.
22.	This person is neat and clean.						
	Are you like this person?	YES	yes	no	NO	22.
23.	This person is a good athlete.						
	Are you like this person?	YES	yes	no	NO	23.
24.	This person is often picked as captain of a team.						
	Are you like this person?	YES	yes	no	NO	24.
25.	This person talks to his or her parents about problems.						
	Are you like this person?	YES	yes	no	NO	25.
26.	This person is sometimes mean to smaller boys or girls.						
	Are you like this person?	YES	yes	no	NO	26.
27.	This person is punished at times.						
	Are you like this person?	YES	yes	no	NO	27.
28.	This person is likely to be chosen class president.						
	Are you like this person?	YES	yes	no	NO	28.
29.	This person has little to do after school.						
	Are you like this person?	YES	yes	no	NO	29.
30.	This person is very smart.						
	Are you like this person?	YES	yes	no	NO	30.
31.	This person sings in the shower or tub.						
	Are you like this person?	YES	yes	no	NO	31.
32.	This person does funny things in school.						
	Are you like this person?	YES	yes	no	NO	32.
33.	This person reads a lot of books.						
	Are you like this person?	YES	yes	no	NO	33.
34.	This person worries about getting hurt when he plays games.						
	Are you like this person?	YES	yes	no	NO	34.
35.	This person is teased by others.						
	Are you like this person?	YES	yes	no	NO	35.
36.	This person fools around when he should be studying.						
	Are you like this person?	YES	yes	no	NO	36.
37.	This person is very good in arithmetic.						
	Are you like this person?	YES	yes	no	NO	37.
38.	Becoming class president is important to this person.						
	Are you like this person?	YES	yes	no	NO	38.
39.	This person sleeps late on school holidays.						
	Are you like this person?	YES	yes	no	NO	39.
40.	This person eats a variety of foods.						
	Are you like this person?	YES	yes	no	NO	40.

SCREENING SUMMARY

Teacher _Mallum_   School _Wilson H.S._   District _California City_

Grade _9_   Class _Social Studies_ Period _III_   Date of Screening _November 1960_   Number of pupils in class _32_

Name of Pupil	TEACHER RATING — Behavior Rating of Pupils	PEER RATING — Student Survey COLUMN A	B	C	SELF RATING — self Test	How Screened
Rios, Ricardo	51				31	T S borderline
Nightingale, Lillie	49					T
*Reynolds, Chris	48	9	9	100%		(TP)
Ryan, Bill	48					T
*Heath, Madge	42	16	14	88%	28	(TPS) borderline
*Allgood, Peter		22	19	86%	41	(PS)
Dunn, Mathew		11	9	82%		P
Boiner, Jeff		7	6	86%		P
Salvatore, Vince					32	S
Campbell, Mary					30	S
Davis, Vicky					29	S
Dubrow, Rachel					45	S
Smith, Tom					41	S

INTERPRETING THE RESULTS OF THE SCREENING PROCESS

T HE EFFECTIVENESS and economy of this method of screening children with emotional handicaps is based on combining three perceptions of a child: teacher, peer, and self. In analyzing and using the results, it is well to keep the following facts in mind about these measures.

Experimental Nature of the Screening Process

Although the instruments and procedures described in this *Manual* have been used successfully with thousands of children in hundreds of classrooms, both the instruments and procedures must continue to be used and interpreted as experimental devices. That is, even though they have come through initial experimentation successfully, they must be used only under strictly controlled conditions (in *bona fide* research projects) until still more is known about them. This fact has an important bearing on your interpretation of results.

Most important of all: *the primary purpose of this screening procedure is to help teachers identify those pupils in a class who are likely to have emotional problems and who should be referred to a specialist in mental health for diagnosis and prescription.* Tragic consequences can result if any teacher should assume that the screening process will diagnose the nature or cause of emotional problems, or if any teacher should assume that use of the procedure alone makes *him* a competent therapist. The *only* interpretation that this process will support — and the only interpretation the teacher legitimately can make concerning the performance of an individual pupil — is that the pupil has been screened as needing special attention, or has not been so identified.

Strict adherence to this limit on interpretation is required. Deviation from it is dangerous for pupils and teachers alike. What follows in this section is intended to help the teacher to understand the screening process — *not* to make a clinician of him.

Teacher Perceptions*

The ability of teachers to identify children with poor or good mental health has been a question of much concern and interest to mental health specialists, as well as to educators. A study by Wickman (1) in 1928 seemed to indicate that teachers did not perceive pupil behavior from a mental health point of view. Although Wickman has been careful to point out that the teachers in his study had not been instructed to observe behavior in terms of mental health, this study has been cited for years as evidence of the inability of classroom teachers to recognize the symptoms of emotional problems.

Teachers' ratings of pupil adjustment seem to show closer relationships to sociometric ratings than to intrapersonal data, such as those derived from personality tests. There is also some evidence indicating that teachers, along with other professional personnel, have greater difficulty perceiving the patterns of maladjustment in girls than in boys. Undoubtedly, the manifest overt symptoms in boys permit teachers to be more confident about their perception of acting-out behavior.

What about the teacher's own adjustment and its effect on his perception of children? Teachers have needs and problems; it would be unrealistic to assume that these are deposited in the principal's office while the teacher meets with his class. Teachers with serious personality difficulties are often able, like other persons, to transfer their anxieties or hostilities to children. On the other hand, some teachers with mental health problems may manifest such problems by being unenthusiastic, over-conforming, or rigid.

Most critical effective judgment of the behavior of others, perhaps, is the teacher's level of self-awareness and the extent to which he is able to gain insight into self. A teacher who is fearful of any type of behavioral deviation in his class may be oversensi-

---

*"Perception" as used in this *Manual* refers to the process of assigning meaning to events or relationships by the perceiving individual.

tive to some types of behavior or may deny the seriousness of other types. Another teacher may feel that children need a Prussian kind of control because the teacher's parents employed it successfully with him. When a teacher's personal and emotional difficulties cloud or distort his perception of children, he may resist help or uphold values which will keep him from accepting assistance. In some cases, the teacher may feel hostile toward the whole idea of understanding behavior or rebel against in-service programs aimed at helping him gain insight into children's behavior. Dr. Lyman, the disgruntled, disturbed teacher in *Bus Stop,* summed up this point of view as follows: "Educators have despaired of ever teaching students anything so they have decided the second best thing to do is to understand them . . . I graduated *magna cum laude* from the University of Chicago; I studied at Oxford on a Rhodes scholarship and returned to take my Ph.D. at Harvard. I think I have the right to expect my students to try to understand me." (2)

A study by Gronlund (3) demonstrated that a teacher's ability to judge children accurately was not related to experience, age, education, marital status, or length of time he had been in contact with the class. The only criterion which differentiated the teachers who are poor judges of behavior from teachers who are good judges was voluntary participation in an inservice child development program. Here, the results seemed to indicate that those teachers most interested in understanding children are the teachers who get to know them best.

When a teacher is able to verify or compare his perceptions of children with other information, he may become more interested in understanding children and trying to be a more accurate observer and judge of behavior. An opportunity for verifying or rejecting his judgments on a more scientific basis may also help him to strengthen his relationship with the guidance counselor or clinician and enable him, through this relationship, to gain a better understanding of himself. This is a long way around, but it may be a good road to increasing teaching effectiveness. One of the values of this screening technique lies in its encouragement of a teacher to fit information about a child together in a meaningful pattern and, hopefully, by this means to help him to be an even more effective teacher.

Peer Perceptions

"The Teacher's Worksheet for Scoring Peer Ratings" enables a teacher to evaluate and compare peer perceptions and self perceptions on the same items. The total selections of a child by his peers can be utilized as a rough index of the social impact of that child in the class. The total negative choices can be utilized as a rough index of the negative impact of the child in the class. By dividing the first total into the second, one can get a good approximation of the quality of "visibility" — the extent, or degree, or intensity, of awareness of an individual child by the members of his class. The same analytic process holds for tabulating and evaluating the second section of *A Class Play* and the *Student Survey*. The percentage obtained in Section I (peer perception) can be compared to that obtained in Section II (self perception) for each child as follows:

1. *The child who is seen positively by his peers and who sees himself positively.* This description usually fits a majority of the children in the class.
2. *The child who is seen by his classmates as a negative child but who sees himself positively.* This child may need to distort reality somewhat or may have difficulty in appraising how others see him. Many emotionally handicapped children show this or the next pattern of self-peer relationship.
3. *The child who is seen by his classmates as a negative child and who also sees himself negatively.* Some of these children show delight in playing negative roles. Some are quite realistic in appraising how they are seen by others. Most of these are emotionally handicapped children.
4. *The child who is seen positively by his classmates but who sees himself negatively.* Such relationships are rare but do occur in children who are academically and socially successful but who feel they are not living up to some internalized expectations. Such children may have personality problems which are seldom noted in a typical classroom. In past research studies, few emo-

tionally handicapped children have shown this peer-self relationship.

5. *The child who is not seen by his classmates at all.* This group includes: slow-learning or mentally retarded children; quiet, non-intrusive personalities; and a core of children who have actively withdrawn from the group because of emotional problems. It is well to note the IQ score in analyzing the meaning of a low social-impact score. Children with above average IQ's who are found in this category should be reviewed for possible emotional problems. In addition to IQ score, scores on the "self" instruments should be carefully studied to obtain clues about the absence of peer perception.

6. *A child who is seen by his classmates in a mixture of positive and negative roles.* These children have great role versatility in the eyes of their peers. Often they are children who are mildly irritating but not sufficiently so to provoke hostility or rejection of the child by his peers.

Another factor that may be relevant to an analysis of the results of peer ratings relates to the choices of children who do not perceive their peers as others in the class do. This idiosyncratic perception may be caused by such things as poor reality testing (see below), late entrance into the class, or low intelligence. In any case, the teacher should be aware not only of how a child is chosen but of how he chooses. It is often helpful to discuss results with other teachers who have known the child, or with the school psychologist, guidance counselor, or principal.

In appraising the relationships of peer and self scores on *A Class Play* and the *Student Survey,* one should be aware of a fundamental concept of mental hygiene called "reality testing." "Reality testing" refers to the ability to perceive others and oneself accurately and to be free to test the accuracy of one's inferences about the environment in which one lives. It is often helpful to know to what extent a child sees himself as others do. To what extent does a child need to use fantasy to change the nature of reality? To what extent does a child need to deny the realities of his peer relationships?

Studies by Sears (4), Rogers, Kell, and McNeil (5), and Davids and White (6) may be helpful in understanding the relationships of perceptions elicited by this technique. For example, Sears studied children who experienced continuous success in school as compared to children who had a long history of school failure and found that the former set goals at levels which indicated good reality testing while the latter set their goals with little regard for their possible fulfillment. Rogers and his co-workers found that, in a group of delinquent children for whom there was an adequate amount of diagnostic information, the self-understanding or reality testing factor had the greatest predictive value for later adjustment. A follow-up study by Rogers proved that realistic perception of self was the best predictor of future behavior.

Publications by Taba (7), Jennings (8), and others on the analysis of groups may be helpful to teachers in learning to use this technique. Grambs (9) has listed some of the basic assumptions in the development and understanding of peer rating techniques. In the final analysis, this technique, like any other classroom procedure, can only serve to initiate, verify, or reject hypotheses about children. It provides a point of view for looking at behavior. Along with other reference points, it can give the teacher a more sharply focused picture of what the child really is like.

The effective use of this technique depends, as with other techniques, on the professional skill of the teacher and her willingness to examine the meaning of the results in light of other data. This technique, along with other types of sociometric instruments, adds an important dimension to the total perception of the child. Teachers and others have a tendency to overrate the acceptance by peers of the children they, the teachers, like best and to underrate the status of those they like less. (10) When sociometric choices differ from teacher judgments, the differences in perception should not be regarded as an indication that one or the other perception is wrong. Both perceptions may be right, i.e., accurate. Peers do not perceive one another from the same value systems as their teachers perceive them. A teacher may learn much about herself by comparing other perceptions of a child with her own.

Self Perception

Self perception is the most difficult and least accurate measure used in the screening process. *Thinking About Yourself* and *A Self Test* attempt to measure discrepancy between a *wanted* self and a *perceived* self; *A Picture Game* is aimed at obtaining a measure of the child's perception of his environment as either happy or sad.

When one perceives, one not only "sees"; one interprets and experiences what one has perceived. The *self* of an individual is a learned concept made up of the multitude of relationships and interactions of the individual with other persons. One's concept of self is not fixed and unchanging, however; it can and does vary, depending on the situation in which one finds himself, and the persons with whom he must live — in a community, a job, or in a classroom. Block (11), for example, found that a secretary's concept of herself varied in relation to the person she was with at the time but that a core of self was always present. He found that, if we may speak of the *self* as divisible into parts, about half of the self is flexible, adaptable to change in the circumstances and environment in which one finds himself. The other half remains basically unchanged. It is that part of us which makes us recognizable as the "same persons" whatever change in jobs, personal relationships, or life circumstances we may seek or experience.

One can theorize, then, that someone with a larger store (substantially larger than half, that is) of basic, unchanging *self* perceptions may be unable to adapt readily to changing social and personal conditions. Similarly, a person with only a small store of basic *self* perceptions may shift too easily in response to changing pressures or circumstances. Such a person may be described as lacking stability, or, more precisely, as having little "self."

In any case, the *self* is the standard by which one assesses the environment, other people, and the observer himself. To use still another figure of speech: the self is the window through which we perceive, and the quality of the glass — its transparency or opacity, its freedom from distortion, its color or lack of color — determine how well we perceive the environment and understand the people in it and our relationship to them.

It should not surprise us, therefore, that a child who is asked to communicate about *self* may communicate what we as teachers and adults believe is *not* an accurate self-concept. First, the child may not see himself clearly, especially when he is asked to delineate his concept of self on a pencil-and-paper questionnaire. What is to you confusion and fragmenting of self may be a direct result of the child's inabilty to see himself clearly. Or his self-concept may in part be built on a need to deny problems. Such children may communicate only what they can comfortably reveal.

From the point of view of the teacher, such children may seem "untruthful." But even a denial by a child that he has problems can be a significant fact in understanding the child — if the denial is understood as part of the dynamics of *self* protection. It will be helpful, also, to appraise the extent to which a child is able to communicate how he feels.

As these and other perceptions of the child's self are made available to the teacher, inconsistencies in the child's perceived self may become apparent. Such inconsistencies, it must be remembered, are part of the very structure of self. Understanding this is basic to understanding behavior, for what may appear at times erratic or unpredictable behavior, can become consistent and significant if we can gain even a little insight into the child's self and learn how he perceives the world around him.

It should be emphasized that the psychological processes of children are not necessarily bound by either moral or logical considerations. A child whose experiences tend to persuade him that he is unworthy or inadequate will develop a self which accepts only those perceptions which confirm or are consistent with these feelings. He may refuse to try to do tasks he is obviously equipped to do (obviously to adults, that is). He may avoid the everyday competition with his peers or siblings which is a part of family, classroom, and community living. And to the adult who has not understood that such a child is acting out a role he feels he must, such behavior may seem slothful, illogical, stubborn. Watching two children fail in a task, be it batting a baseball or translating a sentence from French into English, and seeing the two fail in the same way and to the same degree, we may find one child "quitting," becoming sullen, angry, and despondent over his failure, while the other child may bounce back, ready — even eager — to try again. The latter response is very probably an indication of good mental health; the former response, if repeated, may well be an early symptom of emotional difficulty. But to change the unhealthful attitude, to change any basic behavioral pattern for that matter, requires some change in the individual's perception of self.

The relationship between one's perception of self and one's perception of others may help to explain why children who have negative concepts of themselves show up, on sociometric instruments such as those used in the screening process, as isolated from their peers. Sheerer (12) found a definite and relatively high correlation between acceptance of and respect for self and acceptance of and respect for others. Stock (13), in an independent study, confirmed Sheerer's results. Both investigators found a regular increase in acceptance of and respect for self and others in individuals who had had a successful counseling experience. Sullivan described the relationship between a person's perception of himself and his perception of others as follows: "If there is a valid and real attitude toward the self, that attitude will manifest as valid and real toward others. It is not that 'As ye judge, so shall ye be judged,' but 'As you judge yourself, so shall you judge others.'" (14)

A Self Test and *Thinking About Yourself* utilize intra-individual measures of self. The scores obtained are not based on comparing answers to a norm or on how other children have answered the item. The scoring is based on the assumption that the larger the difference between wanted or desired self (Do you *want* to be like him or her?) and present self (*Are* you like him?), the greater is the child's dissatisfaction with his present status. (This is not to suggest that little or no difference is a guarantee of good mental health. On the contrary, some attention should be paid to those children whose present self and wanted self are almost entirely congruent as well as to those who have high discrepancy scores.) It is possible that in responding to the question "Do you want to be like him?," the child may range in his thinking from immediate situational needs to highly developed fantasies. For example, the weaker or more helpless a child's concept of himself is, the more imperious or overwhelming may be the demands of the environment. As a consequence, the desired or wanted self may be built out of a strong need to live in fantasy.

Studies have shown that adults who scored low on acceptance of self also showed high discrepancy between the perceived self and wanted or desired self. (15) (16) One study (17) of the congruence of perceived self and desired self in relation to personality adjustment noted that the correlation between the two aspects of personality (acceptance of self and perception of self) tends to be positive and somewhere between .33 and .46. The results of this study suggest the relevance of measures of self and ideal self as measures of personality maladjustment. Seldom is anyone completely satisfied with himself; similarly, few individuals are completely dissatisfied with themselves. Some children are too frightened to express a wanted self that is any different from self. Others are so disturbed that they cannot help being greatly dissatisfied with the way things are going. An optimum relationship between self and wanted self would depend on many factors, including how much insight the child has about himself.

Children with good reality testing usually feel comfortable about themselves and their future. Children who are disturbed may hesitate to disclose a wanted self different from self, or may, without difficulty express a wanted self even greatly different from self.

The results on other self instruments should be considered along with the results on self-peer ratings. The wanted or desired self on the personality inventory may be a more direct expression of self needs or wishes. A study (18) of the relationship of personality tests and sociometric choices demonstrated that children who were perceived positively by peers had the "best" scores on the personality test, while those with few positive choices and many negative ones had the poorest personality test scores. Children with few or no negative choices on the sociogram as compared with those who had many negative choices had better adjustment scores on the personality test. The investigators found that peer perceptions can be helpful in understanding the results of a personality inventory and, conversely, a child's concept of himself as revealed on a personality inventory can be helpful in understanding his positive or negative valuation by the class.

Distinguishing Between Pathology and Difference

Teachers know from experience that "things are not always what they seem" — that poor work from a student may be no true measure of his ability, that defiance of authority can mask a plea for help, that submissive quiet in a classroom can be the prelude to an epidemic of hilarious mischief. Teachers, like parents, develop a sixth sense, and this, along with their professional training, makes them aware that *interpreting* the results of observations always calls for serious attention and prudence.

This caution is particularly necessary in interpreting the results of the screening instruments you have been using, for a major difficulty in interpretation lies in the need to distinguish between incipient pathology (emotional disorders) and behavioral differences which may be perfectly normal. Marked differences from normal behavior are noted in children with emotional handicaps, but they are also noted in children who *choose* to behave somewhat idiosyncratically.

In distinguishing between two individuals or two groups of individuals who deviate markedly from normal behavior, the key is the *source* of the behavior. The behavior of the emotionally handicapped child is, to the extent of his handicap, a *necessity,* not a matter of choice. His behavioral freedom, his choice of behavioral patterns, is restricted by internal conflicts or by a lack of inner controls. Of this, we are clinically certain.

Socially unconventional behavior may, of course, be thought of as in a sense "determined" also — in the sense that an individual *needs* to prove himself. But it is significant that such an individual is almost always able to choose from among a variety of roles, all of which are clearly perceived, to test his developing self. At any rate, strange or unconventional behavior cannot, in and of itself, be regarded as a sign of an emotional handicap.

Teacher-Peer-Self Thermometer

This process for identifying children who are, or are becoming, emotional problems was designed to secure a "psychological thermometer" that might be used by teachers to help them better estimate the mental health of children in their classes. This "thermometer," like a clinical thermometer, should be easy to read and should indicate with reasonable consistency and accuracy the existence of emotional "fevers" in children. The value of such a thermometer is described by Howe as follows:

"No longer are we looking for some one definitive measure of mental health comparable to a platinum bar, but, rather, for indications of the state of being — that is, for indices. What we seem to need is the kind of measuring device that may be compared to a clinical thermometer on which successive readings can be taken in order to chart deviations from and approximations to the norm of 98.6 degrees. Such a thermometer might yield only one limited and partial kind of measurement, to be sure, but this kind of measurement is better than none — at least, if proper precautions regarding its interpretation are observed." (19)

It must be remembered that thermometers provide only one kind of information about an individual's condition or illness causing the fever. Similarly, the use of the information and process of this study may help a teacher in many ways. It may help him confirm a suspicion about a child or reject a suspicion, or, in some cases, to raise a suspicion. The use of the materials and processes of this study may provide a teacher with more accurate and reliable evidence (more accurate and reliable, that is, than subjective feelings) for deciding that specialized help is needed for some children and for describing the extent of that need for help from specialists. It may also provide the interested teacher or school a base line from which change in individual children can be assessed. For some teachers it can also furnish a standardized, helpful procedure for continuous inquiry into the validity of their own judgments about children.

And for all who have a share in the responsibility for educating children, such instruments as these can help to deepen our insights into others, to clarify our judgments concerning behavior, to enable us to make sounder decisions about how best to do the job we have chosen to do — in short, to help us to be better teachers and administrators; better not so much in techniques and skills, for in these we may be masters, but in knowledge and understanding of human behavior (our own as well as that of others), for in this realm there is no end to the search, no limit to our growth.

CONCLUSIONS AND SUGGESTIONS FOR FURTHER RESEARCH

In GENERAL, the screening procedures described in this *Report* are effective enough to be used further in research applications. The effectiveness of the screening procedures is related to their identification of children with emotional problems and to their assistance in helping teachers learn more about the validity of judgments of children's behavior. There is subjective evidence to suggest that in schools utilizing the screening procedure, a change in the kinds of referrals and in the time of referral may be obtained. The results of the use of the screening procedure by teachers are not only manifested in the children selected, but in the effect of the process on the teacher. In essence, the process becomes one of enabling a teacher to confirm or reject a hypothesis about a child's behavior. These suggestions grow from observations rather than from experimental data, however, and must be interpreted accordingly.

Under Utopian conditions, it would be possible to eliminate the need for this kind of screening process. Under such conditions, schools would have classes of 20 to 25 children, teachers specially trained to recognize early signs of emotional maladjustment, easily available guidance and psychological assistance, and a school climate in which screening activity is a continuous part of the teaching process. Since these conditions are not possible at the present time, some kind of standardized screening process is needed. If the school is to realize its potential as an agency which can reduce the number of children and adults alienated from society, it will need to identify and assist those children upon whom the school can have a positive impact and to reduce their vulnerability to disabling emotional handicaps.

Because of the pressures of time and money, final revisions of the screening instruments were not made until the last few

246

months of the study sponsored by Senate Bill 62 of the 1957 California State Legislature, which authorized the California State Department of Education to study ways of educating emotionally handicapped children.

Although the screening instruments were an integral part of the selection of experimental and control students for these programs, research related to a complete exploration of the reliability and validity of the instruments had to be conducted concurrently with the use of these materials in various programs. The revisions which will be used by research workers represent the best efforts of the authors to incorporate the results of the item studies presented in this report, along with what is considered to be a useful conceptual framework for studying emotional disorders of school children. The characteristics of these revised instruments are only slightly known. While other research workers will be able to use these tests for further exploration of a screening process for identifying emotionally handicapped children, the authors plan to continue validity and reliability investigations, as well as other studies of the instruments, using large samples of pupils.

A number of possibilities for further research have been suggested by the use of these instruments in a variety of school settings. Unanswered questions which may interest future researchers are:

1. To what extent are perceptions of children and by children modified as they go through the grades?

2. To what extent are initial perceptions of children maintained by teachers and peers through the 10 years of elementary and secondary education?

3. To what extent are perceptions by teachers stereotyped by grade level, sex, age, F scale score, Rorschach, and so on?

4. To what extent will differences in relationships between classes and teachers be manifested in total negative perception by peers?

5. What kinds of students selected as EHC by peer and teacher perceptions offer a highly congruent self and ideal self or a highly discordant self and ideal self?

6. What kinds of students are actually referred by teachers as

being in need of help? To what extent is this a function of available services, teacher anxiety, use of screening processes, administrative sanction, and so on?

7. What kinds of children perceive themselves negatively yet are perceived positively by peers and/or teacher?

8. Does the relationship between positive peer perception and IQ follow a reciprocating relationship which results in increased dependence of these variables?

9. In junior and senior high schools, what kinds of classes — *e.g.*, English, social studies, physical education — are most appropriate for obtaining reliable peer, self, and teacher ratings?

10. By which grade does it become apparent that a child's self-concept and his relationship to peers and teacher will be stabilized positively or negatively?

11. How does one differentiate among children who are not perceived on peer instruments? What clues are there in separating the withdrawn, retarded, shy, or non-impressionistic for screening purposes?

12. Can the teacher-peer-self triad be used as an Index of Relatability ⟷ Alienation to measure changes as a result of specific mental health programs?

13. How do hypothetically vulnerable groups of children — *i.e.*, children who have attended child-care centers, or who have one-parent families, etc. — compare with others on teacher-peer-self ratings as they enter the first grade?

14. To what extent are the self measures *(A Picture Game, Thinking About Yourself,* and *Student Survey)* comparable as self measures and how do they differ?

15. Are there class patterns on teacher-peer-self perceptions which can be said to be characteristic of a school, a community, or a grade level?

16. What are the self, peer, and teacher ratings of children being seen in child guidance or psychiatric clinics?

17. In a class where the children have been studied individually and are well-known, which children are missed in the screening who have poor mental health and which are selected who seem to have good mental health?

18. To what extent is academic achievement related to a child's Index of Relatability $\longleftrightarrow$ Alienation?

19. What changes are there, if any, in a teacher's perception of children as the screening procedure is used?

20. To what extent does use of the screening process commit a teacher to take some kind of action?

21. Are there demonstrable changes in the relationship of the teacher to the adminstrator or guidance staff as a result of the use of the screening instruments by the teacher?

22. What types of emotionally handicapped children show poor reality testing, *i.e.,* peer and self selections markedly different from those of classmates?

23. To what extent is grade point average related to positive or negative self perception? Are there differences related to age, sex, and school?

24. What factors in addition to high scores on the Index of Relatability $\longleftrightarrow$ Alienation seem to predispose children to delinquent behavior?

25. What relationship is there between scores on the Index of Relatability $\longleftrightarrow$ Alienation and the socioeconomic class of a child's family?

Mark Twain said, "Everybody talks about the weather, but no one does anything about it." This was probably true in his day, but in our present-day world, we have air-conditioners for the home and car, heating systems handling heat and cold in one unit available at moderate cost for the home buyer, and cloud-seeding rainmakers in many of the nation's agricultural centers. We have not yet found a way to turn the sun off or on, nor have we yet found any way to assure "correct" amounts of rain. Nevertheless, we *are* doing a great deal about the weather. To paraphrase the old favorite, then, everyone talks about early identification of children with emotional handicaps, but no one does much about it. Let us hope that we will soon move to a stage in early identification analagous to our great and promising effort toward weather control.

This report has summarized the efforts of one group of research workers to find a means to identify children who are vulnerable to or handicapped by emotional disturbance — before the problem is one for the mental institution, the court, or the hospital. Mental health specialists have worked hard and valiantly to provide services for adults and children with neuroses and psychoses which require that they should be protected by society. Creative approaches to identifying early enough the most susceptible, the vulnerable, and the unprotected, and to strengthening them to meet the demands of working, playing, and loving, can surely reduce the number that society later must care for in custodial fashion.

REFERENCES

1. Wickman, E. K.: *Children's Behavior and Teacher's Attitudes.* New York, The Commonwealth Fund, 1928.
2. Inge, William: *Bus Stop.* New York, Random House, 1955.
3. Gronlund, Norman E.: *The Accuracy of Teachers' Judgments Concerning the Sociometric Status of Sixth-grade Pupils.* New York, Beacon House, 1951.
4. Sears, Pauline Snedden: Levels of aspiration in academically successful and unsuccessful children. *Journal of Abnormal and Social Psychology, XXXV,* October 1940.
5. Rogers, Carl R.; Kell, B. L., and McNeil, Helen: The role of self-understanding in the prediction of behavior. *Journal of Consulting Psychology, III,* May-June 1948.
6. Davids, Anthony, and White, A. A.: Effects of success, failure, and social facilitation on the level of aspiration in emotionally disturbed and normal children. *Journal of Personality, 26:*77-93, March 1958.
7. Taba, Hilda: *With Perspective on Human Relations.* Washington, D. C., American Council on Education, 1955.
8. Jennings, Helen Hall: Sociometry in group relations. *Intergroup Education in Cooperating Schools.* Washington, D. C., American Council on Education, 1955.
9. Grambs, J. D.: *Group Processes in Intergroup Education.* New York, National Council of Christians and Jews, pp. 25-28. 1953.
10. Gronlund, N. E., *op. cit.*
11. Block, Jack: The assessment of communication. *Journal of Personality, XXI:*272-286, December 1952.
12. Sheerer, E. T.: An analysis of the relationship between acceptance of and respect for others in ten counseling cases. *Journal of Consulting Psychology, XIII:*169-175, June 1949.
13. Stock, Dorothy: An investigation into the interrelationships between the self concept and feelings directed toward other persons and groups. *Journal of Consulting Psychology, XIII:*176-180, June 1949.
14. Sullivan, H. S.: *Conceptions of Modern Psychiatry.* Washington, D. C., William Alanson White Psychiatric Foundation, 1947, p. 3.
15. Bills, E. R.; Vance, E. L., and McLean, O. S.: An index of adjustment and values. *Journal of Consulting Psychology, XV:*257-261, March 1951.
16. Bower, Eli M., and Tashnovian, Peter J.: Q methodology; an application.

    California Journal of Educational Research, VI:200-205, November 1955.
17. Hanlon, Thomas E.; Hofstaetter, Peter R., and O'Connor, James P.: Congruence of self and ideal self in relation to personality adjustment. *Journal of Consulting Psychology, XVIII:*215-220, June 1954.
18. Tindall, Ralph H.: Relationships among indices of adjustment status. *Educational and Psychological Measurement, 15:*152-162, Summer 1955.
19. Howe, Louisa P.: Problems in the evaluation of mental health programs. In Ruth Kotinsky and Helen L. Witmer (Eds.): *Community Programs for Mental Health.* Cambridge, Harvard University Press, 1955, pp. 225-295.

APPENDIX

Computation of Percentage for Peer Ratings

TOTAL NUMBER OF SELECTIONS

	1	2	3	4	5	6	7	8	9	10	11	12	13	14	15	16	17	18	19	20	21	22	23	24	25	26	27	28	29	30	31	32	33	34	35	36	37	38	39	40
1	100	50	33	25	20	17	14	13	11	10	9	8	8	7	7	6	6	6	5	5	5	5	4	4	4	4	3	4	3	3	3	3	3	3	3	3	3	3	3	3
2		100	67	50	40	33	28	25	22	20	18	16	15	14	13	13	12	11	11	10	10	9	9	8	8	8	7	7	7	7	6	6	6	6	6	5	5	5	5	
3			100	75	60	50	43	38	33	30	27	25	23	21	20	19	18	17	16	15	14	14	13	13	12	12	11	11	10	10	10	9	9	9	9	8	8	8	8	
4				100	80	67	57	50	44	40	36	33	31	29	27	25	24	22	21	20	19	18	17	17	16	15	15	14	14	13	13	13	12	12	11	11	11	11	10	10
5					100	83	71	63	56	50	45	42	38	36	33	31	29	28	26	25	24	23	22	21	20	19	19	18	17	17	16	16	15	15	14	14	14	13	13	13
6						100	86	75	67	60	55	50	46	42	40	38	35	33	32	30	29	27	26	25	24	23	22	21	21	20	19	19	18	18	17	17	16	16	16	16
7							100	88	78	70	64	58	54	50	47	44	41	39	37	35	33	32	30	29	28	27	26	25	24	23	23	22	21	21	20	19	19	18	18	18
8								100	89	80	73	67	62	57	53	50	47	44	42	40	38	36	35	33	32	31	30	29	28	27	26	25	24	24	23	22	22	21	21	20
9									100	90	82	75	69	64	60	56	53	50	47	45	43	41	39	38	35	33	32	31	30	29	28	27	26	25	24	24	23			
10										100	91	83	77	71	67	63	59	56	53	50	48	45	43	42	40	38	37	36	34	33	32	31	30	29	29	28	27	26	26	25
11											100	92	85	79	73	69	65	61	58	55	52	50	48	46	44	42	41	39	38	37	35	34	33	32	31	31	30	29	28	28
12												100	92	86	80	75	71	67	63	60	57	55	52	50	48	46	44	42	41	40	39	38	36	35	34	33	32	32	31	30
13													100	93	87	81	76	72	68	65	62	59	57	54	52	50	48	46	45	43	42	41	39	38	37	36	35	34	33	33
14														100	93	88	82	78	74	70	67	64	61	58	56	54	52	50	48	47	45	44	42	41	40	39	38	37	36	35
15															100	94	88	83	79	75	71	68	65	63	60	58	56	54	52	50	48	47	45	44	43	42	41	39	38	38
16																100	94	89	84	80	76	73	70	67	64	62	59	57	55	53	52	50	48	47	46	44	43	42	41	40
17																	100	94	89	85	81	77	74	71	68	65	63	61	59	57	55	53	52	50	49	47	46	45	44	43
18																		100	95	90	86	82	78	75	72	69	67	64	62	60	58	56	55	53	51	50	49	47	46	43
19																			100	95	90	86	83	79	76	73	70	68	66	63	61	59	56	56	54	53	51	50	49	48
20																				100	95	91	87	83	80	77	74	71	69	67	65	63	61	59	57	56	54	53	51	50
21																					100	95	91	88	84	81	78	75	72	70	68	66	64	62	60	58	57	55	54	53
22																						100	96	92	88	85	81	79	76	73	71	69	67	65	63	61	59	58	56	55
23																							100	96	92	88	85	82	79	77	74	72	70	68	66	64	62	61	59	58
24																								100	96	92	89	86	83	80	77	75	73	71	69	67	65	63	62	60
25																									100	96	93	89	86	83	83	78	76	74	71	69	68	66	64	63
26																										100	96	93	90	87	84	81	79	76	74	72	70	68	67	65
27																											100	96	93	90	87	84	82	79	77	75	73	71	69	68
28																												100	97	93	90	88	85	82	80	78	76	74	72	70
29																													100	97	94	91	88	85	83	81	78	76	74	73
30																														100	97	94	91	88	86	83	81	79	77	75
31																															100	97	94	91	89	86	84	82	79	78
32																																100	97	94	91	89	86	84	82	80
33																																	100	97	94	92	89	89	85	83
34																																		100	97	94	92	89	87	85
35																																			100	97	95	92	90	88
36																																				100	97	95	92	90
37																																					100	97	95	93
38																																						100	97	95
39																																							100	98
40																																								100

TOTAL OF EVEN NUMBERED SELECTIONS

253

PUPIL RECORD FOLDER
For TEACHER, PEER, and SELF RATINGS

A RECORD FOLDER should be prepared for every student. Space
is provided for entering the results on:

1. **Teacher Rating** *(Behavior Rating of Pupils)*
2. **Peer Rating** *(Class Pictures, Class Play,* or *Student Survey)*
3. **Self Rating** *(A Picture Game, Thinking About Yourself,* or *A Self Test)*

The purpose of such a record is to enable teachers, administrators, and pupil-personnel workers to note whether present patterns of relationships are consistent with past patterns, whether a child seems to be moving toward more positive relationships with peers, and, in general, to obtain a picture of a child's pattern of development over a period of time.

Marked changes in behavior patterns should be noted as well as patterns which show increasingly negative relationships to teacher, peers, or self. School systems maintaining these "T-P-S Pupil Record Folders" over a period of time will find the information on each child helpful in identifying children who may need individual study and/or assistance.

I. Teacher Rating

How to record Teacher Ratings

To complete the individual record of the teacher's rating, find the pupil's name for Statement A, in one of the boxes on the *Behavior Rating of Pupils*. Place an "A" in the same box on the rating scale. Now, find his name in one of the boxes for Statement B. Place a "B" in that same box on the rating scale. Complete all eight ratings (A through H) in this manner. Keep in mind that ratings are made in relation to other pupils in this class. A professional person looking at the completed rating scale should be able to tell at a glance how a child was rated by his teacher in relation to his peers on each of the eight behavior categories. If you wish to compare ratings by teachers of an individual pupil for a number of consecutive years, colored pencils can be used to differentiate the ratings from year to year.

Statements of Behavior

A This pupil gets into fights or quarrels with other pupils, more often than others.

B This pupil has to be coaxed or forced to work or play with other pupils. He or she will actively avoid having any contact with classmates.

C This pupil has difficulty in learning school subjects.

D This pupil makes unusual or immature responses during normal school activities. His behavior is unpredictable or inappropriate for his age.

E This pupil works extremely hard in learning school subjects to the exclusion of any other interests or activities. This pupil pours all his energies into school work.

F This pupil behaves in ways which are dangerous to self or others. This pupil will get into situations in which he or she may be hurt or frightened.

G This pupil is unhappy or depressed. He or she may cry easily, be inattentive, or daydream.

H This pupil becomes upset or sick often, especially when faced with a difficult school problem or situation.

II. Peer Rating

Data from *"TEACHER'S WORKSHEET FOR SCORING PEER RATINGS"**

Check test used: **Results**   Date: Date: Date:

*Class Pictures*_____Total Selections (Column **A**) _____

*A Class Play*_____Total Even Selections (Column **B**)_____

*Student Survey*_____% of Negative Peer Ratings (Column **C**)_____

No. enrolled in class___% of Negative Self Ratings (Column **F**) _____

III. Self Rating

Data from *"CLASS RECORD SHEET"*
for *A Picture Game,* or *Thinking About Yourself,* or *A self Test*

Check test used: Date: Date: Date:

*A Picture Game*_____

*Thinking About Yourself*_____

*A Self Test*_____

Score:_____

Comments:

_____

_____

_____

_____

_____

_____

_____

_____

_____

_____

*You may, if you wish, staple an individual student's "Score Sheet" from *Thinking About Yourself* or *A Self Test* to this folder for future reference. The pupil's copy of a *Student Survey* and *A Class Play* may also be enclosed.

READING REFERENCES

1. Allensmith, Wesley, and Goethals, George: *The Role of Schools in Mental Health*. New York, Basic Books, 1961.
2. Buhler, Charlotte; Smitter, Faith, and Richardson, Sybil: *Childhood Problems and the Teacher*. New York, Henry Holt, 1952.
3. Caplan, Gerald (Ed.): *Emotional Problems of Early Childhood*. New York, Basic Books, 1956.
4. Caplan, Gerald (Ed.): *Possibilities for Prevention of Mental and Emotional Disorders*. New York, Basic Books, 1961.
5. Erikson, Erik H.: *Childhood and Society*. New York, W. W. Norton, 1950.
6. Freud, Sigmund: *A General Introduction in Psychoanalysis*. New York, Liveright Publishing Corp., 1935.
7. Gibson, William: *The Miracle Worker*. New York, Alfred A. Knopf, 1957.
8. Gurin, Gerald: Veroff, Joseph, and Feld, Sherla: *Americans View Their Mental Health*. New York, Basic Books, 1960.
9. Jahoda, Marie: *Current Concepts of Positive Mental Health*. New York, Basic Books, 1958.
10. Kotinsky, Ruth, and Witmer, Helen L. (Eds.): *Community Programs for Mental Health*. Cambridge, Harvard Univer. Press, 1955.
11. Krugman, Morris (Ed.): *Orthopsychiatry and the School*. New York, American Orthopsychiatric Association, 1958.
12. Lindgren, Henry C.: *Mental Health in Education*. New York, Henry Holt, 1954.
13. Redl, Fritz, and Wattenberg, William: *Mental Hygiene in Teaching*. New York, Harcourt Brace, 1959.
14. Wall, William D.: *Education and Mental Health*. New York, Columbia Univer. Press, 1955.

INDEX